MARK TWAIN

The Development of a Writer

MARK TWAIN

The Development of a Writer

By

HENRY NASH SMITH

THE BELKNAP PRESS OF
HARVARD UNIVERSITY PRESS

Cambridge, Massachusetts

1962

Library of Congress Catalog Card Number 62-19224

PRINTED IN THE UNITED STATES OF AMERICA

FOR JANET

PREFACE

THIS book considers first the problems of style and structure Mark Twain faced at the outset of his career, and then traces his handling of these problems in nine of his principal works. Since questions of technique necessarily involve questions of meaning, I have dealt also with his ethical ideas. The inquiry leads ultimately to the consideration of how his writing reveals a conflict between the dominant culture of his day and an emergent attitude associated with the vernacular language of the native American humorists.

Just as the diction of the humorists contrasted violently with the diction considered appropriate for the upper ranges of literature, vernacular values were at odds with the values cherished by accredited spokesmen for American society. The vernacular perspective was potentially subversive: conservative critics accused the humorists not only of coarseness but of irreverence. This state of affairs placed formidable obstacles in the way of Mark Twain, who presented the paradox of a humorist seeking recognition as a serious writer. His efforts to find an alternative to the prevailing cult of gentility and to define his own role in society appear in his work as a series of difficulties in the management of narrative viewpoint. His degree of success in solving all three problems can be traced in his progress toward the creation of a consistent fictional persona to serve as the protagonist of first-person narratives. Thus his technical innovations might be described with equal accuracy as an ethical, a sociological, or a literary undertaking.

After twenty years of trial and error, from the 1860's to the 1880's, the development of both technique and meaning in Mark Twain's work reaches a climax in *Adventures of Huckleberry Finn,* which is his nearest approach to the full embodiment of vernacular values in fiction. Yet in the very act of discovering how to solve his technical problems Mark Twain became aware that the vernacular protest against the dominant culture did not adequately embody his insight into the meaning of man's social experience. The ideal of the good life represented by Huck and Jim alone on the raft was too special, too vulnerable to sustain his confidence in the possibility of human happiness; it was threatened by every contact with society. He was accordingly faced with the question whether human beings could hope to fulfill themselves within a civilization like that of the United States in his day. *A Connecticut Yankee in King Arthur's Court* (1889) asks this question, and answers it in the negative. Thereafter his significant work treats social experience as a tragic burden and seeks an imaginative escape from it.

The vernacular perspective that figures prominently in my argument is not easy to define. Mark Twain himself never made fully articulate what he was trying to affirm; any explicit statement would falsify his presentational mode of thought. Provisionally, however, one might say that his highest good was freedom from stereotyped attitudes. In a society encumbered by a traditional culture that had hardened into a set of conventions having little relation to the actual experience of its members, he fell back on the integrity of the individual, the capacity to face any situation flexibly and with a minimum of preconceptions. His intellectual position approximates the "horse sense" that Walter Blair has traced through almost two centuries of American humor. Yet Mark Twain's perspective is more than a way of thinking or solving problems; it involves the whole personality. When he asserts in the preface to *The Innocents Abroad* that he has written "honestly," the term covers much the same ground as the word "loyally" in the profound and moving sentence which Montaigne—who also lived in a period of cultural confusion—placed near the end of his *Essays:* "It is an absolute perfection, and as it were divine, for a man to know how to enjoy his being loyally." The deliberately vulgar image that follows this exalted declaration conveys some of the tone of the vernacular protest against a stilted and artificial refinement: "sit we upon the highest throne of the World, yet sit we upon our own taile." The discursive method of Montaigne's essay keeps the elevated and colloquial styles separate. Because *Huckleberry Finn* is a work of fiction, it can fuse them in the imaginative triumph of Huck's debate with his conscience, which expresses the highest intensity of self-awareness in vernacular language.

Although my major emphasis is on Mark Twain's writing, at three points in the study I have attempted to demonstrate the interaction between his ideas and attitudes, and the culture that shaped them. In the

PREFACE

first two chapters I describe certain widespread American preoccupations during the 1860's which provided the principal themes of Mark Twain's early writing. Chapter V, based mainly on newspaper reports of his speech at the Whittier birthday dinner in 1877, indicates the sharp contrast between hostile and favorable public responses to his work. And Chapter VII, devoted to *A Connecticut Yankee,* deals at some length with the political discussion aroused by the book.

ACKNOWLEDGMENTS

My greatest debt is to Leo Marx and Walter Blair, who have read the manuscript of this book in various stages of its long and not always prosperous embryological development and have given me the benefit of a page-by-page and sometimes line-by-line commentary. I owe only a little less to the detailed criticisms of Frederick Anderson, James M. Cox, and John W. Ward.

I could not have written the book without the fellowship granted me at just the right time by the Institute for Advanced Studies in the Behavioral Sciences at Stanford, California, where Ralph W. Tyler presides genially over the best place to work I have ever encountered. I have also received substantial grants-in-aid from the Committee on Research of the Academic Senate, University of California, Berkeley.

I should like to express my thanks to the editors of the *Harvard Library Bulletin* and to the Regents of the University of Wisconsin for permission to use portions of essays that were first published in the *Bulletin* (Spring, 1955) and in *The Frontier in Perspective,* edited by Walker D. Wyman and Clifton B. Kroeber (Madison, 1957). Finally, I am extremely grateful to the Trustees of the Mark Twain Estate for permission to quote several passages from unpublished writings of Mark Twain.

H. N. S.

Berkeley
January 1962

CONTENTS

I

Two Ways of Viewing the World

IN a short dramatic monologue published in a newspaper in 1866 under the title "Sabbath Reflections" Mark Twain depicts a man trying to maintain a state of mind proper to the day despite vexing interruptions. The piece is not finished or profound, but it deals with a theme to which he would return again and again in his later work:

This is the day set apart by a benignant Creator for rest—for repose from the wearying toils of the week, and for calm and serious [Brown's dog has commenced to howl again—I wonder why Brown persists in keeping that dog chained up?] meditation upon those tremendous subjects pertaining to our future existence. How thankful we ought to be [There goes that rooster, now.] for this sweet respite; how fervently we ought to lift up our voice and [Confound that old hen—lays an egg every forty minutes, and then cackles until she lays the next one.] testify our gratitude. How sadly, how soothingly the music of that deep-toned bell floats up from the distant church! How gratefully we murmur [Scat!—that old gray tom-cat is always bully-ragging that other one—got him down, now, and digging the hair out of him by the handful.] thanksgiving for these Sabbath blessings.*

The remarks not enclosed by brackets resemble a soliloquy on the stage in that they are to be imagined as spoken aloud even though no interlocutor is present. The remarks within brackets represent unspoken thoughts, somewhat in the manner of O'Neill's *Strange Interlude*. They express a different level of the speaker's consciousness. The two levels are kept distinct by differences in diction, syntax, and imagery corresponding to the familiar rhetorical categories of high and low. As the speaker's serenity is disturbed by the succession of vulgar noises the language of his paren-

* The notes, which begin on page 191, are keyed to page and line of text.

thetical comments grows more and more violently colloquial until he bursts out in his exclamation about the cat fight.

Mark Twain assumes that his audience will recognize the speaker's two levels of experience. They represent the realm of the ideal, the locus of values, and the realm of everyday reality, the locus of facts. The contrast between them was so familiar to Mark Twain's contemporaries that it seemed axiomatic. Exploiting such a contrast for comic purposes was a convention of native American humor, and even in the crudest efforts the effect depended on the reader's intuitive awareness of a conflict between two ways of viewing the world. Mark Twain is dealing with the issue described twenty years earlier in Emerson's remark that the American people "have their intellectual culture from one country, and their duties from another." The speaker in the sketch is trying to will himself into experiencing emotions prescribed by literary and theological tradition but inappropriate to his actual circumstances. His predicament corresponds to the elaboration of Emerson's thesis in the celebrated lecture on "The Genteel Tradition in American Philosophy" delivered by George Santayana in 1911, a year after Mark Twain's death. America, said Santayana, "is a country with two mentalities, one a survival of the beliefs and standards of the fathers, the other an expression of the instincts, practice, and discoveries of the younger generations." No doubt the same could be said of almost any country at almost any time. But both Emerson and Santayana were talking about a state of affairs that was especially characteristic of the United States in the middle and later nineteenth century.

Santayana uses "genteel tradition" as a synonym for "the hereditary philosophy," and he defines philosophy broadly to include any "distinct vision of the universe and definite convictions about human destiny," whether or not they are systematically set forth. In this sense he could see in the work of the American humorists (among whom he names no one besides Mark Twain) "some indications of a truly native philosophy" because, together with Whitman, they had made the only considerable effort "to escape from the genteel tradition, and to express something worth expressing behind its back." Nevertheless, Santayana concluded that the humorists "only half escape the genteel tradition . . . for they have nothing solid to put in its place."

It is true that the native humorists were not equipped with a philosophy substantial enough to replace the genteel tradition, but their affirmations were of greater consequence than anyone realized fifty years ago. The transformation of American literary taste that was then just beginning to make itself evident has conferred historical importance on what once seemed merely the irresponsible antics of the funny men. During the two or three decades following the First World War, the attitudes Santayana taught us to call genteel virtually disappeared from serious literature. A phenomenon of this magnitude can hardly be ascribed to a single cause, but the twentieth-century repudiation of traditional modes of thought and feeling has found its most characteristic expression in the creation of a standard American prose derived from the colloquial style of Mark Twain and his less talented predecessors among the native humorists.

This style, like all styles, implies a characteristic vision of the universe —in Santayana's term, a philosophy. What was the philosophy Mark Twain discovered in the humorists, and what use did he make of it?

In seeking answers to these questions, we must make a special effort to avoid seeing Mark Twain merely as a spokesman for the emergent energies of the frontier, the West, in opposition to established tradition. Although Van Wyck Brooks's *The Ordeal of Mark Twain* (1920) and Bernard De Voto's *Mark Twain's America* (1932) are necessary starting points for the study of his work, both books are flawed by such a distortion. Brooks is correct in his perception that Mark Twain was hampered by the necessity for accommodating himself to conventional attitudes at variance with his deepest impulses; De Voto is also correct in emphasizing Mark Twain's debt to native American humor and the subversive character of his best work. But both critics draw too sharp a contrast between West and East, between the supposedly primitive frontier environment of Mark Twain's youth and the New England where he lived when he was writing his principal books. Hannibal and the Far West were not so primitive as Brooks imagined; the inhibitions with which Mark Twain struggled were not peculiar to the East, as De Voto implied, but were implanted in him by his boyhood environment more deeply than by any later experience. Nor was his audience predominantly Western. Some Western critics denounced him violently and some of the most enthusiastic praise of his work came from the East. His work was shaped by two opposed forces, but they cannot be neatly identified with different regions. The conflict was rather between the conventional assumptions he shared with most of his countrymen and an impulse to reject these assumptions, also widely shared, that found expression in humor.

If geography has any meaning in this connection, it lies in the fact that

3

spokesmen for the conventional American culture attempted to maintain a connection with Europe. On the other hand, the tradition of humor that shaped Mark Twain's apprenticeship was indigenous insofar as anything in our culture can properly be so called. The cult of oral storytelling in the United States dated from colonial times, and had long given prominence to humorous anecdotes. It had undergone a rapid subliterary development during the two or three decades preceding the Civil War when amateur and later semiprofessional writers both in New England and in the South began to commit oral humor to print on a large scale in newspapers, magazines, and eventually books. In all its varied forms—tales, dialogues, essays, sketches, dramatic skits—the most usual subject matter of this humor was the language and the attitudes ascribed to uneducated characters of inferior social status. Although the humorists often pretended to be illiterate, they were exploiting a contrast between rural simplicity and urban sophistication that has affinities with the tradition of literary pastoral. Uncouth manners and speech could easily become a mask for homely wisdom and rugged honesty that were an implicit indictment of empty elegance and refinement. Thus native humor provided Mark Twain with themes, situations, a style, and above all a point of view hostile to the values ostensibly dominant in American culture.

The most obvious distinction between "straight" and "low" characters in writing of this sort lay in their speech; the exploitation of local dialects was one of the most common sources of comedy. It is therefore appropriate to use the term "vernacular" to designate not only the language of rustic or backwoods characters but also the values, the ethical and aesthetic assumptions, they represent. Here is the focus about which cluster the native instincts and discoveries Santayana discerned in the work of the American humorists.

2

In Mark Twain's "Sabbath Reflections" conventional and vernacular attitudes appear as conflicting impulses in a single character. This shorthand treatment would not have been feasible if both the writer and his readers had not been thoroughly familiar with the general theme. But since he could count on his audience, he could use his device to achieve an effect of some complexity. The pose of serenity that the speaker tries to maintain—significantly attuned to the sound of a church bell—is of course the attitude prescribed by the official culture, whereas the dog, chickens, and cats represent reality as perceived from a vernacular perspective. Mark Twain takes a mischievous pleasure in depicting the breakdown of the prescribed attitude under pressure from the realm of the commonplace. The speaker's effort to conform to the dictates of convention by inducing proper feelings in himself is represented as a comic pretension.

His choice is between trying to protect an illusory ideal and accepting the actual world of experience. In this context the vernacular attitude appears as a species of naturalism. It is inherently opposed to the dominant culture, whose values are confined to an ideal realm. The cult of ideality pervades the writings of the authors, British as well as American, that were most widely read in the United States in the mid-nineteenth century. A convenient source of illustration is the work of Josiah G. Holland, who was in the later 1860's "the most successful man of letters in the United States, measured either by the number of his readers or by the solid pecuniary rewards that had come to him." Holland was an editorial writer for Samuel Bowles's *Springfield Republican,* and one of the most popular lyceum speakers in the country. During the season 1859–60, for example, he traveled almost twenty thousand miles and delivered one hundred and fifty-six lectures and public addresses. At his death the New York *Evening Post* said that "He thought the thoughts of the average American citizen." An interesting light is thrown on regional differences in taste by the editorial writer's further remark that "to the more staid and critical East, it was a constant amazement to see the extent of his fame; but once beyond the Alleghenies his books sold by scores, and perhaps hundreds, where even Longfellow and Whittier sold by twos and threes."

Mark Twain's skill in capturing the tone of the dominant culture becomes evident if "Sabbath Reflections" is placed beside a passage from Holland. With the interruptions eliminated, the Sabbath monologue reads as follows.

This is the day set apart by a benignant Creator for rest—for repose from the wearying toils of the week, and for calm and serious meditation upon those tremendous subjects pertaining to our future existence. How thankful we ought to be for this sweet respite; how fervently we ought to lift up our voice and testify our gratitude. How sadly, how soothingly the music of that deep-toned bell floats up from the distant church! How gratefully we murmur thanksgiving for these Sabbath blessings.

Holland habitually wrote in just such a vein of relentless didacticism. The following passage, for example, appeared in a collection of his lyceum lectures published in 1861 under the title *Lessons in Life*.

Let us suppose that in a country journey we arrive at the summit of a hill, at whose foot lies a charming village imbosomed in trees from the midst of which rises the white spire of the village church. If we are in a poetical mood, we say: "How beautiful is this retirement! This quiet retreat, away from the world's distractions and great temptations, must be the abode of domestic and social virtue—the home of contentment, of peace, and of an unquestioning Christian faith. Fortunate are those whose lot it is to be born and to pass their days here, and to be buried at last in the little graveyard behind the Church." As we see the children playing upon the grass, and the tidy matrons sitting in their doorways, and the farmers at work in the fields, and the quiet inn, with its brooding piazzas like wings waiting for the shelter of its guests, the scene fills us with a rare poetic delight.

This is the tone that Mark Twain's speaker is trying to maintain. Surprisingly enough, Holland also focuses attention on the discrepancy between ideal and real. He continues:

In the midst of our little rapture, however, a communicative villager comes along, and we question him. We are shocked to learn that the inn is a very bad place, with a drunken landlord, that there is a quarrel in the church which is about to drive the old pastor away, that there is not a man in the village who would not leave if he could sell his property, that the women give free rein to their propensity for scandal, and that half of the children of the place are down with the measles.

The contrast established here, even to the hint of comic anticlimax in the reference to the measles, resembles the contrast between Mark Twain's Sabbath reverie and the discordant noises of animals. In such a situation, he considers that the raucous facts discredit the rhapsody. This was the assumption of the writers who would call themselves "realists" in the 1880's and 1890's: the drunken landlord, the quarrel in the church, and the gossiping housewives sound like material for a realistic novel of village life. But Holland's position is the exact opposite of the realists': he is a staunch defender of the doctrine of ideality that would soon become their principal target. "The true poet," he continues, "sees things not always as they are, but as they ought to be. He insists upon congruity and consistency. Such a life should be in such a spot, under such circumstances;

and no unwarped and unpolluted mind can fail to see that the poet's ideal is the embodiment of God's will."

Holland's distinction between the poet's ideal and things as they are is a debased version of the romantic irony that had once been able to engender a major literature. In the course of two generations a mode of vision with genuinely tragic implications had been transformed into a mindless optimism, a device for conjuring away everything disturbing or unpleasant by declaring it contrary to God's will and therefore not truly real. As soon as the doctrine of ideality preached by Holland and such contemporaries as Henry Ward Beecher was subjected to the scrutiny of common sense it became ridiculous, for it had no substance: it was mere empty rhetoric.

Because the target is so vulnerable, the comic effect of the "Sabbath Reflections" is achieved too easily. Mark Twain accepts the divorce between fact and value and bluntly affirms the fact. The burlesque seems to rely on a crude naturalism that is simply an inversion of the doctrine it attacks. When we are invited to prefer a reality defined by barnyard noises to the spurious ideal values of the speaker's reverie, neither alternative seems satisfactory. The reader familiar with Mark Twain's later work will nevertheless be able to detect even here the dim outlines of the imaginative vision that would sustain the powerful affirmations of *Adventures of Huckleberry Finn*. Over a period of years Mark Twain would sharpen his recognition of the weaknesses in genteel pretensions, and the increase in analytical penetration would reveal to him more fully the values he could endorse. What he really objected to was the distorting effect of conventional notions of propriety on the individual's responses to experience. He came to see that the habit of conformity is more stifling to human freedom than any physical constraint because it subjects the most inward thoughts and feelings to control from without.

The speaker in the sketch has acquired from many sermons a stereotyped image of what the "sweet respite" of the Sabbath should be, and he is determined that what should be, shall be. Even in the face of distracting interruptions and the increasing rebellion of his own impulses he bears out his fiction to the end. In his last phrase he insists he is grateful for "these Sabbath blessings" despite the fact that the supposed respite is actually a series of nerve-racking noises. His determination to conform to the dictates of cultural tradition shuts him off from the natural world, which seems to him merely vulgar.

7

If Mark Twain had followed out the implications of the sketch he would have been obliged to specify in what respects the order of experience defined by barking dogs and fighting cats is superior to that defined by the sound of the church bell and meditation on our future existence. It was not—and is not—a simple question, but he would have to find an answer to it before he would be able to write anything of greater consequence than a newspaper sketch.

3

A number of characters appearing briefly in Mark Twain's newspaper articles of the 1860's have traits that can be recognized as vernacular. One is the nameless stage driver in his description of a long cold night ride over the Sierra Nevada in September 1863—the man who was taking "a bottle of nasty rotten medicine" to sustain life for "the folks at the Thirty-five Mile House," and kept Mark Twain from going to sleep and falling off the box by describing the wildly improbable injuries suffered by a former passenger. Another vernacular character is the Virginia City newspaper editor who could not whistle hard tunes but "could swear and make up telegraph news with any man"; who was adept at "commercial seven-up"; and who was "neck and crop and neck and heels for his friends, and blood, hair and the ground tore up to his enemies." The final cadence, with its surrealist syntax, is a particularly apt illustration of the role of language in Mark Twain's effort to establish a new perspective. It imports into the atmosphere of the newspaper office words and images derived from tall tales about backwoods gouging contests. "Neck and crop" and the dialect participle "tore" bring with them the imaginary rural world, the homespun Arcadia that was the constant poetic resource of native humor.

Still another vernacular character is Old Mother Utterback of Arkansas, introduced in a reminiscence of Mississippi steamboating entitled "Captain Montgomery":

Whenever he commenced helping anybody, Captain Ed. Montgomery never relaxed his good offices as long as help was needed.

As soon as he found that no steamboat ever stopped to wood with Old Mother Utterback in the bend below Grand Gulf, Mississippi, and that she was poor and needed assistance, he began to stop there every trip and take her little pile of wood and smile grimly, when the engineers protested that it wouldn't burn any more than so many icicles—and stop there again the very next trip. He used to go ashore and talk to the old woman, and it flattered her to the last degree to be on such sociable terms with the high chief officer of a splendid passenger steamer. She would welcome him to her shabby little floorless log cabin with a royal flourish, and make her six gawky "gals" fly around and make him comfortable. He used to bring his lady passengers ashore to be entertained with Mother Utterback's quaint conversation.

I do not know that this incident is worth recording, but still, as it may let in the light of instruction to some darkened mind, I will just set down the circumstances of one of Captain Montgomery's visits to Mother Utterback and her daughters. He brought some fine ladies with him to enjoy the old woman's talk.

"Good morning, Captain Montgomery!" said she with many a bustling bow and flourish; "Good morning, Captain Montgomery; good morning, ladies all; how de do, Captain Montgomery—how de do—how de do? Sakes alive, it 'pears to me it's ben years since I seed you. Fly around, gals, fly around! You Bets, you slut, highst yoself off'n that candle-box and give it to the lady. How *have* you ben, Captain Montgomery?—make yoself at home, ladies all—you 'Liza Jane, stan' out of the way—move yoself! Thar's the jug, help yoself, Captain Montgomery; take that cob out and make yoself free, Captain Montgomery—and ladies all. You Sal, you hussy, git up f'm thar this minit, and take some exercise! for the land's sake, ain't you got no sense at all?—settin' thar on that cold rock and you jes' ben married last night, and your pores all open!"

The ladies wanted to go aboard the boat, they bade the kind, hospitable old woman good by, and went away. But Captain Montgomery staid behind, because he knew how badly the old lady wanted to talk, and he was a good soul and loved to please her.

Like many other humorous sketches, this is the description of a practical joke. Captain Montgomery exposes the fine ladies to Mother Utterback in order to enjoy their discomfiture. It is a device for confronting genteel and vernacular characters, and the Captain follows an established procedure of the humorists in contriving the situation. Mother Utterback's monologue, in fact, has the air of being a set piece, a classic bit of steamboatmen's folklore set down from memory. Mark Twain associates it with an actual person, and one is tempted to think of Captain Montgomery as a gifted storyteller with a recognized repertory, an artist of the sort who keep an oral narrative tradition alive. Such a hypothesis would help to resolve the problem presented by the punch line about Sal's physical condition, which is bawdier than anything else in Mark Twain's publicly acknowledged writings. The point needs to be made that he was as a rule markedly reticent about sex in print—much more reticent than

9

a number of his predecessors. The backwoods tradition of American humor was faithful to the ancient conception of country matters. George W. Harris' *Sut Lovingood Yarns,* for example, "the nearest thing to the undiluted oral humor of the Middle West that has found its way into print," takes advantage of a thick screen of dialect to engage in a highly explicit treatment of upcountry love-making.

In his writing for Far Western newspapers Mark Twain displays a rather schoolboyish interest in female anatomy, whether of the "clipper-built" Adah Isaacs Menken or of nude Hawaiian maidens in swimming. We know also that he cherished for many years the recollection of such indecent anecdotes as the masterpiece of Jim Gillis which is unfortunately known to posterity only by its title, "The Burning Shame." Yet in view of the tone of conversation in the print shops and pilot houses and mining camps where Mark Twain worked as a young man, it is surprising how infrequent are the passages either in his notebooks or in his published writing that indulge in impropriety about sex. He habitually plays with allusions to drinking and gambling and offensive smells that were by contemporary standards unrefined, but he seldom fails to exhibit a conventional respect for ideal womanhood. When he became a writer of books he abandoned even the mild indecencies of his apprentice days. In the fictive worlds of his later work sexuality has almost no place. His characterization of Joan of Arc, which he sometimes considered his major achievement, presupposes an intensely conventional attitude toward female purity. Despite his attack on many aspects of the cult of ideality, he was farther than Henry James or Howells from anticipating the revolution in attitudes toward sex that has become so conspicuous in American fiction of the twentieth century.

In short, it seems unlikely that the bawdy climax of Mother Utterback's monologue is of Mark Twain's own invention. His imagination did not move freely in this area. The part of the sketch that bears his personal stamp is the details of characterization which he presumably added to the remembered monologue, the rendering of the old woman's warmth and vitality in contrast with the colorless ladies from the boat. In no more words than would go into a short lyric poem Mark Twain endows her with an old-fashioned courtliness sadly eroded by two or three generations of life in the backwoods (she assumes her elegant guests will enjoy a swig of whiskey out of the jug), and with the personal force of a matriarch.

Two Ways of Viewing the World

The effect of "Jim Smiley and His Jumping Frog" (1865), the sketch that won for Mark Twain his first national reputation, also depends upon the rather mysterious charm of the vernacular spokesman, Simon Wheeler. Wheeler is a good-natured derelict "dozing comfortably by the bar-room stove of the dilapidated tavern" in the Mother Lode ghost town of Angel's Camp. He is "fat and bald-headed," with "an expression of winning gentleness and simplicity upon his tranquil countenance." Wheeler's simplicity is evident in the fact that he is dazzled by heroic memories of the "transcendent genius" of both Jim Smiley, owner of the celebrated jumping frog, and the stranger who won the bet by filling Smiley's frog with shot. But this simplicity and even the preposterous story about the frog, which was current in the mining camps, are less significant than Wheeler's gentleness and tranquillity. He shares with Mother Utterback the vernacular traits of basic good will and freedom from the kind of inner conflict suffered by the speaker in "Sabbath Reflections." Left behind in this backwater by the vanished mining boom, he dwells on the elegiac theme of mute inglorious Miltons. Smiley's handicapped dog Andrew Jackson, he says, "would have made a name for hisself if he'd lived, for the stuff was in him, and he had genius—I know it, because he hadn't no opportunities to speak of, and it don't stand to reason that a dog could make such a fight as he could under them circumstances, if he hadn't no talent." Even Daniel Webster, the frog, is an example of great abilities frustrated by circumstance. "Smiley said all a frog wanted was education, and he could do 'most anything—and I believe him." After three months of intensive training Daniel could "nail a fly every time as fur as he could see him." But he was cheated of the triumph he deserved by the stranger's trick.

Wheeler is however not aware of the note of apology in his tale, and the theme is subordinate to the creation of a grotesque fictive world lacking the stresses imposed on men in the real world who must exhibit approved attitudes in order to achieve power and status. Just as Mother Utterback is unconstrained by the embarrassment and guilt with which the traditional culture had surrounded human sexuality, Wheeler is indifferent to the competitive self-consciousness of an acquisitive society. Both characters represent gestures of escape from the pale negations and paler affirmations of the genteel tradition; they are the beginnings of an effort to "express something worth expressing behind its back."

4

Although many of Mark Twain's earliest comic pieces are mere verbal pranks and hoaxes, his treatment of the dominant culture is nearly always hostile. But his attitude changes during his trip to the Sandwich Islands in the spring and summer of 1866. He shows signs of being attracted toward some of the attitudes he had previously satirized. The change in orientation was apparently related to a change in his conception of himself. In his dispatches about Hawaii, especially those written after his return to San Francisco, he began experimenting with a new identity as if he were trying on a ready-made suit of clothes. Yet he had not fully decided to buy it; he still reverted often to earlier attitudes.

The explanation for this wavering is probably to be found in the change of status brought about by his commission as traveling correspondent for the Sacramento *Union*. The new role must be viewed against the background of his life during the previous four or five years. When he had come West in 1861, an unsympathetic observer might have charged with some justice that he was ignominiously running away from the war. In Nevada and California he called himself a Bohemian and adopted in both his life and his writing a pose of gay indifference to national politics or any other serious matters. After he moved from Virginia City to San Francisco in 1864 he worked for a few weeks on the *Morning Call* but he could not force himself to do routine work and soon resigned—or was fired. For more than a year he had no income except what he could pick up as a free-lance contributor to the *Golden Era,* the *Californian,* and other local periodicals. On one occasion he probably spent a night in jail on a charge of being drunk and disorderly. He says in *Roughing It* that for a certain period of two months he "did not earn a penny, or buy an article of any kind, or pay board." He loafed most of the winter of 1864–65 with a group of pocket miners in a ghost town on the Mother Lode. Back in San Francisco, he tried living on his credit again until his friend and former employer Joe Goodman rescued him by contracting to buy a daily letter for the *Territorial Enterprise.* Five months of heroic exertions enabled him to pay his debts but, as he said, he found he was "unspeakably tired" of the regular grind. In this extremity, "fortune favored, and I got a new berth and a delightful one": he persuaded the *Union* to send him to the Sandwich Islands for the purpose of writing up the sugar industry.

This assignment tended to detach him from his irresponsible Bohemianism and make him into a spokesman for respectable opinion. To be sure, he still considered that his primary obligation was to be amusing. But he made intermittent efforts to live up to his new role by representing himself as a relatively dignified traveler and inventing a traveling companion named Brown to take the vernacular point of view. Thus he writes: "In this connection it may not be out of place to insert an extract from a book of Hawaiian travels recently published by a visiting minister of the gospel." Whereupon Brown, who has been looking over the writer's shoulder, retorts, "Well, now *I* wouldn't, if I was you." The narrator's rebuke to him is primly elegant: "I wish you would indulge yourself in some little respite from my affairs and interest yourself in your own business sometimes." Brown, unabashed, launches into a diatribe against "these mush-and-milk preacher travels":

Father Damon [Damien] has got stacks of books shoemakered up by them pious bushwhackers from America, and they're the flattest reading—they are sicker than the smart things children say in the newspapers . . . You just look at Rev. Cheever's book and Anderson's—and when they come to the volcano, or any sort of heavy scenery, and it is too much bother to describe it, they shovel in another lot of Scripture, and wind up with "Lo! what God hath wrought!" Confound their lazy melts!

The narrator's reply stiffly asserts his own gentility:

Mr. Brown, I brought you with me on this voyage merely because a newspaper correspondent should travel in some degree of state, and so command the respect of strangers; I did not expect you to assist me in my literary labors with your crude ideas. You may desist from further straining your intellect for the present.

The relation of the narrator to Brown is another variant on the device of bringing straight and vernacular characters into collision. Although Mark Twain voices through Brown his own criticism of the clergymen's travel books, he is ostensibly identified with the narrator who speaks in the first person. This ironic use of a first-person narrator with genteel attitudes exposed Mark Twain to a temptation he did not always resist. Sometimes, particularly toward the end of the series, he launches into flights of eloquence about the landscape that seem to be seriously intended and are not subjected to Brown's deflation. On such occasions Mark Twain shifts his tacit commitment from one pole to the other of the basic pattern, and adopts the attitudes to be expected in a spokesman for the dominant culture.

He was evidently impelled in this direction by his impulse to accept the point of view of the businessmen in whose behalf he was investigating commercial opportunities in the Pacific. During his four months in the islands he discovered with surprise that his commission from the *Union* made him a man of importance. Soon after his arrival in Honolulu he wrote to his mother and sister that he had dined in the company of the American minister with the King's Chamberlain, "who is related to the royal family, and although darker than a mulatto . . . has an excellent English education and in manners is an accomplished gentleman." The Chamberlain was to call for him next day "with his carriage, and we will visit the King at the palace—both are good Masons—the King is a Royal Arch Mason." This was only the beginning. A few weeks later he could report:

Hon. Anson Burlingame, U. S. Minister to China, and Gen. Van Valkenburgh, Minister to Japan, with their families and suites, have just arrived here *en route*. They were going to do me the honor to call on me this morning, and that accounts for my being out of bed now [he had been ill]. You know what condition my room is always in when you are not around—so I climbed out of bed and dressed and shaved pretty quick and went up to the residence of the American Minister and called on *them*. Mr. Burlingame told me a good deal about Hon. Jere Clemens and that Virginia Clemens who was wounded in a duel. He was in Congress years with both of them. Mr. B. sent for his son, to introduce him—said he could tell that frog story of mine as well as anybody . . . At his request I have loaned Mr. Burlingame pretty much everything I ever wrote [evidently in scrapbooks of clippings] . . . I stopped three days with Hon. Mr. Cony, Deputy Marshal of the Kingdom, at Hilo, Hawaii, last week and by a funny circumstance he knew everybody that I ever knew in Hannibal and Palmyra. We used to sit up all night talking and then sleep all day. He lives like a prince.

Within a few days Burlingame, who was "acknowledged to have no superior in the diplomatic circles of the world," had invited the correspondent to visit him in China. "I expect to do all this," Mark Twain declares, "but I expect to go to the States first—and from China to the Paris World's Fair."

The atmosphere was strikingly different from that of the grubby boarding houses and cheap restaurants of San Francisco, but Clemens was acclimatizing himself rapidly: the beadroll of "Hons." and royal chamberlains and relatives in Congress, the discovery that men of the great world were impressed by the literary renown of the author of "Jim Smiley and His Jumping Frog," the plans to go to New York, to China, to Paris, represent a marked change of tone for the newspaperman who had arrived in Honolulu "unheralded and unsung" and with almost no money in his pocket. The lesson of his experience was plain, and Burlingame made it explicit. Toward the end of his life Mark Twain recalled: "Mr. Burlingame gave me some advice one day which I have never forgotten, and which I have lived by for forty years." The advice was, "Avoid inferiors. Seek your comradeships among your superiors in intellect and character; always *climb.*"

Burlingame's imperative was rich in ambiguities. Superiority in intellect: how could it be measured in post–Civil War San Francisco except in terms of commercial success? What could character mean except the traits that would inspire confidence in a banker? Mark Twain, at any rate, seems to have construed climbing as an increasing identification with the dominant forces in the society, that is with the business community. He comments with satisfaction, for example, on the Hawaiian laws that condemn a native employed on a sugar plantation to two days of hard labor "on the reef" for every day he is absent without excuse from his job. He points out that since "the hire of each laborer is $100 a year—just about what it used to cost to board and clothe and doctor a negro" in the prewar South—the use of native labor on the sugar plantations is even more profitable than was the slave system. Better still is the labor of coolies imported by the Hawaiian government from China who work for $5 a month. The correspondent predicts in oracular tones: "You will have Coolie labor in California some day. It is already forcing its superior claims upon the attention of your great mining, manufacturing and public improvement corporations."

In the same vein he can fall into the accents of the spread-eagle orators who had so often celebrated the American advance westward to California and thence into the Pacific. "To America," he writes, "it has been vouchsafed to materialize the vision, and realize the dream of centuries, of the enthusiasts of the old world." San Francisco will become the Golden Gate to the commerce of the Orient, "the almost exclusive trade of the most opulent land on earth . . . the land where the fabled Aladdin's lamp lies buried—and she is the new Aladdin who shall seize it from its obscurity and summon the geni and command him to crown her with power and greatness, and bring to her feet the hoarded treasures of the earth!"

This geopolitical ecstasy is entirely serious. Of course it is a tissue of clichés, but it is on that account only the more interesting; for it reveals an aspect of Mark Twain's personality that makes itself felt again and again in later years. He had a remarkable capacity for entering imaginatively into modes of experience at second hand. It would give him the power to see the world of his childhood from the quite different perspective of Huck Finn, but at the same time it exposed him to a long series of contagions. His gift of empathy was particularly powerful with respect to language. He apprehended tone and rhythm and imagery as if by instinct, and could apparently write at will in almost any style. Like Walt Whitman, and indeed like most of his contemporaries, he was moved to rapture by what seems now mere demagogic rant. When he read the orators of Manifest Destiny he surrendered himself to the plaster-and-gilt opulence of their lofty utterances and came under the spell of their self-hypnosis. In this mood he could forget the pleasure he had taken in deflating genteel bombast, and for the moment could fall a victim to the malady he had so mordantly ridiculed in others.

On such occasions Mark Twain was capable of describing scenery with all the stereotypes of conventional rhetoric. The connection between cheap Hawaiian labor and the splendors of Manifest Destiny is obvious (he spells it out in dollars and tons of sugar), but that between Manifest Destiny and rhapsodies about landscape may not be so clear. What links them is tone: both are facets of what the dominant culture considered exalted and resplendent. In either case it is a question of conceptions larger than life, ideal images rising above the niggling limitations of everyday routine to the plane of sublimity.

5

The vision of San Francisco as the new Aladdin crowned with power and greatness occurs in the last Hawaiian dispatch but one. For his climax, at the end of the series, Mark Twain used a long description of the volcano Kilauea that he had held back for this purpose from its chronological place in the report of his travels. It reads in part:

For a mile and a half in front of us and half a mile on either side, the floor of the abyss was magnificently illuminated; beyond these limits the mists hung down their gauzy curtains and cast a deceptive gloom over all that made the twinkling fires in the remote corners of the crater seem countless leagues removed—made them seem like the camp-fires of a great army far away. Here was room for the imagination to work! You could imagine those lights the width of a continent away—and that hidden under the intervening darkness were hills, and winding rivers, and weary wastes of plain and desert —and even then the tremendous vista stretched on, and on, and on!—to the fires and far beyond! You could not compass it—it was the idea of eternity made tangible—and the longest end of it made visible to the naked eye!

Mark Twain is experimenting with rhetorical devices for creating the mood prescribed for cultivated observers of the natural sublime. The syntax is artfully managed. After the restraint suggested by the periodic structure of the opening, emotion bursts out in the brief exclamatory second sentence and is given full sway in the paratactic conclusion, broken into short elements set off by dashes that suggest quickened breathing. The diction follows a similar pattern, progressing from the abstract formality of "magnificently illuminated" by way of such bookish phrases as "gauzy curtains," "deceptive gloom," and "countless leagues" and the implications of physical vastness in "width of a continent" and "tremendous vista" to the climactic invocation of the idea of eternity. As is almost invariably the case when Mark Twain is working up a rhetorical effect, he resorts to conspicuous alliteration ("winding rivers, and weary wastes," "to the fires and far beyond," "eternity made tangible").

At the peak of exaltation, however, he suddenly deflates the mood he has created by a comic turn—the deliberately colloquial reference to "the longest end" of eternity. The glowing lava reminds him of hell, which he flippantly indicates as the place where he and his readers will spend the afterlife. The idea is repeated later in the dispatch in a reference to the vapors rising from the crater: "The smell of sulphur is strong, but not unpleasant to a sinner."

The abrupt shift in tone reveals a curious and significant attitude in Mark Twain toward the problem of prose style. He marshals stereotyped procedures for describing an awesome natural phenomenon as easily as if he were a carpenter-builder ordering plaster-of-paris cornices or jigsaw moldboards from a catalogue. Yet he feels self-conscious about his own facility. After all, he has written a good many pieces like "Sabbath Reflections" ridiculing precisely this kind of rhetoric. In order to disavow his pretentiousness he takes refuge in mockery of it. The pattern is illustrated in brief compass by the entry he made in the Visitors' Book of the Volcano House at the time of his visit to Kilauea, which associates the vulgar deflation with Brown but at the same time implies that the author's raptures were the result of drunkenness:

I mused and said "How the stupendous grandeur of this magnificently terrible and sublime manifestation of celestial power doth fill the poetic soul with grand thoughts and grander images; and how the overpowering solemnity"
(Here the gin gave out. In the careless hands of Brown the bottle broke.)

It is amusing, incidentally, how even in this obvious caricature the eloquence of the description carries over into the style of the comic interruption. "In the careless hands of Brown the bottle broke" is periodic in structure, elegantly impersonal in tone (the epithet "careless" is applied to the hands, not to the man himself), alliterative, and noticeably metrical.

If both the rhetoric and the reaction against it are mere stylistic exercises, can we discover what Mark Twain's attitude toward the volcano actually was? The question is ultimately unanswerable insofar as it concerns the mental processes of Samuel L. Clemens, since we can know nothing about them except what he wrote, and he could express himself only by means of established linguistic and stylistic conventions of one kind or another. But a distinction can be made with some confidence between a style worked up according to a formula, and a style using a more spontaneous diction and imagery. The later paragraphs of the description of Kilauea contain a series of homely, nonpoetic images: the floor of the crater "looked like a colossal railroad map of the State of Massachusetts done in chain lightning on a midnight sky"; torrents of lava branched out from holes in the crust "like the 'spokes' of a lady's fan" or "made a long succession of sharp worm-fence angles," crossing and recrossing one another "like skate tracks on a popular skating ground." The molten lava had "about the consistency of mush," and a distant pool of it "looked very little more respectable than a schoolhouse on fire." "We heard a week ago," says Mark Twain even more colloquially, "that the volcano was getting on a heavier spree than it had indulged in for many years, and I am glad we arrived just at the right moment to see it under full blast." A final comparison likens the noise of the volcano to the sounds made by a low-pressure steamer on the Mississippi.

These allusions are derived from firsthand experience; they lack the exotic overtones of such images as "gauzy curtains" and "the camp-fires of a great army," or the imposing dignity of the idea of eternity. In that sense they provide a "natural" medium of description, bringing us as close as we are likely to get to the writer's actual experience of Kilauea. He is making a serious but unself-conscious effort to convey to the reader an exact impression of the spectacle. It is the style of an expert journalist without literary pretensions. The unusually high incidence of imagery is due to the fact that he is describing an unfamiliar phenomenon that he finds imposing. Mark Twain would eventually make a style of this kind, with a simpler syntax, into his normal expository and narrative medium, and it would exert an influence on much American prose of the twentieth century. Now, however, he was still in his apprenticeship, not sure of his role and his audience and uncertain what style he should adopt if he wished to follow the career of a writer as distinguished from that of a journalist. He would have to go through a long period of experimentation before he could discover—or rather, invent and perfect—the style in which he could say exactly what he wanted to say.

6

The next phase of Mark Twain's apprenticeship led him to the lecture platform. Soon after he returned to San Francisco he delivered a discourse on the Sandwich Islands in which the description of Kilauea was a central feature. Although he repeated the lecture perhaps a hundred times over a period of seven years, he was never able to achieve a stable attitude toward his own exalted rhetoric. Sometimes he treated it seriously, sometimes he made fun of it. The Boston *Daily Advertiser,* reviewing the Sandwich Islands lecture, reported on 11 November 1869:

> The audience gets into a queer state after a while. It knows not what to trust: for while much is meant to be seriously taken, the fun is felt to be the real life of the thing; and yet they never know where the fun will come in. Even when Mr. Clemens has made a really fine period, or introduced a brilliant descriptive passage, he takes pains to turn the affair into a joke at the end. As, for instance, after a very graphic and well written description of the great volcanic eruption in the Sandwich Islands, delivered with perfect indifference and almost as with an effort—he paused for just an instant, and then said in the same passionless tone "There! I'm glad I've got that volcano off my mind."

He had several other ways of undercutting his own oratory. He might comment, "Let someone beat that for harnessing adjectives together." He sometimes applauded himself at the end of the passage until the audience joined in. More subtly, toward the end of the description he would pretend to forget a word so as to break the spell in which he held the audience and prevent the tempest of applause that would otherwise have followed. Yet he continued to include the description of Kilauea in his performance, and audiences continued to delight in it. As late as 1873, when he took the lecture to England, the Liverpool *Journal* reported that "perhaps the greatest surprise after all was the sudden introduction at different points of the lecture without any notice or change of manner of two of the most eloquent pieces of descriptive composition that ever fell from the lips of man." One of these was the passage about the volcano.

7

These examples of Mark Twain's apprentice work illustrate Santayana's thesis that in the nineteenth century the United States was a country of two mentalities. Many of the comic devices presuppose a conflict between an established culture having for its focus the notion of ideality, and unrefined impulses originating in everyday experience, the vulgar world of the natural man. In the pastoral situation that Mark Twain took over from earlier humorists he found the means for dramatizing this conflict by bringing straight characters of conventional outlook face to face with vernacular characters who were indifferent or hostile to conventions and proprieties. The conflict could also be expressed through a contrast of styles: elevated rhetoric and diction versus colloquial speech and commonplace images. Although the vernacular impulse was potentially subversive of the traditional culture, Mark Twain did not perceive the issue abstractly. His mind was that of an artist; he thought in presentational rather than discursive terms. Nevertheless, his handling of comic situations and of contrasting styles shows an intuitive awareness of the cultural problem that Emerson and Santayana described. He was feeling his way toward the recognition that the traditional culture was decadent because it had lost the power to relate its values to actual experience.

Despite Santayana's charge that the humorists had no positive values to put in the place of the tradition they were attacking, Mark Twain's vernacular characters at least suggest the possibility of a view of life preferable to the attitudes implied by the notion of ideality—an integrated vision of the universe that could perceive ideal values within the realm of the commonplace. But it is no more than a hint. At the time when Mark Twain left San Francisco for the East, a perceptive observer might have entertained hopes for his development into a major writer, for he had already displayed a remarkable technical ability and flashes of insight, but it would have been reckless to speak of sustained accomplishment. His wavering between acceptance and rejection of conventional attitudes showed he still lacked a stable perspective from which to deal with the conflict of values in American culture.

II

Pilgrims and Sinners

THE *Innocents Abroad* was Mark Twain's first effort to construct a book-length narrative. Since he made it out of dispatches not written according to a preconceived scheme, we can follow the steps he took in attempting to solve his problems of composition. He had had relatively few predecessors in writing about the Far West or Hawaii, but now he was dealing with staple subjects of European and American literature. His sensitivity to the attitudes and styles he encountered in guidebooks and works of travel made it hard for him to find a center and establish a perspective. Furthermore, as newspaper correspondent he had customarily written in a mode that freely mingled straight reporting with fanciful improvisation. The question of genre had hardly occurred to him. As a result, *The Innocents Abroad* is partly a journalist's account of what he saw on his travels, partly an autobiography with strong subjective coloring, and partly, because his artist's imagination responded to the challenge, a fictional narrative, an embryonic novel.

The various kinds of writing shade into one another in a fashion that often baffles analysis. The retailing of guidebook facts such as the dimensions of Milan cathedral or the names of famous people buried in Père Lachaise cemetery may be disregarded here because it has little bearing on Mark Twain's development as an imaginative writer. But this exclusion still leaves a wide range of literary modes to be considered. In the parts of the book that go beyond routine journalism the most useful distinction is between passages in which Mark Twain speaks in his own person and those in which the narrator is to some extent a fictitious character, a narrative persona. The fictional element throws most light on his future development but it occupies a relatively small place in the book, and it is embedded in a great deal of other material that is also aimed at literary effects. The best way to discern the true fiction emerging from this confused matrix is to identify first the other varieties of imaginative writing in the narrative.

Much of Mark Twain's effort in *The Innocents Abroad* went into the composition of set pieces of rhetoric describing historical monuments—the Acropolis, the Sphinx—or celebrated places such as the Sea of Galilee or Jerusalem. This kind of thing was a blind alley into which he was directed by environmental pressures that continued to influence him in some degree throughout his career and therefore deserve notice. After the success of his lecture on the Sandwich Islands at the San Francisco Academy of Music in October 1866 he set out on a lecture tour of California and Nevada. His dispatches about Hawaii to the Sacramento *Union* continued to appear until mid-November. The reputation he acquired through this series and through his lectures encouraged him to put into effect the plan he had formed in Hawaii for a trip around the world. On 15 December he set out for New York with an agreement from the San Francisco *Alta California* to buy fifty letters describing his travels at twenty dollars each, but after he reached New York he decided instead (with the consent of the publishers of the *Alta*) to book passage on the *Quaker City* excursion to the Mediterranean and Palestine. When the steamer sailed in June 1867 he was launched upon the most remarkable period of change he would ever experience. During the next two years he became a nationally famous newspaper correspondent and lecturer with a handsome income. In 1870 he married Olivia Langdon of Elmira. He made a false start by taking the editorship of the Buffalo *Express,* but the surprising success of *The Innocents Abroad* revealed to him his true vocation, and in 1871 he sold his interest in the *Express* at a loss in order to settle in Hartford, the headquarters of his publishers, the American Publishing Company. He was definitely committed to a literary career.

Although Mark Twain may have begun making a book out of his *Quaker City* dispatches soon after he returned from the cruise in November 1867, his concentrated work on it began in January 1868 when he accepted the proposal of Elisha Bliss of the American Publishing Company to publish the book by the highly profitable subscription method. The first draft was written in Washington and San Francisco between January and June 1868, and the manuscript went to Bliss late in July. After a strenuous lecture tour during the autumn and winter of 1868–69, in the intervals of which Mark Twain visited Elmira several times and finally secured the consent of Livy's parents to a formal engagement, he began an extensive revision of his manuscript and a struggle with the proofs that lasted through the spring and summer. Livy helped with the proof-reading during his further visits to Elmira, and he added some passages on these occasions.

Mark Twain's active courtship of Livy had begun after the first draft of the book was finished, but the changes that he made in revision were dictated to a considerable extent by his effort to become the kind of writer he thought she wanted him to be. This was not an easy matter, for the publishers and the public conceived of him primarily as the Wild Humorist of the Pacific Slope, whereas she shared the conventional distaste for the antics of newspaper funny men. An incident in December 1868 reveals the difficulties Mark Twain faced. In a transparent effort to present himself in a better light to the Langdons, he included in a Christmas Eve letter to his mentor and adopted "mother," Mrs. Mary Fairbanks, an eloquent paragraph about the Nativity. Mrs. Fairbanks suggested publishing the passage in her husband's paper, the Cleveland *Herald*—because, as Mark Twain wrote Livy, the "reverent spirit is more to my credit than my customary productions." On 6 January he wrote to Mrs. Fairbanks that Livy "wants me to thank you from her heart . . . & she wants a copy of the paper—poor girl, anybody who could convince her that I was not a humorist would secure her eternal gratitude! She thinks a humorist is something perfectly awful. I never put a joke in a letter to her without feeling a pang. Best girl in the world."

This seems clear enough, but the humorous tone suggests Mark Twain may be exaggerating. It is easy to oversimplify his attitude toward the advice of critics interested in improving his taste. He had welcomed the tutelage of Mrs. Fairbanks during the *Quaker City* cruise with only a touch of irony. She shepherded him to prayer meetings, lectured him "awfully" (as he wrote his mother and sister) "on the quarter-deck on moonlit promenading evenings," corrected his copy, and, according to a fellow passenger, on at least one occasion caused him to discard whole pages. Livy and Mrs. Fairbanks were spokesmen for the dominant culture. They merely put into words what Mark Twain recognized as the imperatives that must govern a journalist wishing to achieve the status of a man of letters. He had deleted "passages, paragraphs & chapters" from his manuscript at the suggestion of Bret Harte, whose review in the *Overland Monthly*, although on the whole favorable, shows concern about the "lawlessness and audacity" of the book, the lack of "moral or aesthetic limitation" in its humor.

2

The Innocents Abroad as finally published in 1869 was irreverent enough to evoke hostile criticism; Mark Twain had not renounced his role of humorist. But his eagerness to rise to the social and cultural level represented by Livy and Mrs. Fairbanks led him to make substantial changes in the *Quaker City* letters as he transformed them into a book. He deleted many phrases of the sort Mrs. Fairbanks regarded as slang, and some entire passages that seemed likely to offend refined readers, notably his burlesque versions of the story of Joseph and the parable of the Prodigal Son. More important, he added many passages in the oratorical manner he had experimented with in his newspaper dispatches. A significantly large number of these come at the ends of the chapters, where they could have been tacked on most easily in proof. An example is the description of the Sea of Galilee at night. In the original dispatch Mark Twain had emphasized the appalling bareness and ugliness of the landscape under the glare of the summer sun, and had attacked earlier travelers for praising it. Presumably his tone seemed disrespectful toward the scriptural associations of the place. The added passage, probably written in response to a suggestion from Livy, diverts attention from the present ugliness of the lake to its illustrious past:

Night is the time to see Galilee . . . Gennesaret with the glittering reflections of the constellations flecking its surface, almost makes me regret that I ever saw the rude glare of the day upon it. Its history and its associations are its chiefest charm, in any eyes, and the spells they weave are feeble in the searching light of the sun. *Then,* we scarcely feel the fetters. Our thoughts wander constantly to the practical concerns of life, and refuse to dwell upon things that seem vague and unreal. But when the day is done, even the most unimpressible must yield to the dreamy influences of this tranquil starlight. The old traditions of the place steal upon his memory and haunt his reveries, and then his fancy clothes all sights and sounds with the supernatural. In the lapping of the waves upon the beach, he hears the dip of ghostly oars; in the secret noises of the night he hears spirit voices; in the soft sweep of the breeze, the rush of invisible wings. Phantom ships are on the sea, the dead of twenty centuries come forth from the tombs, and in the dirges of the night wind the songs of old forgotten ages find utterance again.

Exploiting associations in this fashion was a heritage from eighteenth-century Scottish literary theorists, especially Lord Kames, Hugh Blair, and Archibald Alison. The notion that a writer could endow a landscape with aesthetic value by evoking images of past events connected with it in his mind had been a commonplace of American criticism for fifty years or more. Alison's *Essays on the Nature and Principles of Taste,* for example, first published in 1790, went through nine editions in this country, three of them before 1835; and by the 1830's, the Scottish theories were regularly taught in American colleges. Associationism was important in the history of British aesthetic theory because it directed attention to psychological processes, and it was a vital force in the development of Wordsworth and Coleridge. But on this side of the Atlantic the doctrine tended to remain in a state of arrested development. Although Wordsworth had given a democratic turn to associationism by insisting that images of lowly life had value for poetry, the theory as originally formulated had rested on the assumption that only an upper-class observer well read in history and polite letters could have a mind stocked with the appropriate associations. Lord Kames had stated categorically that "those who depend for food upon bodily labour, are totally devoid of taste." The American critics, mainly Federalists, who domesticated associationism in the early years of the nineteenth century emphasized the conscious conservatism of the theory. In a country where social patterns were fluid and rapidly changing, and competition for status was correspondingly intense, it was inevitable that writers should work Kames's logic backwards: they set about demonstrating their superior sensibility by producing associations considered appropriate for a member of the leisure class. By the 1860's the rhetoric dedicated to this end had become standardized into a peculiarly artificial and invidious exercise.

Mark Twain's effort to redeem the ugliness of Galilee by drawing over it the veil of night and parading fanciful associations in place of the actual scene illustrates the divorce between literature and firsthand experience that was the fatal weakness of the traditional culture. From the point of view he assumes here, aesthetic value has no place in the real world; it belongs to the realm of the supernatural. Spirit voices and ghostly oars are presumed to be more affecting than actual voices and oars. The artificiality of the passage is evident in the movement toward poetic mannerism at the end: the alliteration, the iambic rhythm, the ornate periodic and parallel structure, the self-consciously figurative language in phrases like "dirges of the night wind."

A second passage added during revision (although in San Francisco rather than in Elmira) was the prose aria about the Sphinx. Like the description of Galilee, this proved to be a favorite of reviewers. The "mysterious Sphinx," together with the nearby pyramids, had long been a standard topic in books of travel about the Eastern Mediterranean. A few years after the publication of *The Innocents Abroad,* Mark Twain's friend and neighbor Charles Dudley Warner would remark of the pyramids in his *Mummies and Moslems* that "every visitor seems inclined to measure his own height by their vastness, in telling what impression they produce upon *him*." "I suppose there are more 'emotions' afloat about the pyramids," he said, "than concerning any other artificial objects." A man who undertook yet another description of so celebrated a monument was almost explicitly engaged in a kind of athletic competition (might one say at the running high jump?) with earlier writers.

In a different mood, Mark Twain could have burlesqued his own rhetoric. Some years later he jotted down in his notebook an idea for a comic sketch: "Sent agent to visit great picture or mountain, but it was a failure because he had not had time to 'put up his emotions' . . . Hadn't read up; didn't know what style of emotions the best authorities required for that subject." There is not a trace of irony, however, in the effusion on the Sphinx in *The Innocents Abroad:*

After years of waiting, it was before me at last. The great face was so sad, so earnest, so longing, so patient. There was a dignity not of earth in its mien, and in its countenance a benignity such as never anything human wore. It was stone, but it seemed sentient. If ever image of stone thought, it was thinking. It was looking toward the verge of the landscape, yet looking *at* nothing —nothing but distance and vacancy. It was looking over and beyond everything of the present, and far into the past. It was gazing out over the ocean of Time—over lines of century-waves which, further and further receding, closed nearer and nearer together, and blended at last into one unbroken tide, away toward the horizon of remote antiquity. It was thinking of the wars of departed ages; of the empires it had seen created and destroyed; of the nations whose birth it had witnessed, whose progress it had watched, whose annihilation it had noted; of the joy and sorrow, the life and death, the grandeur and decay, of five thousand slow revolving years. It was the type of an attribute of man—of a faculty of his heart and brain. It was MEMORY—RETRO-SPECTION—wrought into visible, tangible form. All who know what pathos there is in memories of days that are accomplished and faces that have vanished—albeit only a trifling score of years gone by—will have some appreciation of the pathos that dwells in these grave eyes that look so steadfastly back upon the things they knew before History was born—before Tradition had being—things that were, and forms that moved, in a vague era which even Poetry and Romance scarce know of—and passed one by one away and left the stony dreamer solitary in the midst of a strange new age, and uncomprehended scenes.

The Sphinx is grand in its loneliness; it is imposing in its magnitude; it is impressive in the mystery that hangs over its story. And there is that in the overshadowing majesty of this eternal figure of stone, with its accusing memory of the deeds of all ages, which reveals to one something of what he shall feel when he shall stand at last in the awful presence of God.

The stereotyped character of this description goes beyond its use of accepted aesthetic categories, for Mark Twain takes over specific details from earlier writers. Since the passage was written long after the experience it is supposed to record, and since there is no description of the Sphinx in the notebook covering this part of the excursion, one can hardly avoid the conclusion that it was put together deliberately as an exercise in rhetoric. One of the writers to whom Mark Twain seems indebted is a man whose sentimentality he had frequently derided in earlier chapters—William C. Prime. In *Boat Life in Egypt and Nubia* Prime had written:

We . . . ascended Cheops and looked back, up the lordly river, and up the river of time as well, for there is no spot on earth from which man can see so far into the past as from that same summit of Cheops . . . we sat down under the shadow of the sphinx and gazed at his stony countenance, whose calm, almost ineffable smile, seems, among the shifting sands and rifled tombs, now too sneering for a smile, and now too soft, and sad, and mournful for a sneer . . . we looked into a hundred vacant resting-places of the old dead, and pondered much on the power of time and the oblivion with which age wraps nations, as with a grave-cloth and a grave, out of which their voices come in sepulchral tones . . . at length we climbed Cheops once more and swept our eyes over the plain, and up the Nile, and far away over the Libyan desert to the dim horizon that seemed as distant as the days of Moses.

A number of ideas are common to Prime's description and Mark Twain's: the sadness of the face; the notion of looking backward in time as one looks out over the surrounding desert; the succession of nations that have come and gone. The similarity of tone is equally noticeable.

The treatment of the Sphinx in *The Innocents Abroad* resembles even more closely that of the English traveler Alexander William Kinglake in his book *Eōthen,* which had been widely read for twenty years on both sides of the Atlantic. The rhetorical pattern of the long inventory of scenes upon which the Sphinx has gazed through the centuries is particularly suggestive of Mark Twain's reference to "five thousand slow revolving years." Kinglake wrote:

Laugh, and mock if you will at the worship of stone idols, but mark ye this, ye breakers of images, that in one regard, the stone idol bears awful semblance of Deity—unchangefulness in the midst of change—the same seeming will and intent for ever and ever inexorable! Upon ancient dynasties of Ethiopian and Egyptian Kings—upon Greek and Roman, upon Arab and Ottoman conquerors—upon Napoleon dreaming of an Eastern Empire—upon battle and pestilence—upon the ceaseless misery of the Egyptian race—upon keen-eyed travellers—Herodotus yesterday and Warburton to-day—upon all, and more this unworldly Sphynx has watched, and watched like a Providence with the same earnest eyes, and the same sad, tranquil mien. And we, we shall die, and Islam will wither away . . . and still that sleepless rock will lie watching and watching the works of the new, busy race, with those same sad, earnest eyes, and the same tranquil mien everlasting. You dare not mock at the Sphynx.

In addition to the references to the sad face and the procession of empires, Kinglake hints at the identification of the Sphinx with the Deity that Mark Twain uses for his climax, and the idea of its anachronistic survival into a strange modern age.

Yet the description in *The Innocents Abroad* is more elaborate than either of the earlier specimens. Mark Twain develops the idea of the historical sublime in greater detail and makes more concrete the identification of the vast physical landscape with the infinitely receding historical past. Most striking of all (and apparently original with him) is the act of projection which endows the "stony dreamer" with the state of mind suitable for a cultivated observer meditating upon a scene of historical consequence. And the final image of a sinner before an accusing God is worthy of an accomplished pulpit orator.

Even to Mrs. Fairbanks, Mark Twain deprecated this kind of thing as "moralizing." Nevertheless, he brings it off with remarkable skill. He is a virtuoso; we can almost forgive him what he is doing because he is doing it so well. But it is a stunt rather than serious writing. The impression he gives of having persuaded himself for the moment that he means what he is saying cannot in the end conceal the fact that the emotions have been worked up according to a formula. Writing in this fashion proved that he could function as a man of letters, but it proved also that such a function was for him irrelevant.

3

The passages about the Sea of Galilee and the Sphinx were both added in revision. The original dispatches, however, contain a number of passages similar in tone. Indeed, Mark Twain had already begun to exploit historical associations in his letters from Hawaii, as for example in the evocation of a vision of long dead warriors and heathen sacrifices in his description of the "ancient heathen temple" near Honolulu ("If these mute stones could speak, what tales they could tell, what pictures they could describe"). Europe cried aloud for such treatment and the temptation was the greater because guidebooks and the works of earlier travelers provided an inexhaustible store of ready-made associations for historical monuments and ruins, and even collected appropriate quotations. The passages from Bulwer Lytton and Samuel Rogers in *The Innocents Abroad* are probably taken from guidebooks. But Mark Twain's own knowledge of Shakespeare was sufficient to allow him to write of Venice in his letter to the *Alta California*: "It is easy . . . in fancy, to people these silent canals with plumed gallants and fair ladies—with Shylocks in gaberdine and sandals, venturing loans upon the rich argosies of Venetian commerce—with Othellos and Desdemonas, with Iagos and Roderigos—with noble fleets and victorious legions returning from the wars."

When Mark Twain added passages of serious eloquence to *The Innocents Abroad* he was simply expanding an element already present in the original dispatches. In adopting this style he assumed the well-defined identity of the genteel tourist. The role had the advantage of providing a focus for a narrative of travel, and it allowed the writer to display both erudition and sensibility in his thronging memories of the past. But Mark Twain could not bring himself to sustain the role of genteel traveler throughout the book. Even though he could be as eloquent as anyone in the exalted mode, his writer's conscience told him it was dead and empty.

It offered him no challenge; the conventions that went into operation with such ease for him made it impossible to say anything fresh. Worst of all, the ritual of listing historical associations imposed an unbroken solemnity. The mood collapsed at the first suggestion of comedy, and from the time of his first exercises of this kind in the Hawaiian letters Mark Twain had found the temptation to ridicule his own flights of rhetoric almost irresistible.

In the *Quaker City* dispatches the narrator often resorts to comic deflation. His first ride in a Venetian gondola, for example—"the fairy boat in which the princely cavaliers of the olden time were wont to cleave the waters of the moonlit canals and look the eloquence of love into the soft eyes of patrician beauties"—disillusions him because the craft turns out to be merely "an inky, rusty old canoe with a sable hearse-body clapped onto the middle of it," and the gondolier's singing is so hideous he threatens to throw the man overboard. On the lecture platform, when he had delivered his apostrophe to the Sphinx he sometimes "could not resist tacking on a few words about the vandal carelessly whistling in the shadow of the ancient monument." Yet the associations evoked by Europe and Palestine were so rich that he could not dispose of them by mere flippancy. The old world was too important a topic for Americans. In *The Innocents Abroad* he felt obliged to analyze his reactions to the endless succession of places renowned in history, if only to justify his recurrent impatience with the accepted attitude toward them. On reflection he discovered that images of the past have a moral as well as an aesthetic aspect. It was not clear what value for the citizen of an enlightened republic lay in dwelling upon the panorama of crimes recorded in the guidebooks. In Florence, he reports, "we tried indolently to recollect something about the Guelphs and Ghibelines and the other historical cut-throats whose quarrels and assassinations make up so large a share of Florentine history, but the subject was not attractive."

The implication that the history of Europe is but a burden to be cast off by the man of the new world was an important part of Mark Twain's ideology; it will demand consideration later. The problem of Palestine was different, for scriptural history could not be dismissed as a mere chronicle of wickedness. In the end, however, the doctrine of associations failed Mark Twain there also—not because the past called up in his memory was sordid but, paradoxically enough, because it was so resplendent. The Holy Land of actuality, with its desert terrain and its half-starved, disease-ridden people, was too remote from the Holy Land of imagination, which had been the setting for the lives and deeds of patriarchs and prophets and even of the Savior himself. It was yet another demonstration of the lack of connection between actual experience and the realm of ideality. At Ephesus Mark Twain notes:

> One may read the Scriptures and believe, but he cannot go and stand yonder in the ruined theater and in imagination people it again with the vanished multitudes who mobbed Paul's comrades there and shouted, with one voice, "Great is Diana of the Ephesians!" The idea of a shout in such a solitude as this almost makes one shudder.

In the Grotto of the Annunciation at Nazareth the difficulty was even greater:

> It was not easy to bring myself up to the magnitude of the situation. I could sit off several thousand miles and imagine the angel appearing, with shadowy wings and lustrous countenance, and note the glory that streamed downward upon the Virgin's head while the message from the Throne of God fell upon her ears—any one can do that, beyond the ocean, but few can do it here. I saw the little recess from which the angel stepped, but could not fill its void. The angels that I know are creatures of unstable fancy—they will not fit in niches of substantial stone. Imagination labors best in distant fields. I doubt if any man can stand in the Grotto of the Annunciation and people with the phantom images of his mind its too tangible walls of stone.

In the Church of the Nativity in Bethlehem still another distraction interfered with the state of mind dictated by convention. The original dispatch read as follows:

> You cannot think in this place any more than you can in any other in Palestine that would be likely to inspire reflection. Beggars, cripples and greasy monks compass you about, and make you think only of bucksheesh when you would rather think of something more in keeping with the character of the spot.
>
> I was glad to get out of there, and glad when we had trotted through the grottoes where Eusebius wrote, and Jerome fasted, and Joseph prepared for the flight into Egypt, and the dozen other distinguished grottoes, and knew we were done.

Here was the supreme challenge, for the birthplace of the Savior should in theory have aroused the uniquely rich mass of associations. Mark

Twain recognized it as a crucial instance. When he reached this point in his revision he inserted an uncomfortable apology just before the paragraph quoted above:

I have no "meditations," suggested by this spot where the very first "Merry Christmas!" was uttered in all the world, and from whence the friend of my childhood, Santa Claus, departed on his first journey to gladden and continue to gladden roaring firesides on wintry mornings in many a distant land forever and forever. I touch, with reverent finger, the actual spot where the infant Jesus lay, but I think—nothing.

Then, after picking up the remaining page of his dispatch, he adds at the end of his chapter in *The Innocents Abroad* a general comment on the problem of associations that may well have been elicited by objections from Livy and Mrs. Fairbanks:

The commonest sagacity warns me that I ought to tell the customary pleasant lie, and say I tore myself reluctantly away from every noted place in Palestine. Everybody tells me that, but with as little ostentation as I may, I doubt the word of every he who tells it . . . it is the neat thing to say you were reluctant, and then append the profound thoughts that "struggled for utterance" in your brain; but it is the true thing to say you were not reluctant, and found it impossible to think at all—though in good sooth it is not respectable to say it, and not poetical, either.

We do not think, in the holy places; we think in bed, afterward, when the glare, and the noise, and the confusion are gone, and in fancy we revisit alone the solemn monuments of the past, and summon the phantom pageants of an age that has passed away.

To be alone, passive in the darkness, is the posture of the Stony Dreamer. Mark Twain's apology hints at a contradiction in the use of the doctrine of associations in a travel book, a contradiction that became apparent as tourism was organized on a large scale along established routes. When the traveler is conducted by his guides and couriers to the celebrated monument, he finds many other tourists with their guides and couriers, and he cannot attain the requisite state of mind. The purpose of his pilgrimage is frustrated because he needs to be solitary and undisturbed in order to turn his attention entirely inward.

As Mark Twain thought further about his experience in Bethlehem he moved toward the conclusion that one can describe places of historical note only at a distance from them in both space and time. He

33

had almost regretted having seen Galilee in harsh daylight. His disenchanting visit to Bethlehem suggests the devastating reductio ad absurdum that a writer is better off describing places he has never visited, since he has no distracting memories of the prosaic actuality to interfere with the pure poetry of his associations. Mark Twain had apparently reached this point in his revision when he composed the Christmas letter that Mrs. Fairbanks published in the Cleveland *Herald*. Written thousands of miles from Bethlehem and months after Mark Twain's visit to the shrine, the letter supplies the meditations appropriate to the site. When he realizes the trend of his own implicit logic he feels obliged to protest that he is after all glad he saw the place:

Don't you picture it all out in your mind as we saw it many months ago? And don't the picture mellow in the distance & take to itself again the soft, unreal semblance that Poetry & Tradition give to the things they hallow? And now that the greasy monks, & the noisy mob, & the leprous beggars are gone, & all the harsh, cold hardness of *real* stone & unsentimental glare of sunlight are banished from the vision, don't you realize again, as in other years, that Jesus *was* born there, & that the angels *did* sing in the still air above, & that the wondering shepherds *did* hold their breath & listen as the mysterious music floated by? *I* do. It is more real than ever. And I am glad, a hundred times glad, that I saw Bethlehem, though at the time it seemed that that sight had swept away forever, every pleasant fancy & every cherished memory that ever the City of Nativity had stored away in my mind & heart.

4

Despite Mark Twain's recurrent dissatisfaction with the rhetoric of associations, he had discovered that this lecture audiences liked this kind of fine writing and he assumed correctly that readers of *The Innocents Abroad* would have the same taste. Yet he had gained his reputation primarily as a humorist, the successor to Artemus Ward. The edifying descriptions in his lectures came in very well by way of contrast, and reassured conservative members of the audience by adding an element of instruction to an evening otherwise frivolous. But the people read him and came to hear him mainly because they expected him to be funny. In its simplest form, therefore, the problem he faced in composing his book was how to combine serious passages—guidebook information and exalted eloquence—with comic anecdotes.

It was not entirely a matter of meeting the demands of a potential audience; the problem also lay within him. He had to some extent adopted as his own the criteria he ascribed to the reading public. He needed to demonstrate his command of a serious style to himself as well as to others. He analyzed his situation with professional clarity in a letter to his wife written in November 1871 just after he had lectured on Artemus Ward in Bennington, Vermont:

Good house, but they laughed too much.—A great fault with this lecture is that I have no way of turning it into a serious & instructive vein at will. *Any* lecture of mine ought to be a running narrative-plank, with square holes in it, six inches apart, all the length of it, & then in my mental shop I ought to have plugs (half marked "serious" & the other marked "humorous") to select from & jam into these holes according to the temper of the audience.

The narrative-plank of *The Innocents Abroad* was provided by the actual journey, and much of the book undoubtedly does have a structure corresponding to the image of plugs jammed into regularly spaced holes. The descriptions of Galilee and the Sphinx are serious plugs. The humorous plugs are an anthology of all the kinds of comic effects Mark Twain had attempted during his journalistic apprenticeship. In the original dispatches literary burlesque was represented by the Legend of the Seven Sleepers of Ephesus, which plays elaborately but clumsily with the notion that the sleep was drunkenness. For the book Mark Twain added his raucously antisentimental version of the story of Abelard and Heloïse, as well as a Legend of Count Luigi that follows Thackeray's *Legend of the Rhine* in burlesquing a historical novel by Dumas and goes on to a farcical rehash of two plays by Victor Hugo. To this category also belong the amusing Roman playbill and review of a gladiatorial spectacle in the Coliseum, and the various satiric references to William C. Prime's *Tent Life in the Holy Land*. The narrator's ostentatious mourning at the Tomb of Adam, often singled out for praise by reviewers, is a parody of Prime's dithyramb about Jerusalem. Placed as it is close to the serious account of the Holy Sepulcher, the passage seems to embody a covert protest against exploiting the tomb of the Savior as a spectacle for tourists.

In addition to literary burlesques, the comic episodes include a number of anecdotes in the Washoe manner making the narrator the comic butt, such as his encounter with the young woman selling gloves in Gibraltar, his excruciating shave by a French barber, the night expedition to the Acropolis which involves stealing grapes and being pursued by guards, the *Quaker City* crew's ridicule of the pompous address presented by the passengers to the Czar of Russia, jokes about the half-starved horses provided for overland travelers in Palestine, and an irrelevant but extremely funny reminiscence of a wretched hotel in some Middle Western town.

Introduced as they are suggested by places the tourists visit, the humorous and sentimental ornaments for the factual narrative present a rather mechanical symmetry. Sometimes, however, Mark Twain probes deeper into his material to integrate episodes with the narrative as a whole. Just as the historical associations in the set passages of description have a serious thematic relevance to the pilgrimage of an American innocent to the old world, the comic passages furnish a counterstatement: they have a tone of irreverence toward the past that alternates with the reverence of the formal descriptions. The best example is the game of tormenting guides played by the narrator and his cronies. Through their metonymic linkage with monuments and paintings the guides come to represent the past that the tourists are expected to find awe-inspiring. But the guides are unprepossessing creatures with the status of hired servants, and therefore vulnerable to attack as the monuments themselves are not:

All their lives long, they are employed in showing strange things to foreigners and listening to their bursts of admiration. It is human nature to take delight in exciting admiration . . . Think . . . what a passion it becomes with a guide, whose privilege it is, every day, to show to strangers wonders that throw them into perfect ecstasies of admiration! . . . After we discovered this, we *never* went into ecstasies any more—we never admired anything—we never showed any but impassible faces and stupid indifference in the presence of the sublimest wonders a guide had to display.

The ship's surgeon acts as spokesman for the group because he has a special talent for the deadpan manner prescribed by humorous tradition: "he can keep his countenance, and look more like an inspired idiot, and throw more imbecility into the tone of his voice than any man that lives." Whenever the guide shows them a notable object, whether it be a bust of Columbus or an Egyptian mummy, the doctor asks after a judicious pause, "Is he dead?" The question catches the exact blend of ignorance and condescension in the American irreverence toward the past.

The alternation of serious and humorous episodes in *The Innocents Abroad* defines the extremes of awe and mockery, of humility and arrogance between which the narrator oscillates as he confronts the almost overwhelming phenomenon of Europe. In this sense *The Innocents Abroad* has great documentary value: it records a representative American experience. But it falls short of ultimate accuracy because at this stage of his development Mark Twain was not able to conceive an overall structure or even a way of handling separate incidents that could express reverence and irreverence simultaneously. Only a narrative method and a style of this complexity could have done justice to the ambivalence of the tourists. In order to grasp the full meaning of the book one must consider it as a whole, back away from it far enough to allow the seemingly heterogeneous parts to blur into one another. That is, the reader must be content to deal with virtual and putative meanings not fully worked out in the text; he must do some of the writer's work for him. But if he is willing to do this, he discovers an archetypal fable with elements of epic, tragedy, comedy, and farce depicting the return of the American prodigal to his old home.

5

Contemporary reviewers ignored the shifts in tone and point of view in *The Innocents Abroad* that disturb the twentieth-century reader; they praised both the eloquence and the humor. They regarded the serious parts, however, as mere ornaments in a work which they took to be fundamentally an act of irreverence toward Europe and the past (or, more subtly, toward the sentimental veneration of Europe in conventional books of travel) on the part of a writer perfectly representing the average uncultivated American. "The irreverence of the volume appears to be a tip-top good feature of it," Clemens wrote to Bliss when he had seen the reviews. He added, perhaps in deference to his feminine mentors, "though I wish with all my heart there wasn't an irreverent line in it." Yet the irreverence that the reviewers liked was precisely the quality Mark Twain claimed for the book when he said in his preface that he had written "honestly," describing things as the ordinary reader would be likely to see them rather than as he ought to see them. The Boston *Transcript,* for example, said that the author "saw things as they were, not as they have been described by poets and romancers"; the Providence *Herald* remarked that he had "shorn many of the venerable shams of the old world" of their "false charms"; and the Rochester *Chronicle* declared that "Twain's book is valuable for pricking many of the bubbles and exploding the humbugs of European travel."

A reviewer in the Albany *Journal* asserted that although a thousand volumes had described approximately the same route, Mark Twain had performed the seemingly impossible feat of finding something new to say because he "did not consider himself bound to go into ecstasies of worshipful adoration before every traditionary shrine, or to draw between the present and the past, contrasts unfavorable to our own generation in every matter of art, philosophy, architecture—everything relating to aesthetic development." The New York *Times* said more explicitly, though noncommittally, that the author had "no great respect for associations and surroundings—laying wagers on the very top of the Pyramid of Cheops, cracking jokes in the Coliseum, and making the entry into Jerusalem with a hilarity not abated in any perceptible degree." The Syracuse *Standard* undertook an elaborate defense of Mark Twain's treatment of Jerusalem—one of the sections of the book that presumably gave rise to the charges of irreverence:

If we had written just such a book as "The Innocents Abroad," we would consider it the highest praise if we were told that we were not a bit reverent in it. Other travelers have been reverent—reverent over old traditions in which they could not possibly have had the slightest interest; reverent over places which had not the slightest claim to be revered—reverent, in short, over the past, and when they were abreast the present . . . Mark Twain sees just what all of us would see under the same circumstances; and he tells the truth about what he sees. The wit is his own; the phraseology is his own; but the eyes with which he sees are our eyes as well as his. They are not the eyes of the solemn old humbugs through which we have been forced to look so often. And thus the book becomes a transcript of our own sentiments.

The reviewers' comments show that the irreverence of *The Innocents Abroad* gave expression to strong and widely shared feelings in Mark Twain's audience. He had evoked one of the central images in the American tradition: the man of the new world refusing to be cowed by what he does not understand about the old, and sturdily asserting the value of his own country and its institutions. The founders of the Republic had believed, as Jefferson declared, that "Our lot has been cast, by the favor of heaven, in a country and under circumstances, highly auspicious to our peace and prosperity, and where no pretence can arise for the degrading and oppressive establishments of Europe." "Novus ordo seclorum" reads the motto that Jefferson chose for the great seal of the United States. America stood for the new, the rational, and the useful as well as for liberty and justice. If it lacked the complexities and overtones generated by two thousand years of history and was therefore barren of aesthetic interest, so much the worse for art. Mark Twain was dealing in axiomatic assumptions when he contrasted the dreamlike unreality of the European past with the American workaday world of technology and progress. At Pompeii, he says, as he went "dreaming among the trees" he was shocked to hear the irreverent and unpoetical blast of a locomotive whistle summoning passengers "in the most bustling and business-like way." The locomotive was Italian, and he had encountered other unpoetical innovations in Europe, such as gleaming railway stations and smoothly paved highways. But his adherence to the popular belief was unshaken: such marvels properly belonged to the new world, along with republican institutions, whereas history and poverty and tyranny—and art—belonged to the old.

This pattern of ideas was so familiar in the United States that it could serve as the stock in trade of such a run-of-the-mill journalist as J. Ross Browne. Since the travels described by Browne in *Yusef; or The Journey of the Frangi. A Crusade in the East,* a compilation of dispatches to the Washington *National Intelligencer* published in 1855, cover much of the same ground later to be covered by the *Quaker City* excursion, this book offers a useful means of identifying conventional ideas in *The Innocents Abroad.* After inspecting the ruins of antiquity in Sicily, Browne frames an apostrophe to the "mighty kings and chieftains" of the past:

Listen to a few plain facts. I am going to address you solemnly in your tombs, and post you up concerning the nineteenth century. Tourists have so long sung your praises that I mean to make a martyr of myself by telling you the truth.

It is quite true, as enthusiastic travelers say, that your temples, and castles, and palaces are splendid specimens of architecture . . . But you were a barbarous people at best . . . If the Coliseum at Rome had accommodated fifty millions of people instead of fifty thousand, would it have taught them the blessings of peace and good government, or disseminated useful knowledge among them? If all your palaces were built of pure gold instead of marble, would it have caused the thousands of human beings that you were continually embroiling in war to entertain a more fraternal spirit toward each other? . . . We don't build pyramids and coliseums, but we build railroads. The smallest steamboat that paddles its way up the Hudson is greater than the greatest monument of antiquity, and does more to promote the civilization and happiness of mankind; the wires of our electric telegraphs carry more power in them than all the armies you ever brought into battle.

Browne's arrogance has an essentially political rationale. It is supported by an ideology of republicanism that is indistinguishable from American nationalism because he considers the United States to be the unique embodiment of republican institutions. The ideology also has corollaries that may be called democratic in the sense of supporting the image of the self-educated average man against a cultivated elite. Although as a passenger on the relatively luxurious *Quaker City* Mark Twain could not imitate Browne's ostentatiously plebeian method of traveling cheaply in rough outdoor clothing, much of *The Innocents Abroad* is permeated by an ideology quite similar to Browne's. When Mark Twain first tried to find a unifying theme for a lecture about his travels he invented a generic figure called "the American Vandal" representing "the roving, independent, free-and-easy character of that class of traveling Americans who are *not* elaborately educated, cultivated, and refined, and gilded and filigreed with the ineffable graces of the first society." The Vandal, in other words, is to be distinguished from "the best class of our countrymen" who go abroad and then write books about their travels. The name calls attention not only to the Vandal's barbarous ignorance but also to his refusal to be impressed by the buildings and paintings he is supposed to admire. He says the Last Supper is "a perfect old nightmare of a picture and he wouldn't give forty dollars for a million like it."

Mark Twain adds: "and I endorse his opinion." Later he remarks that he "and three other Vandals" made the excursion to the Acropolis. He glides easily from speaking of the Vandal in the third person to uttering similar opinions in his own person. Yet his relation to the figure of the Vandal is ambiguous. He reserves for himself the function of evoking historical associations of Venice and Athens that are beyond the Vandal's ken. Furthermore, the lecture ends on a patronizing note:

I could have said more about the American Vandal abroad, and less about other things, but I found that he had too many disagreeable points about him, and so I thought I would touch him lightly and let him go. If there is a moral to this lecture it is an injunction to all Vandals to *travel*. I am glad the American Vandal *goes* abroad. It does him good. It makes a better man of him. It rubs out a multitude of his old unworthy biases and prejudices.

Although the Vandal is not mentioned in *The Innocents Abroad*, the reviewers read the book as if it related the adventures of a protagonist conceived on exactly similar lines. But this was an oversimplification fostered by the aggressive nationalism that was so prominent in the years immediately following the victory of the North in the Civil War. Mark Twain's attitude was more complex than the critics recognized. Despite moments in which he seemed to enter fully into the attitudes he ascribed to the Vandal, in the end he repudiated the Vandal's philistine self-importance. There is a note of ironic disdain in the letter he wrote for the New York *Herald* on the day of his return, containing a rapid summary of the *Quaker City* excursion:

None of us had ever been anywhere before; we all hailed from the interior; travel was a wild novelty to us, and we conducted ourselves in accordance with the natural instincts that were in us, and trammeled ourselves with no ceremonies, no conventionalities. We always took care to make it understood that we were Americans—Americans! When we found that a good many foreigners had hardly ever heard of America, and that a good many more knew it only as a barbarous province away off somewhere, that had lately been at war with somebody, we pitied the ignorance of the Old World, but abated no jot of our importance . . . The people stared at us everywhere, and we stared at them. We generally made them feel rather small, too, before we got done with them, because we bore down on them with America's greatness until we crushed them.

Although most newspaper reviewers identified the narrator of *The Innocents Abroad* with the average uncultivated American, it is important to recognize that in his role of Vandal the narrator is not a vernacular figure comparable to Mother Utterback or Simon Wheeler. The Vandal represents an ideology—a set of dogmatic principles backed by some of the most powerful political, economic, and social imperatives in American culture. Mark Twain's experimental use of the Vandal in his lectures shows that he was not yet clear in his own mind about the vernacular system of values. His truly vernacular characters do not have an ideology. They are not self-important or aggressively patriotic; they are indifferent to republican principles because they are not interested in abstract ideas of any kind. On the contrary, the vernacular perspective deflates the rhetoric of Manifest Destiny as effectively as it discredits the clichés of refinement and ideality. One of Mark Twain's earliest contributions to the Virginia City *Territorial Enterprise,* unfortunately now lost except for its magnificent opening sentence, was a burlesque of a Fourth-of-July oration delivered by a Nevada politician, beginning: "I was sired by the Great American Eagle and foaled by a continental dam!"

A few months after the publication of *The Innocents Abroad* he would describe a speech by another Nevada politician as follows:

And now the General, with a great glow of triumph on his face, got up and made a mighty effort; he pounded the table, he banged the lawbooks, he shouted, and roared, and howled, he quoted from every thing and every body, poetry, sarcasm, statistics, history, pathos, and blasphemy, and wound up with a grand war-whoop for free speech, freedom of the press, free schools, the Glorious Bird of America and the principles of eternal justice! [Applause.]

6

Unable to identify himself comfortably with the image of the Vandal, Mark Twain continued his efforts to conceive a narrator for *The Innocents Abroad*. His use of newspaper dispatches made it all but inevitable that the book would be written from the point of view of a character in many respects identical with the author. His actual situation as an untutored observer of the monuments of the mighty past placed him in a position analogous to that of the American humorists' low character confronting a representative of the traditional culture. Like his fellow passengers, he felt himself to be in an inferior position in Europe. His impulse to protect himself against the crushing weight of history led him to pretend he cared nothing about pictures and statues and mummies. But his situation could not be translated satisfactorily into fictional terms as long as his adversary was merely an abstraction, or so easy a victim as a professional guide. Not until the later stages of the journey did Mark Twain discover an antagonist who adequately represented the forces of convention and conformity. During the horseback trip through Palestine he became intensely irritated with the aggressive piety of three older men among the party of eight. He focused on them the hostility he had felt all along toward the self-chosen elite of the *Quaker City* excursion who forbade quadrilles on shipboard because dancing was sinful, imposed on the cruise a regimen of "solemnity, decorum, dinner, dominoes, devotions, slander," and made the supposed pleasure cruise resemble "a funeral excursion without a corpse." His bitterness was deep and lasting. The fragment of a farce he wrote soon after his return has for its theme the spiteful gossip of certain elderly passengers about the men who spend their time drinking wine and playing cards. And only a year or two before Mark Twain's death he wrote beside the author's portrait in a presentation copy of Stephen W. Griswold's *Sixty Years with Plymouth Church*:

"Here is the real old familiar Plymouth-Church self-complacency of 40 years ago. It is the way God looks when He has had a successful season."

In the Palestine letters Mark Twain consistently applies to the three censorious elders the name "pilgrims" which he sometimes used to designate all the ship's company. The other five overland travelers are called "the sinners." His resentment of the pilgrims sprang primarily from their exemplification of what he elsewhere described as "the most malignant form of Presbyterianism,—that sort which considers the saving one's own paltry soul the first & supreme end & object of life." He is rancorous in relating how they compelled the whole party to cover three days' distance in two, despite the suffering of the wretched horses, in order to avoid traveling on the Sabbath. "We pleaded for the tired, ill-treated horses, and tried to show that their faithful service deserved kindness in return, and their hard lot compassion. But when did ever self-righteousness know the sentiment of pity? What were a few long hours added to the hardships of some overtaxed brutes when weighed against the peril of those human souls?"

Mark Twain is annoyed also by the pilgrims' resolute twisting of fact in order to demonstrate the fulfillment of scriptural prophecies and by their general sourness of disposition, which under strain tended to break out in bickerings and mutual recriminations. "They have never heard a cross word out of our lips toward each other—but *they* have quarreled once or twice. We love to hear them at it, after they have been lecturing us. The very first thing they did, coming ashore at Beirout, was to quarrel in the boat." He adds, rather unconvincingly: "I have said I like them, and I do like them—but every time they read me a scorcher of a lecture I mean to talk back in print."

The most detailed account of the relation between pilgrims and sinners is Mark Twain's comment on the pilgrims' haggling over the price demanded for a sail on the Sea of Galilee. The effort costs them their only opportunity to hire a boat. The boatmen simply sail away, and the stinginess of the pilgrims is shown to be stronger than their professed eagerness to embark on the sacred waters.

How the pilgrims abused each other! Each said it was the other's fault, and each in turn denied it. No word was spoken by the sinners—even the mildest sarcasm might have been dangerous at such a time. Sinners that have been kept down and had examples held up to them, and suffered frequent lectures, and been so put upon in a moral way and in the matter of going slow and being serious and bottling up slang, and so crowded in regard to the matter of being proper and always and forever behaving, that their lives have become a burden to them, would not lag behind pilgrims at such a time as this, and wink furtively, and be joyful, and commit other such crimes—because it would not occur to them to do it . . . But they did do it, though—and it did them a world of good to hear the pilgrims abuse each other, too. We took an unworthy satisfaction in seeing them fall out, now and then, because it showed that they were only poor human people like us, after all.

When Mark Twain reached the account of this incident in his revision he was evidently struck by the possibilities for expanding the characterization of the pilgrims within a nascent fictional pattern. He recognized in their foolish enthusiasm at the prospect of "skimming over the sacred waters of Galilee" exactly the traits he found irritating in William C. Prime and other authors of books about Palestine who insisted on the beauty of a landscape that no ingenuity could make attractive "to one's actual vision." The books, he declares, simply express the preconceptions of their authors. Presbyterian travelers "found a Presbyterian Palestine, and they had already made up their minds to find no other"; they "entered the country with their verdicts already prepared." The pilgrims likewise see only what the books have instructed them to. "I can almost tell, in set phrase, what they will say when they see Tabor, Nazareth, Jericho, and Jerusalem—*because I have the books they will 'smouch' their ideas from.*"

Later on Mark Twain contrives an obviously fictitious episode to illustrate his point. Observing the barefooted and homely Arab girls at the Fountain of the Virgin in Nazareth, the three pilgrims comment one by one in almost identical language on their "Madonna-like beauty." They are quoting Prime's preposterous remark about an Arab maiden he saw at the same fountain: "A Madonna, whose face was a portrait of that beautiful Nazareth girl, would be 'a thing of beauty,' and 'a joy forever.'"

The process of converting the pilgrims into fictional characters is incomplete, but in bracketing them with Prime Mark Twain is evidently working toward a generic image of the genteel tourist. For example, there appears to be a connection between the habit of rhapsodizing about Palestine and a certain underlying brutality. He says that Prime "went through this peaceful land with one hand forever on his revolver, and the other on his pocket-handkerchief. Always, when he was not on the point of crying over a holy place, he was on the point of killing an Arab." The pilgrims, who have already shown great callousness toward their horses, are impressed by Prime's bloodthirsty attitude toward the natives. They read *Tent Life* "and keep themselves in a constant state of Quixotic heroism. They have their hands on their pistols all the time, and every now and then, when you least expect it, they snatch them out and take aim at Bedouins who are not visible, and draw their knives and make savage passes at other Bedouins who do not exist."

If Mark Twain had completely transformed *The Innocents Abroad* into a work of fiction, he might have brought the pilgrims to life as an adumbration of what we have learned to call the authoritarian personality. Even in its embryonic state, the insight toward which he was groping is valid, and it enables the reader to see what the book is really about. The conflict between pilgrims and sinners is, at least potentially, a conflict between two irreconcilable systems of value. The pilgrims' cult of pious respectability is revealed as essentially self-centered. At bottom it is a competitive striving for status. The sinners, who refuse to enter the race for salvation on these terms, enjoy a comradeship that on its own casual level is a kind of love. The point is worth making because this is the germ that, fifteen years later, would flower in the unpretentious peace and happiness of Huck Finn and Jim on their raft—just as the bondage of the pilgrims to the pressures of cultural conformity foreshadows Mark Twain's depiction of the depraved and joyless towns along the river.

7

Mark Twain recognized that the antagonism between sinners and pilgrims gave concrete form to much of his subversive feeling about the dominant culture, and in his revision of the dispatches he tried to develop the antagonism into a narrative pattern for the book as a whole. His emphasis on the pilgrims' use of Prime as their guide through the Holy Land brings this section of *The Innocents Abroad* into closer relation with the chapters devoted to Europe. And he added to Chapter 11 a brilliant anticipation of the pilgrim-sinner episodes in the description of a bird seen in the Marseilles Zoo, "a sort of tall, long-legged bird with a beak like a powder-horn, and close-fitting wings like the tails of a dress-coat":

This fellow stood up with his eyes shut and his shoulders stooped forward a little, and looked as if he had his hands under his coat-tails. Such tranquil

45

stupidity, such supernatural gravity, such self-righteousness, and such ineffable self-complacency as were in the countenance and attitude of that gray-bodied, dark-winged, bald-headed, and preposterously uncomely bird!

"We stirred him up occasionally," continues the narrator, "but he only unclosed an eye and slowly closed it again, abating no jot of his stately piety of demeanor or his tremendous seriousness. He only seemed to say, 'Defile not Heaven's anointed with unsanctified hands.' We did not know his name, and so we called him 'The Pilgrim.' Dan said: 'All he wants now is a Plymouth Collection.'" This is a powerful image, condensing into a paragraph the emotional weight of the conflict developed through some two hundred pages in the last section of the book. Yet it is still only an emblem. It provides the material for a short lyric but has no narrative or dramatic substance because the figure of the bird, however rich in symbolic import, provides no role for the sinners except to stir him up occasionally and make witticisms about him. Mark Twain still had to face the problem of finding a pattern for the book as a whole.

His effort to employ the antagonism of sinners and pilgrims as a focus obliged him to discard a rudimentary narrative plan with which he had begun his dispatches. In the first few letters of the series he had used for comic effects the vulgar Mr. Brown who had traveled to Hawaii and New York in company with the first-person narrator. Brown's presence tended to force the narrator into the contrasting role of genteel traveler, in accordance with the familiar pastoral confrontation of straight and vernacular characters. But the role of sinner which the narrator takes in opposition to the pilgrims places him at the opposite end of what has been called the "character-axis" of the Mr. Twain–Mr. Brown relation. The sinner, in other words, would have to occupy the same position as Brown, who thus becomes superfluous, and Mark Twain eliminates him from *The Innocents Abroad*. Getting rid of Brown was also desirable because much of his behavior was too crude to be appropriate for the book. The narrator as sinner took over such of Brown's functions as were relevant to the revised plot but he did not fall into Brown's extremes of coarseness. The remarks and exploits of Brown that were still usable were assigned to a character from the Far West named Blucher who is something like a ghost of Brown, or else were distributed among the narrator and his cronies. Blucher in turn all but disappears after the first few chapters, apparently because it became clear that he too was superfluous in the new scheme of things.

46

Having decided to get rid of Brown, Mark Twain proceeded to write four introductory chapters in which, not having to cope with pre-existing dispatches, he was free to present his narrator as a fictional character. It was an interesting moment in his development as a writer, for he was putting to use for the first time a momentous technical discovery. He had never before introduced a narrator clearly less sophisticated than himself without the apologetic framework device that he had taken over from the tradition of native humor. This innovation set him upon the line of development that would lead, with many detours, to be sure, through *Roughing It* to *Adventures of Huckleberry Finn*. But in *The Innocents Abroad* he evidently has only a muffled premonition of the uses to which the device of a fictional narrator can be put. The margin of freedom Mark Twain could exploit was, of course, severely restricted by the character already established for the narrator in the newspaper dispatches. Unless he was prepared to write the whole story afresh—and the pressure of time ruled out this alternative—he could not make his fictional narrator different from himself in any significant outward feature. The narrator would have to be approximately the same age, he would have to be acceptable as a member of the upper middle class group of *Quaker City* tourists, he could not differ significantly from the author in his speech. These limitations prevented anything like the bold venture of using an illiterate outcast boy to tell the story.

Nevertheless, the nascent intention to make the narrator a fictional character is unmistakable. Mark Twain endows him with a well-intentioned but almost childish innocence. The narrator expects the cruise to be highly glamorous: he thinks the tourists will "sail away in a great steamship with flags flying and cannon pealing, and take a royal holiday beyond the broad ocean, in many a strange clime and in many a land renowned in history!" This is not vernacular language and it does not clearly point toward the conflict between sinners and pilgrims that presumably gave rise to the idea of creating a fictional narrator. Mark Twain had in mind a rather simple stratagem based on the general theme of his summary letter to the New York *Herald*. He would expose a simple-minded narrator to disillusionments such as the funereal gloom legislated on shipboard by the pilgrims, the tedium of Old Masters, the poverty and degradation of foreign countries, the ugliness of Palestinian landscape, and the constant importunities of guides and beggars.

The narrator's exposure to disillusionment is foreshadowed in his comments on the official prospectus of the cruise, which he quotes in full. Mark Twain invites the reader to smile at such engaging naïveté. The effect he achieves by a mere arrangement of items from the published itinerary displays extraordinary skill:

> What was there lacking about that program, to make it perfectly irresistible? Nothing, that any finite mind could discover. Paris, England, Scotland, Switzerland, Italy—Garibaldi! The Grecian Archipelago! Vesuvius! Constantinople! Smyrna! The Holy Land! Egypt and "our friends the Bermudians"! People in Europe desiring to join the Excursion—contagious sickness to be avoided—boating at the expense of the ship—physician on board—the circuit of the globe to be made if the passengers unanimously desired it—the company to be rigidly selected by a pitiless "Committee on Applications"—the vessel to be as rigidly selected by as pitiless a "Committee on Selecting Steamer." Human nature could not withstand these bewildering temptations. I hurried to the treasurer's office and deposited my ten per cent.

The narrator's humility and his assumption that he belongs to the class of sinners are revealed in his fear of the "critical personal examination" he must undergo before he can be signed on as a passenger. The notion of a tribunal sitting in judgment on applicants has strong Calvinist associations. When he is at last "duly and officially accepted as an excursionist," he remarks: "There was happiness in that, but it was tame compared to the novelty of being 'select.'" He says later, with a wonderful scrambling of Scripture, that he had prepared himself "to take rather a back seat in that ship, because of the uncommonly select material that would alone be permitted to pass through the camel's eye of that committee on credentials," and he drops in occasionally at the booking office to find out "how many people the committee were decreeing not 'select,' every day, and banishing in sorrow and tribulation." Such allusions prepare for the theological overtones of the antagonism between pilgrims and sinners. The idea of the cruise had originated within the congregation of Henry Ward Beecher's Plymouth Church in Brooklyn. Mark Twain is mildly satiric in having the narrator observe that he paid the balance of his passage money when it was announced that "the Plymouth Collection of Hymns would be used on board the ship."

The folly of expecting the cruise to be a gay affair of flying flags and pealing cannon is emphasized in the description of the ship's departure:

> Groups of excursionists, arrayed in unattractive traveling-costumes, were moping about in a drizzling rain and looking as droopy and woebegone as so

many molting chickens. The gallant flag was up, but it was under the spell, too, and hung limp and disheartened by the mast . . . Two very mild cheers went up from the dripping crowd on the pier; we answered them gently from the slippery decks; the flag made an effort to wave, and failed; the "battery of guns" spake not—the ammunition was out.

The narrator's naïveté is illustrated further by a series of misadventures on the first day at sea, when he finds himself continually falling afoul of this or that regulation. He lights a cigar in an area where smoking is prohibited, is politely but firmly rebuked when he picks up a spyglass and a sextant belonging to the officers, and in a final regression to childishness incurs a reprimand for carving the railing with his pocketknife.

The introductory section ends with a sharp thrust at the pilgrims. The executive officer is annoyed at their persistent prayers for fair winds,

when they know as well as I do that this is the only ship going east this time of the year, but there's a thousand coming west—what's a fair wind for us is a *head*-wind to them—the Almighty's blowing a fair wind for a thousand vessels, and this tribe wants him to turn it clear around so as to accommodate *one*,—and she a steamship at that! It ain't good sense, it ain't good reason, it ain't good Christianity, it ain't common human charity. Avast with such nonsense!

This mariner recalls the Captain Edgar Wakeman whom Mark Twain had met in 1866 and would later develop into the protagonist of "Captain Stormfield's Visit to Heaven." He serves here to establish firmly the linkage between colloquial speech and true charity in the unregenerate, and between conspicuous piety and selfishness in the pilgrims. But the fact that a more clearly vernacular spokesman had to be imported to make the speech reveals the fatal weakness in the characterization of the narrator. He is too bland for this kind of criticism and hardly a promising adversary of the pilgrims.

8

The conception of the narrator presented in the introductory chapters proved to be of little use to Mark Twain in his effort to find a means of organizing his book. Once the voyage is under way, the theme of disillusionment announced at the outset is largely forgotten. The innocent enthusiast who was cowed by the Committee on Applications has nothing in common with the sardonic sinner of the overland journey through

Palestine, and neither of these characters is identical with the practical joker in the Washoe manner who serves as narrator in the French and Italian sequences. Whether or not this tormenter of guides is Mark Twain himself is not clear; perhaps he is, perhaps, indeed, he is as accurate a portrait of Mark Twain as the book contains. On the other hand, Mark Twain is also represented to some extent by the narrator who adopts the attitude of the Vandal in triumphantly demonstrating the inferiority of the old world to the new and castigating his fellow countrymen who pretend to a knowledge of art that no American could attain without expatriating himself. In any case, the narrator's effort to certify his own gentility by producing trains of historical associations for celebrated sites in Europe and the Holy Land cannot be made congruous with the other roles he assumes.

Yet it would be wrong to conclude from these technical difficulties that *The Innocents Abroad* does not have at its center a coherent story about the experiences of an important character. Mark Twain's imaginative insight showed itself at this stage in his career (and often later) to be more reliable than his command of the technique of extended narrative. The "I" who appears in the book under so many guises and is seen from so many different perspectives, like the subject of a cubist portrait, possesses an identity after all. He represents the meaning that Mark Twain, with his gift for recognizing mythical elements in his own experience, was able to extract from the confusions of the *Quaker City* excursion. The writer cannot bring this "I" into being at the level of novelistic specification but the character has a kind of virtual reality on a different level: he exists in the dimension of romance that Richard Chase has found in the greatest American works of fiction.

The protagonist of *The Innocents Abroad* is an American Adam resembling in many respects his contemporary, the protagonist of *Leaves of Grass*. But he has the advantage of performing a more determinate action. His voyage back to the old home across the Atlantic embodies a greater quantity of historical and psychological reality than does the rather vague passage to India that is offered to Whitman's hero as an alternative to settling down on a farm in the Middle Western Garden of the World. The story of Mark Twain's innocent is profoundly true to the spirit of nineteenth-century American culture. The hero is not defeated by the forces of tyranny and superstition, nor does he lose his way in the labyrinthine corridors of history. It is appropriate for him to make a good many jokes, good and bad, along the way, and even to wear a variety of masks, although this plurality of identities frustrates the writer's effort to subdue him to the uses of art. The insidious question that the travelers ask their guides, "Is he dead?" dispels every menace because it rules out of account the whole sordid record of the past and spreads before the American Adam an enticing tabula rasa.

At the same time, the story has an undercurrent of sadness and disillusionment originating in this very escape from the past. It was a little disconcerting to make the pilgrimage and to find the tomb empty. For the moment, Mark Twain was willing to have it so; his conclusion that the past was only a dream, a figment of his imagination more vivid at a distance of several thousand miles than in the immediate presence of the cold stone of the monuments, released him to make his next search for meaning, in *Roughing It,* into specifically American and Western circumstances. But the question of what significance the European past might have for the American present was not finally settled for him. It remained as a preoccupation that would demand later repetitions of this first excursion (particularly in *A Connecticut Yankee in King Arthur's Court*), and they would not all end on such a lighthearted note as does the pilgrimage of the *Quaker City* innocents.

III

Transformation of a Tenderfoot

AFTER describing his eastward pilgrimage to the old world, Mark Twain next chose for a subject his journey to the West. He told his sister that his new book would be "like the 'Innocents' in size and style"; and at first glance *Roughing It* does seem neatly symmetrical with *The Innocents Abroad*. In England the second part of it was published separately under the title *The Innocents at Home*. The two books deal with the two poles of nineteenth-century American culture: the Europe from which the first colonists had come, and the beckoning West toward which for two centuries and more they and their descendants had been moving. The sections of *Roughing It* that describe the overland journey and the narrator's experiences as a prospector show a marked advance toward the structural firmness of fiction; the management of narrative viewpoint reinforces the meaning Mark Twain had discerned in his material. But the sections about his work as a reporter in Virginia City, San Francisco, and the Sandwich Islands present inconsistencies in the characterization of the narrator that recall similar difficulties in *The Innocents Abroad*. The trouble arises from the same source: in these later chapters Mark Twain could draw once again on his scrapbooks, and the temptation to fall back on summaries of his own writing proved too strong to be resisted.

The first half of *Roughing It* is a striking demonstration of Mark Twain's ability to recognize the representative aspects of his own experience. He was intuitively aware that in crossing the plains and mountains to the Pacific coast he had duplicated the experience of generations of his countrymen. The depth of his insight becomes clear if one compares his account of the overland journey with such earlier narratives of Far Western travel as Irving's *A Tour on the Prairies* (1835) and Francis Parkman's *The Oregon Trail* (1849). As Irving and Parkman represent themselves, they have much in common with the narrator of *The Innocents Abroad:* they have come to see the sights, they are prototourists. They are not personally involved in what they see. In *A Tour on the Prairies* Irving attempts to add aesthetic interest to his rather humdrum observations by adorning them with stereotyped images and allusions that have nothing to do with the West. Parkman came with a more serious purpose: he wanted to study wild Indians in order to equip himself to write his history of the struggle between France and England in North America that had ended in 1763. But he had little interest in the trans-Mississippi West or in the American emigrants crossing the plains. To him they were only rude peasants suffering from jaundice and clad in garments of homespun. He observed the Indians as an anthropologist, the Pikes and Mormons as a Boston Brahmin—that is, from without, and often from above.

In the opening sequence of *Roughing It* Mark Twain also adopts a narrative persona resembling that of the tourist presented at the beginning of *The Innocents Abroad*. But the naïveté of the persona is deliberately exaggerated for the purpose of burlesquing it. The narrator says he originally intended merely to spend three months in Nevada on a pleasure jaunt. His head is filled with adolescent dreams of "Indians, deserts, and silver bars." The reader quickly realizes, however, that the narrative technique in this book is more complex than that of Irving and Parkman; Mark Twain is not simply reporting fact or reciting elegant associations, but writing an imaginative interpretation of his experience in the Far West. When the narrator speaks in the first person, the pronoun "I" links two quite different personae: that of a tenderfoot setting out across the plains, and that of an old-timer, a veteran who has seen the elephant and now looks back upon his own callow days of inexperience. Both are present in the narrative from the start. The contrast between them, which is an implied judgment upon the tenderfoot's innocence and a corresponding claim for the superior maturity and sophistication of the old-timer, is the consequence of precisely that journey which the book will describe. Thus, in a sense, the whole plot is implicit in the management of point of view from the first paragraph.

This narrative method has several consequences. First, the movement in space that provided the pattern for all accounts of Far Western travel acquires here for the first time a moral significance. The West is no longer mere spectacle, mere landscape or potential wealth or theater of Manifest Destiny, but a source of transforming experience. The traveler who enters that strange region does not face the dangers of the early explorers (although he does run some risks), but on the other hand he is certain to be made into a different person, as they were not. Furthermore, it is affirmed implicitly from the outset in the management of the narrative that the criterion of judgment, the standard by which good is distinguished from bad and wisdom from foolishness, is no longer to be found in the settled society which the traveler is leaving behind but in the Far West toward which his journey is taking him.

In other words, the narrative plan of *Roughing It* is a means of exploring the values that come into being when the constraints of ordered social life are relaxed in the chaos of frontier conditions. Like *The Innocents Abroad, Roughing It* contains bursts of eloquence showing that the narrator has not cut himself loose entirely from literary conventions. But *Roughing It* is more coherent than *The Innocents Abroad.* For one thing, the American West offers neither paintings by Old Masters nor sites hallowed by historical associations to tempt the narrator into stereotyped responses. And the narrator of *Roughing It,* unlike the pilgrim to Europe and the Holy Land, is transformed by his journey; it brings about a cumulative change in his outlook on life.

2

The basic situation which *Roughing It* develops is presented in condensed form in Chapter 5. Three days out of St. Joseph, Missouri, the passengers on the stagecoach see their first coyote:

He was not a pretty creature, or respectable either, for I got well acquainted with his race afterward, and can speak with confidence. The coyote is a long, slim, sick and sorry-looking skeleton, with a gray wolf-skin stretched over it, a tolerably bushy tail that forever sags down with a despairing expression of forsakenness and misery, a furtive and evil eye, and a long, sharp face, with slightly lifted lip and exposed teeth.

This is not at first glance an attractive portrait; but the moral universe of *Roughing It* is somewhat paradoxical, and the reader must be prepared to discover that the sad-looking coyote is really a triumphant figure, endowed with almost supernatural powers. The coyote explains indirectly what the narrator calls "the gladness and the wild sense of freedom that used to make the blood dance in my veins on those fine overland mornings."

The coyote's hidden power begins to appear when you "start a swift-footed dog after him . . . especially if it is a dog that has a good opinion of himself, and has been brought up to think he knows something about speed." The coyote seems to make no effort at all, yet the dog cannot come closer than the twenty feet which the coyote chooses to leave as a proper interval between them. The dog

begins to get aggravated, and it makes him madder and madder to see how gently the coyote glides along and never pants or sweats or ceases to smile; and he grows still more and more incensed to see how shamefully he has been taken in by an entire stranger, and what an ignoble swindle that long, calm, soft-footed trot is; and next he notices that he is getting fagged, and that the coyote actually has to slacken speed a little to keep from running away from him—and *then* that town-dog is mad in earnest, and he begins to strain and weep and swear, and paw the sand higher than ever, and reach for the coyote with concentrated and desperate energy. This "spurt" finds him six feet behind the gliding enemy, and two miles from his friends.

But presently the coyote turns and smiles blandly, with a polite apology for having to hurry away: "and forthwith there is a rushing sound, and the sudden splitting of a long crack through the atmosphere, and behold that dog is solitary and alone in the midst of a vast solitude!" Thereafter, the dog takes no interest in chasing coyotes.

This anecdote embodies a view of the relation between vernacular and conventional values. It involves a tenderfoot (that is, a representative of the dominant culture) with a higher opinion of himself than he can make good in the Far Western environment; a veteran who looks disreputable by town-bred standards but is nevertheless in secure command of the situation; and the process by which the tenderfoot gains knowledge, quite fresh and new knowledge, at the cost of humiliation to himself. The anecdote announces a reversal of values as the traveler passes from the accustomed life of towns to the strange life of the Far West. The attitudes brought from back home are shown to be ridiculous in comparison with the coyote's secret—a secret that seems actually to release him from the laws of nature. It is true that the exact content of the vernacular values is not made clear; they are somewhat hypothetical, they are suggested rather than specified. Yet the coyote with his ambiguous smile is perhaps the more impressive because of the air of mystery that surrounds him.

The narrator's physical journey out beyond the frontier is also a withdrawal from the society of which he was originally a member: it is an act of alienation, a voluntary exile. At the same time, he enters a very different community—a psychological and sociological process which corresponds to the physical journey westward. In this sense the narrator can be said to undergo an initiation. He exchanges the silk hat and kid gloves with which he set out for the costume of the mining camps: "a damaged slouch hat, blue woolen shirt, and pants crammed into boot-tops."

3

Near the end of the opening section of *Roughing It* Mark Twain placed three chapters summarizing the narrator's initiation. The sequence consists of two parts: the snowstorm episode (Chapters 32–33), sometimes reprinted under the title "Fruits of Our Reform," and the fake trial arranged as a practical joke on Attorney General Buncombe, sometimes called "The Facts of the Great Landslide Case" (Chapter 34).

In the first episode the narrator and two companions are returning to Carson City from the Humboldt mining district when they find themselves lost in a snowstorm at night. They all believe they will freeze to death before morning. Mark Twain establishes himself and his companions in the role of tenderfeet by describing their reliance on information derived from books. Needless to say, this proves to be useless in the emergency:

> We could find no matches, and so we tried to make shift with the pistols. Not a man in the party had ever tried to do such a thing before, but not a man in the party doubted that it *could* be done, and without any trouble—because every man in the party had read about it in books many a time and had naturally come to believe it, with trusting simplicity, just as he had long ago accepted and believed *that other* common book-fraud about Indians and lost hunters making a fire by rubbing two dry sticks together.

At the moment when they are forced to acknowledge failure in their efforts to make a fire, they discover their horses have left them: "We gave them up without an effort at recovering them, and cursed the lying books that said horses would stay by their masters for protection and companionship in a distressful time like ours."

Reliance on bookish clichés about how to survive in the desert, however, is merely the superficial aspect of the helplessness of the travelers in a strange environment. Mark Twain has in mind a more sweeping demonstration of the irrelevance of the attitudes they have brought with them from "the States." The imminence of death raises them to the peak of ethical awareness which is possible for them within their conventional horizon. The first man, a Prussian called Ollendorff,

got out his bottle of whisky and said that whether he lived or died he would never touch another drop. He said he had given up all hope of life, and although ill-prepared, was ready to submit humbly to his fate; that he wished he could be spared a little longer, not for any selfish reason, but to make a thorough reform in his character, and by devoting himself to helping the poor, nursing the sick, and pleading with the people to guard themselves against the evils of intemperance, make his life a beneficent example to the young, and lay it down at last with the precious reflection that it had not been lived in vain. He ended by saying that his reform should begin at this moment, even here in the presence of death, since no longer time was to be vouchsafed wherein to prosecute it to men's help and benefit—and with that he threw away the bottle of whisky.

The parody of pulpit rhetoric and of that favorite fare of nineteenth-century audiences, the self-dramatization of the reformed reprobate, looks forward to classical moments in *Huckleberry Finn:* Huck's Pap, for example, shedding tears as an inexperienced philanthropist talks to him about "temperance and such things," and saying that "he'd been a fool, and fooled away his life; but now he was a-going to turn over a new leaf and be a man nobody wouldn't be ashamed of."

Mark Twain's ultimate target in the snowstorm scene is the lack of a sense of proportion and the invulnerable self-deception that characterized the crusades for moral reform generated periodically within evangelical Protestantism during the nineteenth century. The travelers' acceptance of their fate—potentially, of course, a state of mind worthy of an Oedipus at Colonos or a Lear—comes out as a burlesque of the exhibitionism of such platform favorites as E. Z. C. Judson and John B. Gough. And the spurious emotion is depicted with the precision of a master of style: in its words ("not . . . in vain," "even here in the presence of death," "no longer time was to be vouchsafed"); in its syntax, especially the arrangement of parallel and subordinate elements and the very pauses for breath that convey the unmistakable melody of cant; in its perfect sense of gesture and timing ("with that he threw away the bottle of whisky").

Ballou, the next speaker, casting aside his pack of cards,

said he never gambled, but still was satisfied that the meddling with cards in any way was immoral and injurious, and no man could be wholly pure and blemishless without eschewing them. "And therefore," continued he, "in doing this act I already feel more in sympathy with that spiritual saturnalia necessary to entire and obsolete reform."

The rhetorical pattern is similar to that of Ollendorff's remarks but there is a cunning variation in the verbal ornaments. The direct quotation intensifies the satire with two splendid jewels of language: "spiritual saturnalia" and "obsolete reform." "Obsolete" is an authentic malapropism (for "absolute"); but "saturnalia" is something else, perhaps a step beyond malapropism, since it is not clear what word of vaguely similar sound the speaker might have intended. "Saturnalia" is nevertheless a forceful allusion to the orgies of sentimentality that customarily accompanied the moments of high resolve Mark Twain intends to satirize. These locutions are in character for Ballou; he has already found alkali water "too technical" for him, and described the predicament of the party when they realized they were lost in the snowstorm as "perfectly hydraulic."

It is now the narrator's turn:

I threw away my pipe, and in doing it felt that at last I was free of a hated vice and one that had ridden me like a tyrant all my days. While I yet talked, the thought of the good I might have done in the world, and the still greater good I might *now* do, with these new incentives and higher and better aims to guide me if I could only be spared a few years longer, overcame me and the tears came again.

Only two or three years earlier Mark Twain had written to Livy: "I am in earnest in my determination to be *everything* you would have me be . . . I bring to this resolve the consciousness of that faith & strength & steady purpose which has enabled me to cast off as many slavish habits & utterly lose all taste or desire for them . . . Once a Christian, & invested with *that* strength, what should I fear?" It is astonishing that he can now use in this fashion phrases ("new incentives and higher and better aims," "free of a hated vice") so closely resembling those he had written to his fiancée.

After these flights of rhetoric, as often before, Mark Twain provides a deliberate shock of anticlimax. The chapter ends with the three wayfarers drifting off into "the warning drowsiness that precedes death by freezing." The next chapter begins as the snow-covered narrator regains consciousness next morning, to hear Ballou demand: "Will some gentleman be so good as to kick me behind?" For "there in the grey dawn, not fifteen steps from us, were the frame buildings of a stage-station, and under a shed stood our still saddled and bridled horses!" But the undercutting of the ecstasies of renunciation is not complete until the three friends return shamefacedly to their abandoned vices, shake hands, and agree "to say no more about 'reform' and 'examples to the rising generation.'"

This is the crisis of the initiation, the moment when the neophytes finally cast off their last connection with the way of life they must leave behind. The next chapter presents the narrator as a full-fledged member of the group he refers to as "the boys," apparently the entire adult male population of Carson City, capital of the territory. This group is the nearest approach in *Roughing It* to a concrete illustration of what a vernacular community might be like. Even so, it is a little shadowy. Mark Twain is unable to give full imaginative body to the system of values his narrator discovers as an alternative to the traditional culture.

The first version of the sketch called "The Facts of the Great Landslide Case," contained in a dispatch to the San Francisco *Call* published 20 August 1863, gives the name of an actual Attorney General, Benjamin P. Bunker, to the victim of the practical joke and dates the incident in 1861. But the anecdote has a distinct air of the tall tale about it; and the greatly expanded version published nine years later in *Roughing It* is essentially a piece of fiction. The conflict is between a self-important newcomer, a tenderfoot who, like the town-bred dog that set out to overtake the coyote, has an exaggerated opinion of his own merits; and "the older citizens" of the territory who "look down upon the rest of the world with a calm, benevolent compassion, as long as it keeps out of the way—when it gets in the way they snub it." The victim, now called Buncombe, is told that Tom Morgan's ranch has slid down the mountainside and covered Dick Hyde's. According to Hyde, "Morgan was in possession and refused to vacate the premises—said he was occupying his own cabin . . . and he would like to see anybody make him vacate." Buncombe is delighted to take a case in which victory seems certain. His "impassioned effort" before the fake tribunal is a burlesque of the kind of oratory that was admired in the courtrooms of the early nineteenth century.

Ex-Governor Roop, who presides over the trial, takes the deadpan role of the native humorist, and destroys the pretensions of the traditional culture by producing a solemn exaggeration of the rhetoric in which its most cherished values were clothed. He burlesques both the pompousness of the law and the cant of a decadent Calvinist orthodoxy. After prolonged reflection, Roop begins by admitting that the overwhelming weight of the evidence is in favor of the plaintiff Hyde.

But, gentlemen, let us beware how we allow mere human testimony, human ingenuity in argument and human ideas of equity, to influence us at a moment so solemn as this. Gentlemen, it ill becomes us, worms as we are, to meddle with the decrees of Heaven. It is plain to me that Heaven, in its inscrutable wisdom, has seen fit to move this defendant's ranch for a purpose. We are but creatures, and we must submit.

The decision is flat: "the plaintiff, Richard Hyde, has been deprived of his ranch by the visitation of God!" Buncombe is of course outraged; he returns that evening to remonstrate with Roop; and only after many days does he realize he has been the victim of a hoax.

What is at issue here is not so much the doctrine of the secret decrees of God as the effrontery of self-appointed spokesmen who arrogate to themselves the function of interpreting these decrees to ordinary mortals. From the unregenerate point of view, such censors claim to have a blank check signed by the Almighty. The point of the anecdote is the same as that of the description of the Pilgrim Bird in the Marseilles zoo: it derides the authority of those professing to have a special insight into the mind of God. And the repudiated authority is associated with the burlesque eloquence that was Mark Twain's forte. Roop's flourish, delivered with an outrageous air of biblical simplicity—"I warn you that this thing which has happened is a thing with which the sacrilegious hands and brains and tongues of men must not meddle"—is a lawyer's version of what the Pilgrim Bird had seemed to say: "Defile not Heaven's anointed with unsanctified hands."

4

With Roop's speech Mark Twain has arrived at the core of meaning in the story. The narrator who set out across the plains as a tenderfoot has become a member of the vernacular community of the mining camps. At this point, however, the style and point of view undergo a marked change. When the narrator abandons the life of a prospector and goes to work as a reporter on the Virginia City *Territorial Enterprise,* Mark Twain can begin to draw upon his clippings from the *Enterprise* and other California and Nevada newspapers.

Transformation of a Tenderfoot

The narrator who speaks in the second half of *Roughing It,* insofar as he has a coherent identity, is the man who had written the newspaper stories pasted in the scrapbooks that lay on Mark Twain's desk. He is not the character who has been shown undergoing the transformation from tenderfoot to old-timer. While Mark Twain was a prospector with his shoulder literally to the wheel of the heavy wagon in the sands of the Forty Mile Desert, or taking his turn with his partner Calvin Higbie at pick and shovel work, or lying awake to decide how he would spend the fortune he thought he had made in the strike of the blind lead, he was a member of the community of miners, one of "the boys." As a reporter for the *Territorial Enterprise* he became an observer, a bystander rather than a participant in the life of the mining community.

The change is aptly illustrated by his change of costume. Whereas the tenderfoot crossing the plains found himself discarding kid gloves and top hat, the miner who walked the sixty miles from Esmeralda to Virginia City to report for work on the *Enterprise* "coatless," with "slouch hat, blue woolen shirt, pantaloons stuffed into boot-tops, whiskered half down to the waist, and the universal navy revolver slung to [his] belt," now changes back. The miner's costume was too "rusty-looking" for a city editor. "I secured a more Christian costume and discarded the revolver. I had never had occasion to kill anybody, nor ever felt a desire to do so, but had worn the thing in deference to popular sentiment, and in order that I might not, by its absence, be offensively conspicuous, and a subject of remark." The more Christian costume considered appropriate for an editor was the boiled shirt and black broadcloth that would not have seemed out of place in Boston or New York. The careless dress that would cause comment after Mark Twain went East was a habit acquired during his period as a down-and-out Bohemian in San Francisco, not a mannerism of Virginia City journalists.

When the narrator of *Roughing It* begins to adopt the point of view of the newspaper articles he sometimes speaks as a neutral observer, but he also sometimes identifies himself with the responsible citizens of Virginia City as against the propertyless miners and prospectors. The consequences of this shift in perspective—which was no doubt quite unconscious —are illustrated in the often-reprinted anecdote of Buck Fanshaw's funeral. The sketch exploits the familiar contrast between colloquial and pedantic speech, but the narrator no longer has the point of view of one of the boys. The pronoun "we" does not designate here a group that could function as a unit in contriving a practical joke on the fatuous tender-foot Buncombe, but a society in which the boys constitute only one class, characterized as "the roughs" or "the vast bottom-stratum of society." And although "we" denotes the entire population of Virginia City, the narrator is distinctly ironic in his attitude toward the roughs. He stands apart from and above them; he identifies himself with the men "of high social standing and probity." "I cannot say which class we buried with most éclat in our 'flush times,' the distinguished public benefactor or the distinguished rough—possibly the two chief grades or grand divisions of society honored their illustrious dead about equally."

Buck Fanshaw was a hero of the roughs: he had "killed his man," "held a high position in the fire department," maintained a dashing mistress, was "a very Warwick in politics," and "kept a sumptuous saloon." Scotty Briggs, who ceremoniously invites the young clergyman to conduct the service, is so closely associated with Fanshaw that he must be regarded as a slightly less resplendent variant. The narrator takes evident pleasure in the richness of Scotty's "short-haired" slang, but it is the pleasure of an A. B. Longstreet in the dialect of his Georgia crackers. The adjective "weighty" in the following passage, for example, establishes a marked psychological distance between Scotty and the narrator. "Scotty was a stalwart rough, whose customary suit, when on weighty official business, like committee work, was a fire-helmet, flaming red flannel shirt, patent-leather belt with spanner and revolver attached, coat hung over arm, and pants stuffed into boot-tops." So attired, Scotty naturally "formed something of a contrast to the pale theological student" with whom he carried on his frustrating colloquy. The minister's impossibly stilted language comes out as follows: "Had deceased any religious convictions? That is to say, did he feel a dependence upon, or acknowledge allegiance to a higher power?" Scotty's manner is represented by his exhortation, "Just go in and toot your horn, if you don't sell a clam."

Mark Twain implies that he had the tale from the clergyman, much later: "in after days it was worth something to hear the minister tell about it." The sequel to the anecdote also seems to bear the imprint of the minister:

Scotty Briggs, in after days, achieved the distinction of becoming the only convert to religion that was ever gathered from the Virginia roughs: and it transpired that the man who had it in him to espouse the quarrel of the weak out of inborn nobility of spirit was no mean timber whereof to construct a Christian. The making him one did not warp his generosity or diminish his courage; on the contrary it gave intelligent direction to the one and a broader field to the other. If his Sunday-school class progressed faster than the other classes, was it matter for wonder? I think not. He talked to his pioneer small-fry in a language they understood!

The narrator is now fully identified with the point of view of an upper class that considers itself to be custodian of the official values. The situation grows complex in the remainder of the paragraph, for Mark Twain must be thinking of his own burlesque of the story of Joseph, omitted from *The Innocents Abroad* because of its extreme irreverence:

It was my large privilege, a month before he died, to hear him tell the beautiful story of Joseph and his brethren to his class "without looking at the book." I leave it to the reader to fancy what it was like, as it fell, riddled with slang, from the lips of that grave, earnest teacher, and was listened to by his little learners with a consuming interest that showed that they were as unconscious as he was that any violence was being done to the sacred proprieties!

"Large privilege" at the beginning of this passage and the reference to "the sacred proprieties" at the end convey an attitude of tolerant but condescending amusement toward Scotty that Mark Twain is confident the reader will share. It is the attitude with which picturesque examples of natural goodness among the lower classes had long been regarded in popular fiction and drama—an attitude superficially similar to Mark Twain's sympathy with vernacular characters in his earlier work but in fact quite different because it affirms rather than challenges traditional assumptions about social status. He has almost certainly imported into his anecdote a stock character from the contemporary stage: Mose, the volunteer fire laddie of New York, hero of the "Bowery B'hoys." Mose had figured in more than twenty plays since he was introduced to a ravished public in 1848 in Ned Buntline's novel, *The Mysteries and Miseries of New York*. In the same year Francis S. Chanfrau had scored a hit as Mose in Benjamin A. Baker's play, *A Glance at New York*, in which the hero, clad in red flannel shirt with his trousers tucked into his boots, distinguished himself by his readiness for a "muss" and his loyalty to his friends. "The fire-boys may be a little rough outside," he announces, "but they're all right here. [*Touches breast.*]" It is interesting that Mose's slang baffles a character who in turn addresses him in grandiloquent language he cannot understand. Sam P. Davis maintains in his *History of Nevada* that many of the volunteer firemen of Virginia City were immigrants from New York; in any case the theatrical cliché had made the transit, for Davis says that "these men, though rough, were not depraved or vicious, and they always arrayed themselves on the side of law and order whenever an issue was made with lawlessness and disorder."

5

Mark Twain is led to pick up such a stereotype from the theater because the fictional narrative persona built up in the first half of *Roughing It* has disintegrated. Henceforth his attitudes are quite unstable. On one page he is a spokesman for the official culture, on the next he veers back toward a burlesque of it, on a third he resorts to straightforward, neutral exposition of such matters as the operation of a stamping mill or the technique of pocket mining. The narrator is no longer projected as a distinct character but becomes more or less identified with what Mark Twain remembers about himself with the assistance of the newspaper clippings.

He had encountered a problem that has made it all but impossible, even down to the present, to write serious fiction about the early West. Identification with a vernacular point of view implied that man is naturally good; if he were released from the perversions of a highly developed society he would reveal his spontaneous benevolence. Freedom from restraint would permit the flowering of individuality into varied and possibly alarming forms, but no harm would come of it—only aesthetic pleasure for the observer, and perhaps the rudiments of a better scheme of values. Mark Twain's file of clippings reminded him again and again of facts that proved this assumption false: removal of the restraints of settled community life produced the spectacular phenomenon of the Western bad man, the killer. When the topic had come up in the chapters devoted to the desperado Slade, Mark Twain's tone had been curiously ambiguous. He seemed not to know whether he feared the man, or admired his courage and skill, or hated him for his brutality, or despised him for the cowardice that might possibly be the basic trait of the desperado. Now, taking up the desperado as a type, he speaks with conventional astonishment about the universal respect accorded such men by "this sort of people" —evidently not the writer's sort:

In Nevada, for a time, the lawyer, the editor, the banker, the chief desperado, the chief gambler, and the saloon-keeper, occupied the same level in society, and it was the highest . . . I am not sure but that the saloon-keeper held a shade higher rank than any other member of society . . . To be a saloon-keeper and kill a man was to be illustrious . . . "There goes the man that killed Bill Adams" was higher praise and a sweeter sound in the ears of this sort of people than any other speech that admiring lips could utter.

The pompous moralist has been aroused in Mark Twain. Recalling that Nevada juries would seldom convict a murderer, he embarks upon a digression about the folly of excluding from jury service all those who had read about a crime or formed an opinion about it. He is outraged that in a certain trial in Virginia City, "a minister, intelligent, esteemed, and greatly respected; a merchant of high character and known probity; a mining superintendent of intelligence and unblemished reputation; a quartz-mill owner of excellent standing, were all questioned . . . and all set aside." These are the people with whom he now identifies himself, and he records with disdain that the jury actually impaneled consisted of "two desperadoes, two low beer-house politicians, three bar-keepers, two ranchmen who could not read, and three dull, stupid, human donkeys!"

Except for the violence of the language, this might have been written by Timothy Dwight or Lyman Beecher. Its remoteness from the vernacular point of view is measured by the fact that Simon Wheeler's natural habitat was a barroom. Mark Twain maintains the tone of civic virtue in a chapter containing long quotations from the scrapbook about shootings and "desperate affrays" in Virginia City, and retraces the line of reasoning that led solid citizens in a hundred frontier towns to organize themselves as vigilantes. He is then reminded of how Captain Ned Blakely hanged the mate of a trading ship who had killed a member of Blakely's crew in the remote Chincha Islands.

In this fashion Mark Twain has worked his way around a circle and once again seems to be on the point of identifying himself with a vernacular character. But Blakely, like Scotty Briggs, turns out to be a stereotype from the popular stage. The Captain

sailed ships out of the harbor of San Francisco for many years. He was a stalwart, warm-hearted, eagle-eyed veteran, who had been a sailor nearly fifty years—a sailor from early boyhood. He was a rough, honest creature, full of pluck, and just as full of hard-headed simplicity, too. He hated trifling conventionalities—"business" was the word, with him. He had all a sailor's vindictiveness against the quips and quirks of the law, and steadfastly believed that the first and last aim and object of the law and lawyers was to defeat justice.

The reference to "all a sailor's vindictiveness" presupposes the existence of a stock character—the British Tar prominent in melodramas on the order of Douglas Jerrold's *Black-Eyed Susan* (1829). Any playgoer in the mid-nineteenth century knew that a sailor was poorly educated, hardened by lifelong exposure to wind, weather, and the dangers of the deep, profane in speech (offstage), ready with his fists, but at heart loyal and virtuous. No other meaning can be attached to the characterization of Blakely as a "warm-hearted, eagle-eyed veteran," and "a rough, honest creature, full of pluck." "Pluck" is a particularly suggestive word: was it ever used except by writers in the school of Horatio Alger?

If any doubt remains concerning Blakely's derivation from the stereotypes of popular drama and fiction, it can be dispelled by noticing the smug satisfaction with which Mark Twain ascribes to him physical brutality in the service of Right. When the bully (another stereotype) comes aboard Blakely's ship, Blakely "backed him against the mainmast, pounded his face to a pulp, and then threw him overboard. Noakes was not convinced. He returned the next night, got the pulp renewed, and went overboard head first, as before. He was satisfied." It should be said in Mark Twain's defense that this kind of thing is rare in his work—a fact which makes it all the plainer that here he is borrowing an effect rather than creating it himself. But as it stands the passage is exactly on the plane of television Western serials, and is well on the way toward Mickey Spillane. It has no meaning except the sadistic gratification offered by the image of someone's face being beaten to a pulp, and the illusory comfort of believing the Good Guy can always whip the Bad Guy. One is not surprised that Mark Twain's next chapter (although without overt connection) is devoted to the burlesque sensation novel supposedly serialized in the *Weekly Occidental*.

Another of the clichés Mark Twain picks up in describing Blakely is the term "stalwart." The same adjective had been applied to Scotty Briggs (he was "a stalwart rough," who had, however, as we remember, "a warm heart, and a strong love for his friends"). And it would be applied later in *Roughing It* to Jim Blaine, narrator of the celebrated story of the old ram. The word calls up a cluster of sentimental attitudes that formed a part of the popular culture. It is a shorthand designation for the formula by which crude, impulsive strength could be transformed from a threat to established values into a means of defending them. The unrefined character is shown to be a loyal defender of basic principles of justice even though he outrages the niceties of etiquette.

Although Mark Twain succumbs in part to melodramatic formulas, a close examination reveals hints of more complex feeling in his attitude toward these characters. Scotty Briggs perhaps conforms too closely to the stereotype to be interesting, but Captain Ned Blakely had some spark of life in him beneath the clichés. He was to undergo a thirty-year evolution in Mark Twain's mind that would transform him ultimately into the magnificent Captain Stormfield who visited heaven; and Jim Blaine is only lightly touched by the blight of melodrama.

6

Blaine's story of the old ram is provided with a framework much like that of "Jim Smiley and his Jumping Frog." The narrator says that "the boys" worked up his expectations about a yarn always told by Blaine when he was drunk to exactly the right degree. The story has a vernacular atmosphere not found elsewhere in the Virginia City chapters. It threatens to get out of hand, however, by turning into wild slapstick: "old Miss Wagner" borrows from "old Miss Jefferson" a glass eye which does not fit tightly in its socket; Miss Wagner also borrows Miss Higgins' wooden leg; we hear of a corpse that "riz up in his shroud" at the funeral in order to win a bet with the undertaker; a missionary and his wife are eaten by cannibals; and a man is snatched up by the machinery in a carpet factory and woven into fourteen yards of carpet. These macabre flourishes point toward the animated cartoons of our day. Their violence is a discharge of pent-up emotion without target or aim; a milder equivalent, perhaps, for the more direct aggressions of Sut Lovingood or Simon Suggs. Miss Wagner's trouble with the glass eye and the carnivorous carpet machine are not so much brutal as grotesque. Yet it is not easy to share Mark Twain's fondness for this kind of material, which has retained only a minimum of comic force.

The true center of Jim Blaine's narrative lies elsewhere. When Mark Twain discussed it many years later he dealt mainly with the material about the Irish hod-carrier who falls from a ladder and injures Blaine's Uncle Lem. He said that Jim Blaine was concerned with the question "whether the falling of the Irishman . . . was an accident, or was a special providence." This is familiar ground: the caricature of the doctrine of special providences links the monologue with Roop's speech at the Buncombe trial. Blaine remarks:

People said it was an accident. Much accident there was about that. He didn't know what he was there for, but he was there for a good object. If he hadn't been there the Irishman would have been killed . . . Uncle Lem's dog was there. Why didn't the Irishman fall on the dog? Becuz the dog would 'a' seen him a-coming and stood from under. That's the reason the dog warn't app'inted. A dog can't be depended on to carry out a special prov'dence. Mark my words, it was a put-up thing. Accidents don't happen, boys.

In describing the most effective technique for telling the story orally, Mark Twain quotes (with minor changes) the statement that the dog would have seen the man falling, and adds:

A pause *after* the remark was absolutely necessary with any and all audiences because no man, however intelligent he may be, can instantly adjust his mind to a new and unfamiliar, and yet for a moment or two apparently plausible, logic which recognizes in a dog an instrument too indifferent to pious restraints and too alert in looking out for his own personal interest to be safely depended upon in an emergency requiring self-sacrifice for the benefit of another, even when the command comes from on high.

The motives assigned to animals in Mark Twain's work are often, as here, instances of projection: a means of expressing what is in his mind or the minds of his characters but is felt to be disreputable or scandalous. Mark Twain's analysis of the dog's attitude makes a useful distinction between the exalted altruism that was ideally supposed to control human actions and the motives operative in the vernacular scheme of things. The vernacular character is free of malice or aggression but he does not feel obliged to sacrifice himself for the sake of another. This healthy egoism has no pretensions to moral grandeur, but it implies an ethical code that is workable in actual experience.

Although Blaine is said to be "stalwart," the epithet proves to be an inadvertence. He offers violence to no one, and his dominant characteristics place him with the Simon Wheelers of this world. Even his drunkenness is tranquil, serene, symmetrical; his face, like Wheeler's, is red and serious; and his monologue, a stream of linked associations, evokes a community, a cast of characters, a way of life that beneath the bizarre surface are pastoral and benign. When Miss Wagner's glass eye is out of position her guests show a politeness worthy of Mother Utterback: "somebody

68

would have to hunch her and say, 'Your game eye has fetched loose, Miss Wagner, dear'—and then all of them would have to sit and wait till she jammed it in again."

Blaine, like Mother Utterback, has a trace of aristocracy in his background (there is a vestigial concern with genealogy in his mention of the Hogadorns, "old Maryland stock," and "the Western Reserve Hagars; prime family"). Yet the society evoked by his stream of consciousness has grown plebeian in the course of migration to the interior. We hear of deacons and Dorcas societies and prayer meetings, of barrels of flour and flapjacks, and even of the great further move westward from Illinois that has brought Blaine to Nevada. A high concentration of animal images, including the superb name of the Hogadorns, further undercuts whatever pretensions to pride of place may be implicit in the emphasis on family connections. Yet the animals mentioned are all domesticated—teams to draw wagons, horses that trot in harness, heifers and fillies grazing in a pasture. And the practical joke on the narrator that is described in the framework surrounding Blaine's story, like that involved in "Jim Smiley and his Jumping Frog," is devoid of brutality. This may be due in part to the fact that the vernacular flavor of "The Story of the Old Ram" belongs to the rural Middle West rather than to the canebrakes and forests of the Old Southwest.

7

In *Roughing It* Mark Twain began a self-scrutiny that would last almost two decades. He did not, of course, have an explicit program; he was trying to find ways of giving literary form to intuitions that always reached farther than his means of expression. But the line of his development can best be indicated by saying that he searched his memory for images which could embody the affirmations implicit in a vernacular system of values. Nevada seemed a promising place to begin his inquiry. Yet the fact was—and the newspaper clippings must have reminded him of this if he had forgotten it—that he had grown bored with Nevada rather quickly. After less than two years in Virginia City, he recalled, "I began to get tired of staying in one place so long . . . I wanted to see San Francisco. I wanted to go somewhere. I wanted—I did not know *what* I wanted. I had the 'spring fever' and wanted a change, principally, no doubt." It will be recalled that later he also "got unspeakably tired" of his job as San Francisco correspondent for the *Enterprise* and "wanted another change."

After he left San Francisco for New York he returned to the West only once, on a business errand. His actual experience in Nevada and California had not satisfied him, and his memories of it failed to provide him with adequate symbols for the unformulated satisfactions he wished to celebrate in fiction.

IV

Discovery of the River and the Town

AFTER Mark Twain used his Sandwich Islands dispatches to pad out the later chapters of *Roughing It* he had no other series of newspaper articles left in his scrapbooks. He was accordingly at a loss concerning the subject for his next book. In 1872–73 he visited England twice, partly to lecture but mainly in order to collect materials for a book about that country. The project did not thrive, and instead he embarked on the collaboration with his Hartford neighbor Charles Dudley Warner that resulted in *The Gilded Age*. This novel contains one of Mark Twain's most memorable characters, the flamboyant Colonel Sellers with his grandiose schemes for making a fortune, but the authors could find no way to construct a plot except by stringing together threadbare devices borrowed from popular fiction. The experience did nothing to help Mark Twain find out how to write his own books. Not until the autumn of 1874 did he come upon an idea with real promise for his development as a writer. It was a revival of the plan for a "Mississippi book" he had considered as early as 1866. He had apparently laid the project aside until (as he wrote Livy just after finishing *Roughing It*) he could "spend 2 months on the river & take notes." This comment, significantly, occurs in the same letter in which he sets forth the formula for his lectures as a narrative plank with serious and humorous plugs inserted in it. He conceived of a book as a longer discourse with an identical structure. He thought he needed a factual narrative as a basis, and if he could not set out from a pre-existent series of newspaper dispatches he believed he must make an actual journey —to England, to the Mississippi—in order to get the material for it.

He was weaned from this conviction almost by accident as a result of Howells' urgent invitation to contribute to the *Atlantic Monthly*. Since a magazine article was not a book, it might be simply a reminiscence. On 24 October 1874 he wrote to Howells:

> I take back the remark that I can't write for the Jan. number. For Twichell & I have had a long walk in the woods & I got to telling him about old Mississippi days of steamboating glory & grandeur as I saw them (during 5 years) *from the pilot house.* He said "What a virgin subject to hurl into a magazine!" I hadn't thought of that before. Would you like a series of papers to run through 3 months or 6 or 9?—or about 4 months, say?

The memories might proliferate to the length of a book: "Old Times on the Mississippi," which ran to seven installments in the *Atlantic* in 1875, would eventually be brought out in England as a volume by itself. But so long as Mark Twain thought he was merely writing a series of articles he could get along without the documentary framework. It is noteworthy that later, when he decided to make a book for publication in America out of "Old Times," he still felt obliged to return to the river on a trip of observation, and also buttressed his reminiscences with wide reading in works of history and travel. (Of course, he was motivated in part by his belief that a book to be sold by subscription must be a big one.)

"Old Times" confirms the discovery Mark Twain had made in the first part of *Roughing It* that his recollections, subjected over a period of time to the unnoticed shaping of imagination, were richer literary material than his deliberate observations; and further that the pattern his imagination discovered in his memories—or imposed on them—provided a far better structure than the narrative plank of his lectures and *The Innocents Abroad.* More important still, in "Old Times" he gained access to a layer of experience buried deeper in the past than his memories of the overland journey of 1861, buried in fact as deep as his childhood.

By analogy with the Matter of Troy or the Matter of Britain in medieval romance, we may say that the reminiscences of piloting in "Old Times" belong to the Matter of the River. But the series opens with a passage belonging to the even richer Matter of Hannibal, the childhood memories that were to provide the vocabulary of images he would use in *Tom Sawyer* and *Huckleberry Finn,* and all his later writing of major importance. "When I was a boy," begins the first installment of "Old Times"—

> When I was a boy, there was but one permanent ambition among my comrades in our village on the west bank of the Mississippi River. That was, to be a steamboatman . . .

Discovery of River and Town

Once a day a cheap, gaudy packet arrived upward from St. Louis, and another downward from Keokuk. Before these events, the day was glorious with expectancy; after them, the day was a dead and empty thing. Not only the boys, but the whole village, felt this. After all these years I can picture that old time to myself now, just as it was then: the white town drowsing in the sunshine of a summer's morning; the streets empty, or pretty nearly so; one or two clerks sitting in front of the Water Street stores, with their splint-bottomed chairs tilted back against the walls, chins on breasts, hats slouched over their faces, asleep—with shingle-shavings enough around to show what broke them down; a sow and a litter of pigs loafing along the sidewalk, doing a good business in watermelon rinds and seeds; two or three lonely little freight piles scattered about the "levee"; a pile of "skids" on the slope of the stone-paved wharf, and the fragrant town drunkard asleep in the shadow of them; two or three wood flats at the head of the wharf, but nobody to listen to the peaceful lapping of the wavelets against them; the great Mississippi, the majestic, the magnificent Mississippi, rolling its mile-wide tide along, shining in the sun; the dense forest away on the other side; the "point" above the town, and the "point" below, bounding the river-glimpse and turning it into a sort of sea, and withal a very still and brilliant and lonely one.

Into this stillness comes the steamboat. The whole town springs into life and makes for the wharf to watch the landing and envy passengers and crew—not only the captain, "calm, imposing," standing by his signal bell, but the feverishly cursing mates and even the deck hand who "stands picturesquely on the end of [the landing-stage] with a coil of rope in his hand." Ten minutes after the steamer casts off, "the town is dead again, and the town drunkard asleep by the skids once more."

As has often been pointed out, this reminiscence of Mark Twain's boyhood hints at nearly all the materials of *Tom Sawyer* and *Huckleberry Finn*: the sleepy villagers; the eager fantasies of the boys; the Negro drayman (a slave, yet possessing an identity and even a reputation—he is "famous for his quick eye and prodigious voice") who announces "S-t-e-a-m-boat a-comin'!"; the bland summer sunshine; the squalor suggested by the wandering sow and her litter; Pap Finn, as yet merely the anonymous town drunkard; and in dramatic contrast, the surrounding forest and the great river itself. Brief as it is, the passage also suggests the variety of Mark Twain's attitudes toward the Matter of Hannibal. He is tenderly ironic about the resplendent primary colors of the boys' dreams of glory. He is nostalgic about "that old time," quietly humorous in his thumbnail sketch of the clerks broken down by the labor of whittling shingles, delicately aware of "the peaceful lapping of the wavelets," and responsive with

73

shortened breath and iambic rhythm to "the majestic, the magnificent Mississippi."

The emotions expressed here are much more intense and more diverse than are the emotions about Nevada expressed in *Roughing It*. After all, Mark Twain did not see the Far West until he was twenty-six years old and already had two careers behind him, as journeyman printer and as steamboat pilot. The Matter of Hannibal, on the other hand, occupied the deepest level of his memory. It was almost endlessly suggestive for him, but it presented difficulties commensurate with its possibilities. Before he could use the material in fiction he must define his attitude toward it; and this meant nothing less than establishing his own identity in relation to it by working out a continuity between his adult life in Hartford and his remote childhood in the small town on the west bank of the river, thirty years in the past.

For an understanding of *Tom Sawyer,* the most important feature of the passage about Hannibal in "Old Times" is its mixture of intimacy and detachment. The author is both inside and outside the image. The town is present to his imagination "just as it was then"; at the same time it is unattainably remote, for it represents a lost innocence. The man who is setting down his recollections belongs to a great world which the villagers do not know exists. And not only his knowledge and experience, but his sensibility is wider than theirs. It is he, not they, who responds aesthetically to the forest and the river, and who finds an exotic charm in their somnolent daily routine. These attitudes determine the most conspicuous traits of St. Petersburg in *Tom Sawyer*—its pastoral tranquillity and the serene beauty of the natural setting. As Walter Blair says, St. Petersburg is a place "of quiet delight bathed in summer air fragrant with the aroma of meadows, woodlands, and flowers." But the description of Hannibal in "Old Times" contains darker, uglier hints as well. The author's detachment-and-involvement includes a suggestion of moral condemnation and aesthetic revulsion implicit in his references to the vegetating clerks, the town drunk, and the decaying melon rinds, which foreshadow Pokeville and other squalid river towns in *Huckleberry Finn*.

Mark Twain has in fact at least three different attitudes toward the Matter of Hannibal that are likely to be aroused in sequence or simultaneously whenever he touches upon any part of it. One is a simple, unquenchable pleasure in the act of recall which seems to obliterate time by restoring his childhood to him. This recovery of the past is often tinged with a facile melancholy like that of Stephen Foster's songs, but sometimes it is a pure act of the imagination. These are the moments that have earned an almost mythical status for the Matter of Hannibal and have made Mark Twain's boyhood an international possession. The two other attitudes are always in some degree self-conscious and sophisticated: they are a tendency to make Tom a vehicle for burlesquing romantic literature, and a sense of moral outrage that gives rise to satire.

Only the first of the three attitudes could conceivably further Mark Twain's effort to discover in the Matter of Hannibal positive values that might be called vernacular. Tom Sawyer's fantasies, for example, are a burlesque of melodramatic fiction, but they make him also a comic butt and rule out any real identification of the author with him. Consider the psychological distance between author and characters in the following passage from the first installment of "Old Times."

When a circus came and went, it left us all burning to become clowns; the first Negro minstrel show that ever came to our section left us all suffering to try that kind of life; now and then we had a hope that, if we lived and were good, God would permit us to be pirates.

"Burning," "suffering," and the hope of divine favor are caricatures of what the boys can actually be imagined as feeling. They are made comically naïve; and while we know what Mark Twain means, the tone places both him and the reader at an elevation from which life in Hannibal seems merely quaint or amusing.

Direct satire, hinted at in the reference to the clerks' exhaustion, also interposes a barrier between the author and his material. Even nostalgia for a vanished past, while it seems to place a high valuation on the images welling up in the writer's memory, tends to seal them off from the actual world by emphasizing their remoteness, their inaccessibility. Nostalgia makes the past seem supremely desirable but blurs its actual features. The only mode of access to the past that can avoid lowering it to the status of a fantasy in the mind of some person in the present is the recovery of it in art by incorporating it in a medium sufficiently controlled to eliminate the artist's approval or disapproval, his nostalgia or his revulsion.

2

Colonel Sellers is a fictional portrait of Clemens' uncle, James Lampton, and thus derives from the Matter of Hannibal. *The Gilded Age* also contains an interesting section about the river in the account of the journey of the Hawkins family from Tennessee to Missouri. But "Old Times" and *Tom Sawyer* are the earliest works in which Mark Twain used the memories of his childhood and youth as the substance of long narratives. Here he made his first intensive effort to discover the meaning of these segments of his experience. The material had so much latent meaning for him that the two works exert an almost magical charm, but they are minor achievements in comparison with what he was able to do later with similar material in *Huckleberry Finn*. The opportunity was so great and Mark Twain's gifts as a writer so remarkable that one can hardly avoid speculating about the reasons for the relative inferiority of these first attempts.

The root of the matter is his attitude toward his material. "Old Times" is weakened by the fact that the writer, especially toward the end, tends to look down on people and incidents from a position of superiority. As long as he views things through the eyes of the green cub his familiar procedures serve him well. He can construct a fictive world in which the narrator remembers himself as a tenderfoot and in some measure a comic butt, and persons of exalted status like the pilot Bixby or even the captain and mates of the vessel, seen from below, take on a heroic glamour. The narrator accepts the hierarchic pattern of his world, but the gradations of status depend so directly on technical competence that the less rational values of society at large are of no moment. As he attains higher status within the world of steamboatmen, however, he sometimes adopts the quite different and even unrelated value system of the world outside.

A "big rise" in the river, he says in one of the later installments, brought a new world under his vision, for then the boats could pass through chutes behind islands that were too shallow in low water. A suspicious gentility creeps into his description of the woodland solitudes thus made accessible: the "grassy nooks and vistas glimpsed as we swept by," "the spendthrift richness of the forest foliage," the "tender willow thickets." One is not surprised that to an observer using diction of this sort the people living along the backwaters should seem less attractive than the natural setting:

Behind other islands we found wretched little farms, and wretcheder little log cabins; there were crazy rail fences sticking a foot or two above the water, with one or two jeans-clad, chills-racked, yellow-faced male miserables roosting on the top rail, elbows on knees, jaws in hands, grinding tobacco and discharging the result at floating chips through crevices left by lost teeth; while the rest of the family and the few farm animals were huddled together in an empty wood-flat riding at her moorings close at hand.

The narrator is quite implacable toward these creatures. To say that the men were "roosting" on the fences degrades them to the level of animals. The hyphenated modifiers have almost the force of profanity. He adds that the chronic malarial chills of the bottom-dwellers are "a merciful provision of an all-wise Providence to enable them to take exercise without exertion." And even the recurrent floods are "kindly dispensations, for they at least enabled the poor things to rise from the dead now and then, and look upon life when a steamboat went by."

The passage has the tone of A. B. Longstreet's *Georgia Scenes* in the 1830's or even of William Byrd's disdainful description of Carolina backwoodsmen in his *History of the Dividing Line* a century earlier. Mark Twain had ordinarily followed the example of later humorists like George W. Harris, creator of Sut Lovingood, who tended to identify with their vernacular characters instead of patronizing or deriding them. While it is conceivable or even probable that a cub pilot might console himself for his degraded position in the status system aboard the steamboat by vaunting his superiority to everyone on shore, the description of the jeans-clad miserables marooned by the flood is written from a point of view strikingly at variance with that of earlier episodes in "Old Times." The difference lies in the fact that Mark Twain momentarily abandons the ironic perspective of a man looking back on his experiences as a callow youth. He has forgotten the cub pilot whose adventures he is supposedly relating; he speaks directly, in his own person. The loss is twofold. He not only adopts a conventionally derisive attitude toward representatives of an uncultivated and poverty-stricken lower class, but obliterates the fictive world that he had brought into being earlier in the narrative.

3

In one of the later installments of "Old Times" Mark Twain tries to explain exactly how he was changed by the process of "learning the river." Although the discussion ostensibly concerns the technical knowledge acquired by a pilot, the imagery and diction broaden the issue into an analysis of the whole scope of conventional aesthetic theory. The passage bears so directly on Mark Twain's thinking about the problem of values that it deserves extensive quotation. As his training at the hands of Bixby proceeded, he says, "The face of the water . . . became a wonderful book—a book that was a dead language to the uneducated passenger, but which told its mind to me without reserve, delivering its most cherished secrets as clearly as if it uttered them with a voice. And it was not a book to be read once and thrown aside, for it had a new story to tell every day." The knowledge acquired by learning the river was very somber: "the passenger who could not read this book saw nothing but all manner of pretty pictures in it, painted by the sun and shaded by the clouds, whereas to the trained eye these were not pictures at all, but the grimmest and most dead-earnest of reading-matter." Thus "a peculiar sort of faint dimple" on the surface of the water, merely charming to the passenger, meant to the pilot something "hideous": "a wreck or a rock was buried there that could tear the life out of the strongest vessel that ever floated."

After such knowledge, Mark Twain asks in effect, what forgiveness? "I had made a valuable acquisition. But I had lost something, too. I had lost something which could never be restored to me while I lived. All the grace, the beauty, the poetry, had gone out of the majestic river!" He illustrates the point by a description of "a certain wonderful sunset which I witnessed when steamboating was new to me."

A broad expanse of the river was turned to blood; in the middle distance the red hue brightened into gold, through which a solitary log came floating, black and conspicuous; in one place a long, slanting mark lay sparkling upon the water; in another the surface was broken by boiling, tumbling rings, that were as many-tinted as an opal; where the ruddy flush was faintest, was a smooth spot that was covered with graceful circles and radiating lines, ever so delicately traced; the shore on our left was densely wooded, and the somber shadow that fell from this forest was broken in one place by a long, ruffled trail that shone like silver; and high above the forest wall a clean-stemmed dead tree waved a single leafy bough that glowed like a flame in the unobstructed splendor that was flowing from the sun. There were graceful curves, reflected images, woody heights, soft distances; and over the whole scene, far and near, the dissolving lights drifted steadily, enriching it every passing moment with new marvels of coloring.

I stood like one bewitched. I drank it in, in a speechless rapture.

Discovery of River and Town

This passage elaborates one element of the contrast announced at the beginning: it is a "pretty picture," the misleading appearance seen by the untrained eye. The note of artificiality in the language is emphasized by the reference to "dissolving lights." For this technical term shows that Mark Twain means to compare the scene to a painting in one of the panoramas of the river exhibited by itinerant showmen, often with ingenious lighting effects. A trained pilot would not have been deceived by the beautiful surface of the water. He would have said to himself:

That floating log means that the river is rising, small thanks to it; that slanting mark on the water refers to a bluff reef which is going to kill somebody's steamboat one of these nights, if it keeps on stretching out like that; those tumbling 'boils' show a dissolving bar and a changing channel there; the lines and circles in the slick water over yonder are a warning that that troublesome place is shoaling up dangerously; that silver streak in the shadow of the forest is the 'break' from a new snag, and he has located himself in the very best place he could have found to fish for steamboats.

Because the expert's knowledge is so disenchanting, "Since those days, I have pitied doctors from my heart. What does the lovely flush in a beauty's cheek mean to a doctor but a 'break' that ripples above some deadly disease? Are not all her visible charms sown thick with what are to him the signs and symbols of hidden decay?"

In short, the initiation of the cub pilot duplicates human experience in general. To possess any kind of exact knowledge is to be aware of a reality that is hidden from the ignorant or inexperienced. What they see is called, significantly, a "picture"—the term which both Mark Twain and his reviewers applied to the passages of ornate description in his lectures and books, for example the descriptions of Kilauea and of the Sphinx. The picture on the surface of the water is "the romance and beauty," "the grace, the beauty, the poetry" of the river. It is conveyed by means of such words as blood, gold, sparkling, opal, silver, flame, splendor: all terms drawn from the conventional aesthetic vocabulary. The "graceful curves" and "soft distances" are particularly suggestive of a genteel sensibility; they prepare us to learn that the coloring of the sunset consisted of "marvels," and that the observer "stood like one bewitched." The false beauty of the sunset belongs to the realm of the supernatural, the miraculous, the magical—that is, the realm of the ideal.

Even more orthodox is the final comparison of the sunset to the flush brought by disease to the cheek of a beautiful woman. Mark Twain seldom advances so far into the labyrinth of the official aesthetics. The analogy not only confers on beauty, romance, and poetry the stigma of falsity, but suggests that the falsity is specifically feminine. Furthermore, it expresses a deep fear of femaleness by implying that woman's beauty is a snare, masking "some deadly disease" or "hidden decay."

In discussing the sunset Mark Twain succumbs to the cliché of heart versus head always lurking in the theory of ideality. He professes to yearn for an innocence of vision that knowledge and experience have destroyed. But the elegant posture he has talked himself into is merely a stereotype. His contention that he has lost the power to perceive the beauty of the sunset is nonsense, even on his own showing. For in the very act of demonstrating what a precious faculty has been stripped away from him he writes a description of the sunset displaying that faculty in a high state of development. The ability to have this ritualized kind of aesthetic experience is of dubious value, but in any case Mark Twain has not lost it. It should be noted finally that he organizes the discussion of the sunset within his familiar pattern of exalted rhetoric followed by a deliberate deflation. As in earlier uses of the pattern, he implies that the rhetoric is false, the prosaic reality true. But just as he can identify himself with upper-class contempt for backwoodsmen, so here he is distressed by the loss of the power to share the conventional aesthetic experience of the sunset.

Or rather, he says he is distressed by the loss, and for the moment no doubt persuades himself that he is. But nearly everything else in "Old Times" can be brought forward as evidence that he enjoyed the pilot's skill and the pilot's function, and that learning the river brought him benefits more than offsetting any hypothetical impairment of sensibility. He took great pleasure, for example, in contrasting the inspired idiocy of the cub with the masterly skill of an expert. When the narrator confesses he thought Bixby was identifying landmarks along the bank merely to be entertaining, the teacher's wrath has a Homeric grandeur, and Mark Twain's description of it is alive with uninhibited delight:

He raged and stormed so (he was crossing the river at the time) that I judged it made him blind, because he ran over the steering-oar of a trading-scow. Of course the traders sent up a volley of red-hot profanity. Never was a man so grateful as Mr. Bixby was; because he was brimful, and here were subjects who could *talk back*. He threw open a window, thrust his head out, and such an irruption followed as I never had heard before. The fainter and farther away the scowmen's curses drifted, the higher Mr. Bixby lifted his voice and the weightier his adjectives grew. When he closed the window he was empty. You could have drawn a seine through his system and not caught curses enough to disturb your mother with.

This is not vernacular diction in the sense of being dialect, but on the other hand it is certainly not the exalted language of sublime description. It is a middle style, the voice neither of Jim Blaine nor of the genteel tourist who viewed the crater of Kilauea, but of a man familiar with the world of commonplace things who assumes that the reader lives in the same world. The diction is not limited to a backwoods vocabulary: "weightier adjectives," "subjects," "thrust his head," and "raged and stormed" are hardly even colloquial. Yet the narrator's emotions (such as his delight in profanity as a fine art), the homely images introduced without self-consciousness (seining for fish, a blacksmith's red-hot iron, a brimful bucket), and the shrewd but sympathetic perception that Bixby could not really relieve himself by swearing at a cub who was forbidden to swear back were material new to literature at the level of the *Atlantic Monthly*. The sensibility that Mark Twain regrets having lost was of no moment in comparison with the sensibility that enabled him to recognize the possibilities in such material and create a style capable of doing justice to them. Without invoking any of the traditional literary devices, he can create wonderfully bizarre effects: "You might reasonably have in mind disturbing your mother with profanity, but in that case Bixby would have been of no use to you." The imagined situation perfectly illustrates a vernacular attitude.

4

The germ of *The Adventures of Tom Sawyer* was an unfinished sketch called "Boy's Manuscript" apparently written in 1870, that is, during the first year of the writer's married life. This is a literary burlesque, possibly suggested by David Copperfield's courtship of Dora. But the comic device of reducing the principals of a story to children was familiar on the popular stage; even as far west as Carson City, Mark Twain had seen the R. G. Marsh troupe of Juvenile Comedians, whose entire repertory consisted of burlesques of this sort. The "Boy's Manuscript" translates the story of an adult courtship (possibly with some reference to Mark Twain's own) into the vocabulary provided by the Matter of Hannibal.

Instead of the conventional flower given by the woman to her lover, Mark Twain's hero, Billy Rogers, receives from his beloved a piece of molasses candy. He wears it next his heart until it melts and sticks to him so that he cannot get his shirt off. Billy Rogers became Tom Sawyer as the book unfolded in the author's mind, and the original love story was modified somewhat by a narrative pattern depicting Tom's growth toward maturity. But the childish love affair remains as a central component of what conventional plot the novel has. Tom's wanderings, intended and actual, are motivated by his despair over being rejected by Becky Thatcher. After their first quarrel he contemplates suicide, then decides to run away in order to become a pirate, but meets Joe Harper and falls to playing Robin Hood instead. After a later rejection Tom actually embarks on his career as a pirate to the extent of escaping to Jackson's Island with Huck Finn and Joe Harper.

The repetition of plot material in these two sequences suggests that Mark Twain found Tom's amorous experiences deficient in variety and exciting incident. He supplements the burlesque love story with two sub-plots: the rivalry between Tom and his half brother Sid (which is itself a burlesque of Sunday-school stories about the Bad Boy and the Good Boy), and the melodramatic sequence of events set in motion when Tom and Huck by accident become witnesses of the midnight grave-robbing and Injun Joe's murder of young Dr. Robinson. This material might be one of Tom Sawyer's fantasies except that we are expected to take it seriously. It is another example of Mark Twain's susceptibility to infection from "wildcat literature."

Neither the love story nor the Injun Joe subplot provides a good framework for the Matter of Hannibal, and the rivalry of Tom and Sid serves merely to introduce such boyish crimes as Tom's swimming without permission. Nothing comes of the hint that Sid picks up about the murder of Dr. Robinson from Tom's talk in his sleep. The Matter of Hannibal gets into *The Adventures of Tom Sawyer* primarily through episodes having little connection with the plot. Yet these are the passages for which the book is remembered: the whitewashing of the fence, the Sunday school and church services, examination day at school.

The structural problems of the novel, like those of Mark Twain's earlier books, reflect the instability of his attitudes toward his material. He was not clear in his own mind whether he was writing a story for boys or a story about boys for adults. The burlesque love story presupposes a grown-up audience; it depends for its effect on the reader's perception of the comic parallels between Tom's behavior and that of an adult. Tom's fantasies about pirates and robbers and Robin Hood, again, are relatively meaningless unless the reader can enjoy the ironic contrast between the glamorous fantasy world of romance and the everyday reality of life in St. Petersburg. Both these modes of burlesque interpose a considerable psychological distance between the novelist and his characters, and make it difficult for him to do justice to whatever values may be latent in the Matter of Hannibal. Thus at the end of the whitewashing episode Mark Twain remarks patronizingly that Tom

had discovered a great law of human action, without knowing it—namely, that in order to make a man or a boy covet a thing, it is only necessary to make the thing difficult to attain. If he had been a great and wise philosopher, like the writer of this book, he would now have comprehended that Work consists of whatever a body is *obliged* to do, and that Play consists of whatever a body is not obliged to do.

The incident is reduced to an exemplum illustrating a generalization that has nothing to do with the story. Something tells the writer he is on the wrong tack and he confuses things further by mocking at himself.

His uncertain attitude is even more apparent in his efforts to lend importance to the Injun Joe subplot. When the half-breed is found dead of hunger and thirst just behind the iron door Judge Thatcher has had installed at the entrance to the cave, Mark Twain inserts a serious version of Jim Blaine's rumination about special providences, with touches reminiscent of the rhapsody on the Sphinx in *The Innocents Abroad*:

In one place near at hand, a stalagmite had been slowly growing up from the ground for ages, built by the water-drip from a stalactite overhead. The captive had broken off the stalagmite, and upon the stump had placed a stone, wherein he had scooped a shallow hollow to catch the precious drop that fell once in every three minutes with the dreary regularity of a clock-tick—a dessert-spoonful once in four-and-twenty hours. That drop was falling when the Pyramids were new; when Troy fell; when the foundations of Rome were laid; when Christ was crucified; when the Conqueror created the British empire; when Columbus sailed; when the massacre at Lexington was "news." It is falling now; it will still be falling when all these things shall have sunk down the afternoon of history and the twilight of tradition and been swallowed up in the thick night of oblivion. Has everything a purpose and a mission? Did this drop fall patiently during five thousand years to be ready for this flitting human insect's need? and has it another important object to accomplish ten thousand years to come?

5

The emphasis on Injun Joe's thirst is implausible in view of numerous earlier references to water in the cave; Tom and Becky had encountered him near a spring. Furthermore, such a burst of eloquence is quite out of keeping with the tone of the book. It serves no purpose except to demonstrate that the narrator can produce the kind of associations held in esteem by the dominant culture. The diction of the novel often has a similar effect. Take for example the introduction to the whitewashing incident:

Saturday morning was come, and all the summer world was bright and fresh, and brimming with life. There was a song in every heart; and if the heart was young the music issued at the lips. There was cheer in every face and a spring in every step. The locust trees were in bloom and the fragrance of the blossoms filled the air. Cardiff Hill, beyond the village and above it, was green with vegetation, and it lay just far enough away to seem a Delectable Land, dreamy, reposeful, and inviting.

The elegantly archaic verb form "was come"; the genteel impersonality of "the lips"; "fragrance" in place of "odor"; the literary allusion in "Delectable Land"; and the telltale reference to dreams, all mark this as polite prose. The imagery and the tone are intended to establish a mood of peace and joy as a foil to Tom's "deep melancholy" over being sentenced to whitewash the fence: "Life seemed to him hollow, and existence but a burden." But the rhetorical effect is overdone.

Another illustration of the psychological distance between the writer and his material is the description of the superintendent's address to the pupils in the Sunday school, with satirical comments like the following.

When a Sunday-school superintendent makes his customary little speech, a hymn-book in the hand is as necessary as is the inevitable sheet of music in the hand of a singer . . . at a concert—though why, is a mystery: for neither the hymn-book nor the sheet of music is ever referred to by the sufferer.

The patronizing air is maintained:

The latter third of the speech was marred by the resumption of fights and other recreations among certain of the bad boys, and by fidgetings and whisperings that extended far and wide, washing even to the bases of isolated and incorruptible rocks like Sid and Mary.

In themselves, the witty understatement of "recreations" and the equally witty comparison of Sid and Mary to rocks with waves breaking against them are amusing, but they represent a kind of exhibitionism on the part of the writer.

Fortunately, Mark Twain is sometimes able to get rid of his self-consciousness and render Tom's experience directly, without comment or moralizing. Such a moment comes during the church service that follows the Sunday-school scene just quoted. The minister is inviting the attention of the Almighty to a long list of persons in need of divine guidance.

In the midst of the prayer a fly had lit on the back of the pew in front of [Tom] and tortured his spirit by calmly rubbing its hands together, embracing its head with its arms, and polishing it so vigorously that it seemed to almost part company with the body, and the slender thread of a neck was exposed to view; scraping its wings with its hind legs and smoothing them to its body as if they had been coat-tails; going through its whole toilet as tranquilly as if it knew it was perfectly safe. As indeed it was; for as sorely as Tom's hands itched to grab for it they did not dare—he believed his soul would be instantly destroyed if he did such a thing while the prayer was going on. But with the closing sentence his hand began to curve and steal forward; and the instant "Amen" was out the fly was a prisoner of war. His aunt detected the act and made him let it go.

The language used in describing the fly is easy and effective without being either high or low: it is an almost imperceptible medium of communication. The insect is not a symbol, but the minuteness with which it is described conveys with admirable force Tom's agony of boredom during the prayer. He seizes upon any distraction that offers itself as a relief from his suffering. The austere language in which the fly is depicted is quite different from Mother Utterback's richly colloquial speech. At its best this prose is devoid of vernacular color as well as of all other idiosyncrasies. But Mark Twain could not have achieved such a command of his medium if he had not learned how to free himself from the preoccupation with eloquence that permeated the American literary tradition, and the means of his emancipation had been the skeptical attitude toward ornate rhetoric developed in his repeated exposures of it to comic juxtaposition with vernacular speech.

The description of Tom's secret journey back to St. Petersburg from Jackson's Island is a comparable example of the spare, flat rendering of experience. The series of declarative statements imparts an appropriate forward motion to the prose and engenders a mood of expectancy. Mark Twain carefully refrains from telling us what Tom is about. There is no reason why the information should be withheld except that the writer wishes to fix the reader's attention by something like suspense. Perhaps the result is impressive because it simulates the inner movement of our feelings in many actual situations: we recognize a strong current impelling us in a general direction, but we do not know what the exact outcome or destination will be. It may be also that stripping away rhetorical ornament fosters vividness by suggesting that the actual situation absorbs all the writer's attention. The passage sounds like Hemingway. Whatever the means by which the effect is achieved, it is an all but complete recapture of the past:

A few minutes later Tom was in the shoal water of the bar, wading toward the Illinois shore. Before the depth reached his middle he was halfway over; the current would permit no more wading, now, so he struck out confidently to swim the remaining hundred yards. He swam quartering upstream, but still was swept downward rather faster than he had expected. However, he reached the shore finally, and drifted along till he found a low place and drew himself out. He put his hand on his jacket pocket, found his piece of bark safe, and then struck through the woods, following the shore, with streaming garments. Shortly before ten o'clock he came out into an open place opposite the village, and saw the ferry-boat lying in the shadow of the trees and the high bank. Everything was quiet under the blinking stars. He crept down the bank, watching with all his eyes, slipped into the water, swam three or four strokes, and climbed into the skiff that did "yawl" duty at the boat's stern. He laid himself down under the thwarts and waited, panting.

Presently the cracked bell tapped and a voice gave the order to "cast off." A minute or two later the skiff's head was standing high up, against the boat's swell, and the voyage was begun. Tom felt happy in his success, for he knew it was the boat's last trip for the night. At the end of a long twelve or fifteen minutes the wheels stopped, and Tom slipped overboard and swam ashore in the dusk, landing fifty yards down-stream, out of danger of possible stragglers.

The information that the current swept Tom downstream faster than he expected lends a peculiar vividness to the passage. Since this had no effect on the outcome of the trip, it does not need to be reported for the sake of logic or coherence. The narrator's remark has the artless, circumstantial air of a witness determined to tell everything he remembers without presuming to judge what is relevant and what is not. The same comment could be made about the statement that the skiff's head stood up high, and the epithet "blinking" applied to the stars: that was the way they looked, although their appearance had no bearing on Tom's mission.

Another moment of almost completely unself-conscious recovery of the past—a moment that must lie close to the emotional center of the Matter of Hannibal for Mark Twain—comes a few pages later, but still in the Jackson's Island sequence:

> After breakfast they went whooping and prancing out on the bar, and chased each other round and round, shedding clothes as they went, until they were naked, and then continued the frolic far away up the shoal water of the bar, against the stiff current, which latter tripped their legs from under them from time to time and greatly increased the fun. And now and then they stooped in a group and splashed water in each other's faces with their palms, gradually approaching each other, with averted faces to avoid the strangling sprays, and finally gripping and struggling till the best man ducked his neighbor, and then they all went under in a tangle of white legs and arms, and came up blowing, sputtering, laughing, and gasping for breath at one and the same time.
>
> When they were well exhausted, they would run out and sprawl on the dry, hot sand, and lie there and cover themselves up with it, and by and by break for the water again and go through the original performance once more. Finally it occurred to them that their naked skin represented flesh-colored "tights" very fairly; so they drew a ring in the sand and had a circus—with three clowns in it, for none would yield this proudest post to his neighbor.

The language here is again almost without color, but what coloring it has is colloquial. "Whooping" and "prancing" are applied more often to animals than to human beings, and the actions they describe are distinctly indecorous. "Round and round" belongs to colloquial rather than exalted diction, and so does "chase" in the sense of "pursue." (One would prefer, incidentally, to omit "latter" in the last clause of the sentence.) "Averted faces" is somewhat literary in place of "faces turned away," but "ducked," "sputtering," "sprawl," and "break for the water" are drawn from a basic oral vocabulary. The writer is directing more attention to his subject than to his diction; it subordinates itself to the actions described.

As in the description of the fly, the minute detail with which the scene is rendered gives it an air of meaning more than it seems to on the surface. The lavish particularity testifies to the value the author attaches to what he is describing. It would never have occurred to Mark Twain to say that natural facts are symbols of spiritual facts, but the memory of such a frolic had for him thirty years later a significance comparable to what Emerson tried to express in metaphysical terms. Although the value is perhaps too deeply buried ever to be brought to the surface and given precise statement, it is value just the same, and it is not derived from the sources or supported by the sanctions acknowledged in the traditional culture. In contrast with the revulsion against the body implicit in the notion of refinement or ideality, this scheme of values lays stress on sensory experience—of sunlight, water, bodily movement, and physical contact with other human beings—and on impulse rather than schedules as a guide to behavior.

6

The images of Tom in church or Tom whooping and prancing along the sand bar remain in the reader's mind after Mark Twain's struggles with plot and subplot and point of view are forgotten. They belong to his primary alphabet of symbols. Their importance for his subsequent career requires us to examine them with care.

Tom is a kind of embryonic Everyman. In church and school he confronts institutions that seem to him alien and at times hostile; on Jackson's Island he enjoys comradeship with his fellows and he responds to the physical environment. Natural man beleagured by society, but able to gain happiness by escaping to the forest and the river: this is undoubtedly an important aspect of the meaning that thousands of readers have found in the novel. In situations of this sort nineteenth-century writers were likely to be led by the heritage of Romantic thought to identify themselves with the virtuous hero and to ascribe evil exclusively to society. The signs of such a tendency on the part of Mark Twain himelf can be discerned in *Tom Sawyer*. But the church and the school are not truly evil, they are merely inconvenient and tedious; Tom doesn't really intend running away for good; his playing pirate is a child's fantasy, and can with perfect appropriateness have its climax in the boys' return:

Suddenly the minister shouted at the top of his voice: "Praise God from whom all blessings flow—SING!—and put your hearts in it!"

And they did. Old Hundred swelled up with a triumphant burst, and while it shook the rafters Tom Sawyer the Pirate looked around upon the envying juveniles about him and confessed in his heart that this was the proudest moment of his life.

As the "sold" congregation trooped out they said they would almost be willing to be made ridiculous again to hear Old Hundred sung like that once more.

Here Tom is fully integrated with the community (which is identical with the congregation in the church); the community is completely harmonious within itself; and the general exultation finds expression in the singing of a Christian hymn at the command of the minister. The official culture of St. Petersburg could hardly receive a more absolute affirmation.

It is the absence of a basic conflict between Tom and the society of the village that obliges Mark Twain to look elsewhere for the conflict he considered essential to the plot of a novel. He solves his problem by introducing evil in the form of Injun Joe, whose mixed blood labels him an outsider. Tom and Huck fear him, and Tom is sufficiently aggressive to testify against him in court, but a direct collision is out of the question and Injun Joe has to be destroyed unintentionally by Judge Thatcher when he seals up the mouth of the cave.

While acknowledging, at least tacitly, the artificiality of this subplot, Bernard De Voto emphasized its importance in contributing to *Tom Sawyer* "murder and starvation, grave-robbery and revenge, terror and panic, some of the darkest emotions of men, some of the most terrible fears of children." He believed such materials were an important aspect of the book's fidelity to human experience. It is an idyll, he pointed out, but it is enclosed in dread; and this keeps it true to the world of boyhood. The argument has weight. Yet a melodramatic villain tends to evoke a melodramatic hero, and Mark Twain does not entirely resist the temptation. He evades the naïve moral categories of the Sunday-school books by making Tom a boy who is "bad" according to their standards yet "good" according to more profound criteria. The demonstration, however, is not enough to give Tom real depth of character. The reader is evidently meant to see Tom's badness as nothing more than endearing mischief, indicative of a normal amount of imagination and energy; it is not bad at all. Mark Twain has written the Sunday-school story about the Good Little Boy Who Succeeded all over again with only a slight change in the hero's make-up and costume.

If the Matter of Hannibal is to be explored by means of a plot involving a protagonist of this sort, two basic situations are possible. We may have the naturally good hero enjoying a triumphant and harmonious relation with his society (Tom in church while the Doxology is being sung), or the naturally good hero at odds with his society (Tom suffering during the minister's prayer). The first of these alternatives could yield nothing except an endorsement of conventional values. The second alternative was more promising; it at least offered a built-in conflict and a point of view adapted to satire of existing institutions. But *Tom Sawyer* shows how dangerous the idea of the hero's natural goodness was as literary material. It constantly threatened to become merely a stereotype because of the difficulty of imagining a kind of goodness basically different from that endorsed by the accepted value system. Francis Parkman, for example, wishing to praise his French-Canadian guide across the plains, Henry Chatillon, said he had a "natural refinement."

Mark Twain would ultimately need a hero more hostile toward the dominant culture than Tom Sawyer was—Tom, the devotee of the "rules," the exponent of doing things by the book, the respectable boy who took out his impulses toward rebellion in harmless fantasies of escape. It is appropriate that *The Adventures of Tom Sawyer* ends with Tom made wealthy by the treasure he has found, acclaimed as a hero, and basking in the approval of both his sweetheart and her father. His last act is to persuade Huck to return to the Widow Douglas' and be "respectable." No doubt this wind-up of the plot was dictated by "the exigencies of romantic literature" which Mark Twain later said accounted for the death of Injun Joe in the cave. In the brief Conclusion he almost explicitly confesses that the conventions of the novel as he has adopted them in *Tom Sawyer* have proved to be poorly suited to his materials.

This perception was probably aided by the fact that even before he had finished the book he had recognized the solution for several of his technical problems. It lay in using Huck Finn as a narrative persona. The outcast Huck was far more alienated than Tom from conventional values. Telling a story in Huck's words would allow Mark Twain to exploit fully the color of vernacular speech. At the same time, the use of a narrator who was also a principal actor in the story would virtually compel the writer to maintain a consistent point of view.

In a fashion that recalls Cooper's discovery of unexpected possibilities in Leatherstocking while he was writing *The Pioneers,* Mark Twain seems to grow suddenly aware of Huck's potential importance only a few pages before the end of *Tom Sawyer*. Huck performs his first significant act in Chapter 29 by giving the alarm to Mr. Jones and his sons, who frustrate Injun Joe's plot against the Widow Douglas. The conversation between Huck and the Joneses is reported at surprising length. Mark Twain has evidently become interested both in the workings of Huck's mind and in his speech; he exhibits him in the process of inventing a cover story— an activity that would become almost compulsive in *Adventures of Huckleberry Finn*. Huck's impulse to run away when he learns that the townspeople have gathered to honor him and Tom in a great civic ceremony and his sufferings under the regimen imposed on him by the well-intentioned Widow Douglas are not merely prophetic of the sequel, they merge imperceptibly with the opening chapters that Mark Twain would begin to write as soon as he had finished *Tom Sawyer*. Indeed, Tom figures too prominently for the taste of most readers in both the opening and the closing chapters of the later novel. But the differences between the two books—aptly illustrated by the contrast between the tone of the chapters of *Huckleberry Finn* in which Tom appears and the tone of those in which he does not—greatly outweigh the similarities. *Tom Sawyer* provides relatively little opportunity to deal with the problem of values to which Mark Twain had devoted so much attention in his early work; *Huckleberry Finn* is his major effort in this direction.

V

The California Bull and the Gracious Singers

IN the summer of 1876, when Mark Twain plunged into the opening sequence of *Huckleberry Finn* while he was reading proof for *Tom Sawyer*, his conception of his role as a writer was in some ways even more ambiguous than it had been eight years earlier when he began composing *The Innocents Abroad*. He was still considered to be primarily a humorist, a disciple of Artemus Ward; yet he had also displayed a surprising ability to hold his own in the *Atlantic Monthly,* which Howells accurately characterized as "the most scrupulously cultivated of our periodicals."

Since its founding in 1857, the *Atlantic* had served as the principal organ for the literary culture of New England, and its best-known contributors —Emerson, Longfellow, Whittier, Holmes, Motley, Lowell—embodied for the general public the ideal of the man of letters. Such authors were regarded with a veneration now hardly conceivable. Rebecca Harding Davis said that when she first visited New England as "a young woman from the backwoods" (that is, West Virginia), she considered Emerson "the first of living men," "the modern Moses who had talked with God apart and could interpret Him to us." "When I heard him coming into the parlor at the Wayside," she continued, "my body literally grew stiff and my tongue dry with awe." In a celebrated passage in his *Literary Friends and Acquaintance,* Howells recounts his similar pilgrimage from the backwoods of Ohio to Boston and Cambridge and Concord.

It was Howells, of course, who had brought Mark Twain into the *Atlantic.* Howells had been appointed to the staff of the magazine in 1865 because he seemed "alert to new developments in literature." An equally important qualification was his respect for the New England literary tradition. His dislike of tension and controversy led him to minimize the differences between old and new attitudes; throughout his long life he continued to venerate the famous writers of an earlier generation, especially Emerson. Yet he realized that they belonged to the past. His own interest in the novel was basically foreign to their world. His doctrine of "realism" in literature owed much to Emerson's ideas, but nothing to his practice. In the 1870's Howells knew better than most Americans that a new era in literature was beginning. He had persuaded the publishers of the *Atlantic,* for example, to offer Bret Harte the unprecedented sum of $10,000 for twelve contributions to the magazine. The investment had turned sour because Harte's work failed to live up to its earlier promise, but now Howells was backing another writer from California: Mark Twain. He had given favorable notices to *The Innocents Abroad* and *Roughing It* (and had been shocked as well as amused by Mark Twain's remark that when he saw the review of *Roughing It* he was "as uplifted and reassured by it as a mother who has given birth to a white baby when she was awfully afraid it was going to be a mulatto"). He had solicited contributions from Mark Twain for the *Atlantic,* and while he had rejected some inferior offerings, by the end of 1875 he had published eight or ten pieces, including "A True Story" and the seven installments of "Old Times on the Mississippi." He was putting Mark Twain up for election to the Academy at some risk to his own standing among New England intellectuals.

Because the *Atlantic* represented the apex of civilization and refinement, whereas the Far West stood for "barbarism," Mark Twain's relation to the magazine was to say the least problematical, both for him and for Howells. A hostile critic remarked icily in 1877 that Mark Twain's appearance in the *Atlantic* "was in the beginning considered an innovation." In 1874, when Mark Twain submitted the first installment of "Old Times on the Mississippi," Howells had welcomed it and asked for more, but he thought he detected "a sort of hurried and anxious air" in the prose as if the writer were under some constraint. "Don't write *at* any supposed Atlantic audience," he advised, "but yarn it off as if into my sympathetic ear." Although Mark Twain's reply may not have been entirely accurate, it underscored the special character both he and Howells ascribed to the readers of the magazine: "It isn't the Atlantic audience that distresses me; for *it* is the only audience that I sit down before in perfect serenity (for the simple reason that it don't require a 'humorist' to paint himself stripèd & stand on his head every fifteen minutes)."

This amounts to saying that as a contributor to the *Atlantic* he might hope to escape the label of humorist and be taken simply as a writer. But the assertion was oversanguine. A widely publicized incident involving his relation to the magazine three years later shows both Howells and Mark Twain taking his role of humorist for granted, with unhappy consequences. The furor arose over a speech delivered by Mark Twain at a dinner given by the publishers of the *Atlantic* to commemorate Whittier's seventieth birthday. The speech itself and the widespread discussion of it in the press provide an opportunity to examine in some detail Mark Twain's relation to the dominant culture a decade after he had achieved a national reputation.

The *Atlantic* dinner was held at seven o'clock on the evening of 17 December 1877 at the Brunswick Hotel in Boston. Fifty-eight men—contributors to the magazine and members of its staff—sat down to a feast on the heroic scale of our ancestors. At a quarter past ten o'clock the doors were opened, additional guests (including ladies) who had been waiting in the halls were admitted, and the speeches began. Henry O. Houghton, publisher of the magazine, made a short address of welcome and introduced Whittier as guest of honor. Whittier excused himself from speaking and asked Longfellow to read a sonnet composed by Whittier for the occasion. Houghton then introduced Howells as toastmaster, and Howells introduced Emerson, who "with much feeling" recited Whittier's "Ichabod." After Howells had made a short speech, Holmes read a new poem of his own and Charles Eliot Norton responded gracefully to a toast to Lowell, who was absent as Minister to Spain. Howells read several letters from guests unable to be present. He then introduced Mark Twain in a fashion which he later thought peculiarly ironic because it praised the speaker for qualities conspicuously absent from the sketch he was about to deliver:

And now, gentlemen, I will not ask the good friend of us all, to whom I am about to turn, to help us to forget these absent fellow-contributors, but I think I may properly appeal for oblivion from our vain regrets at their absence to the humorist, whose name is known wherever our tongue is spoken, and who has, perhaps, done more kindness to our race, lifted from it more crushing care, rescued it from more gloom, and banished from it more wretchedness than all the professional philanthropists that have live[d]; a humorist who never makes you blush to have enjoyed his joke; whose generous wit has no meanness in it, whose fun is never at the cost of anything honestly high or good, but comes from the soundest of hearts and the clearest of heads. Mr. Clemens, gentlemen, whom we all know as Mark Twain, will address you.

The uncharacteristically involved syntax of this introduction suggests that Howells felt uneasy. It is true that he was by nature shy and dreaded any kind of public appearance. But the uneasiness here goes beyond his chronic dislike of making speeches. Perhaps without fully realizing it, he was worried about what his protégé might do, and was uttering a kind of secular prayer. Mark Twain was being put under instruction not to shock the august company by making fun of cherished ideals. Since the occasion was intended to honor Whittier and, through him, the vocation of literature as represented by the contributors to the *Atlantic,* Howells' admonition had an obvious reference to the role of the man of letters in New England and therefore in American culture.

Mark Twain had recognized that the topic was inevitable. His carefully prepared speech, which Howells had not seen, was a little extravaganza exploiting the contrast between the literary life represented by Whittier and the other venerable figures at the head table, and that represented by Mark Twain in his role of the Wild Humorist of the Pacific Slope. We recall that this is the man who had confessed to Mrs. Fairbanks, "There is a fascination about meddling with forbidden things."

Mark Twain said in his speech that some years earlier, when he had just begun to acquire a local reputation as a writer on the Pacific Coast, he "started on an inspection-tramp through the Southern mines of California." Being "callow & conceited," he "resolved to try the virtue of [his] nom de plume."

I knocked at a miner's lonely log cabin in the foot-hills of the Sierras just at nightfall . . . A jaded, melancholy man of fifty, barefooted, opened to me. When he heard my nom de plume, he looked more dejected than before.

Nevertheless, the miner admitted his guest, and after a time explained his somber mood:

"You're the fourth—I'm a-going to move." "The fourth what?" said I. "The fourth littery man that's been here in twenty-four hours—I'm a-going to move." "You don't tell me!" said I; "who were the others?" "Mr. Long-fellow, Mr. Emerson, & Mr. Oliver Wendell Holmes—dad fetch the lot!"

Further conversation reveals that "Mr. Emerson was a seedy little bit of a chap—red-headed. Mr. Holmes was fat as a balloon—he weighed as much as three hundred, & had double chins all the way down to his stomach. Mr. Longfellow was built like a prize fighter . . . They had been drinking—I could see that." The visitors are prolific in quotations, or misquotations, from the famous authors mentioned. "Holmes" inspects the cabin with disapproval, and exclaims: "Build thee more stately mansions,/O my Soul!" "Longfellow" begins to recite lines from *Hiawatha:*

> Honor be to Mudjekeewis!
> You shall hear how Pau-Puk-Kee-wis—

but the host breaks in with, "Begging your pardon, Mr. Longfellow, if you'll be so kind as to hold your yawp for about five minutes, & let me get this grub ready, you'll do me proud." After supper the intruders begin a game of euchre, with remarks adapted from well-known poems. When "Emerson" does not like the hand dealt him, for example, he says:

> They reckon ill who leave me out;
> They know not well the subtle ways
> I keep. I pass, & deal *again!*

Later he points at the host and says,

> Is yonder squalid peasant all
> That this proud nursery could breed?

And next morning when "Longfellow" leaves he steals the host's boots, remarking:

> Lives of great men all remind us
>   We can make our lives sublime;
> And departing, leave behind us
>   Footprints on the sands of Time.

Mark Twain, in his capacity of straight character, hastens to explain the deception to the miner: "Why my dear sir, *these* were not the gracious singers to whom we & the world pay loving reverence & homage: these were impostors." But as so often happens in Mark Twain's anecdotes, the miner, the vernacular character, turns the tables on his interlocutor: "Ah —impostors, were they? are *you?*"

The basic impulse here is similar to that which would lead Mark Twain two years later to link General Grant with the image of a baby trying to put its toe in its mouth. He is reducing exalted personages to a low status and is incidentally concocting a literary burlesque of their work. He was almost certainly unaware of any hostile feeling toward "the gracious singers" whom he joined the world in honoring, but the speech goes far beyond the hint of disrespect, quickly effaced, in the joke about Grant. It is clearly an act of aggression against the three poets as representatives of the sacerdotal cult of the man of letters. Mark Twain is quite sincere in his implied confession that he himself feels like an impostor in the role of a contributor to the *Atlantic* (just as he felt "like a barkeeper entering the Kingdom of Heaven" whenever he read Jane Austen). His very candor lends devastating force to the implication that the literary giants of New England may also somehow be fraudulent.

2

Mark Twain's unconscious antagonism toward the literary Titans caused him to feel uneasy while he was delivering his speech and alerted him to the faintest signs of disapproval from the audience. In reminiscences dictated many years later he said that the expression on his hearers' faces "turned to a sort of black frost. I wondered what the trouble was. I didn't know. I went on, but with difficulty . . . always hoping—but with a gradually perishing hope—that somebody would laugh, or that somebody would at least smile, but nobody did." Before he had finished, he recalled, the audience "seemed turned to stone with horror" at the affront to the revered poets who were seated at the head table. His recollection was that the next speaker was unable to utter more than a few sentences before he "slumped down in a limp and mushy pile," and the program "ended there. Nobody rose. The next man hadn't strength enough to get up, and everybody looked so dazed, so stupefied, paralyzed, it was impossible for anybody to do anything, or even try." Howells (in this version) could only lead away Mark Twain and his successor on the program, the young Wisconsin novelist W. S. Bishop, to suffer in the privacy of a hotel room.

Howells likewise recalled later that Mark Twain's speech was greeted with a "silence, weighing many tons to the square inch," which "deepened from moment to moment, and was broken only by the hysterical and blood-curdling laughter of a single guest, whose name shall not be handed down to infamy." Even after Mark Twain's death, Howells considered the speech to have been a "bewildering blunder," a "cruel catastrophe." He continued:

After the scope of the burlesque made itself clear, there was no one there, including the burlesquer himself, who was not smitten with a desolating dismay . . . Nobody knew whether to look at the speaker or down at his plate. I chose my plate as the least affliction, and so I do not know how Clemens looked, except when I stole a glance at him, and saw him standing solitary amid his appalled and appalling listeners, with his joke dead on his hands. From a first glance at the great three whom his jest had made its theme, I was aware of Longfellow sitting upright, and regarding the humorist with an air of pensive puzzle, of Holmes busily writing on his menu, with a well-feigned effect of preoccupation, and of Emerson, holding his elbows, and listening with a sort of Jovian oblivion of this nether world in that lapse of memory which saved him in those later years from so much bother. Clemens must have dragged his joke to the climax and left it there, but I cannot say this from any sense of the fact. Of what happened afterward at the table . . . I have no longer the least remembrance. I next remember being in a room of the hotel, where Clemens was not to sleep, but to toss in despair, and Charles Dudley Warner's saying, in the gloom, "Well, Mark, *you're* a funny fellow."

Accounts published in Boston newspapers next day show that Mark Twain and Howells had simply invented the notion of a public scandal. Many in the audience laughed at the speech, although some doubtless did not. Howells was correct in saying that Emerson paid little attention to it. Although Whittier, Longfellow, and Holmes may have felt uncomfortable, they seemed to observers in the room to be politely amused. The program was not interrupted, but continued under Howells' direction along its prearranged course for an hour or more after Mark Twain's speech. The gloomy retreat and private condolences of Mark Twain, Howells, Bishop, and Warner came only at the end of the program, toward one o'clock, when the party broke up.

It may be conjectured that Mark Twain was upset because delivering his speech in the presence of the three poets who are mentioned in it made him aware, for a moment, of his latent hostility toward these representatives of literature as a New England institution. Howells, not protected by Mark Twain's psychic censor, no doubt perceived the aggression even more clearly. And one cannot resist the idea that in some degree he shared it.

Despite the fact that Boston sophistication had put a good face on the incident, and at least one qualified reader of the speech in the papers (Francis J. Child) had found it delightful, Mark Twain and Howells knew that some buried force in the humorist had broken from control. He wrote Howells afterwards that he must have been insane when he wrote the speech "& saw no harm in it, no disrespect toward those men whom I reverenced so much." Howells, apologizing for him to Charles Eliot Norton, wrote: "before he had fairly touched his point, he felt the awfulness of what he was doing, but was fatally helpless to stop. He was completely crushed by it, and though it killed the joy of the time for me, I pitied him; for he *has* a good and reverent nature for good things, and his performance was like an effect of demoniacal possession." The abject letter of apology Mark Twain wrote to his three victims ten days later, when Howells had given permission, emphasizes the divorce between conscious and unconscious motives. He interprets his behavior in highly moralistic terms, calling himself a savage by nature with imperfect control over his base impulses, yet innocent of intent to do wrong:

Hartford, Thursday, 27th [December 1877]
To Mr. Emerson, Mr. Longfellow, & Dr. Holmes:
Gentlemen: I come before you, now, with the mien & posture of the guilty —not to excuse, gloss, or extenuate, but only to offer my repentance. If a man with a fine nature had done that thing which I did, it would have been a crime—because all his senses would have warned him against it beforehand; but I did it innocently & unwarned. I did it as innocently as I ever did anything. You will think it is incredible; but it is true, & Mr. Howells will confirm my words. He does not know how it *can* be true, & neither does any one who is incapable of trespassing as I did; yet he knows it *is* true. But when I perceived what it was that I had done, I felt as real a sorrow & suffered as sharp a mortification as if I had done it with a guilty intent. This continues. That the impulse was innocent, brings no abatement. As to my wife's distress, it is not to be measured; for she is of finer stuff than I; & yours were sacred names to her. We do not talk about this misfortune— it *scorches;* so we only think—and think.
I will end, now. I *had* to write you, for the easement of it, even though the doing it might maybe be a further offense. But I do not ask you to forgive what I did that night, for it is not forgivable; I simply had it at heart to ask you to believe that I am only heedlessly a savage, not premeditatedly; & that I am under as severe punishment as even you could adjudge to me if you were required to appoint my penalty. I do not ask you to say one word in answer to this; it is not needful, & would of course be distasteful & difficult. I beg you to consider that in letting me unbosom myself you will do me an act of grace that will be sufficient in itself. I wanted to write such a letter

as this, that next morning in Boston, but one of wiser judgment advised against it, & said Wait.

With great & sincere respect

I am
Truly Yours
Sam¹ L. Clemens

There is no reason to doubt the candor of this painful letter. Mark Twain had indeed been a victim of demonic possession. His unconscious had uttered a truth under the guise of burlesque that was much more frightening to him than to the targets of his derision, for he was obscurely aware of his own guilt, whereas they were protected by their self-confidence and by the public image of them against having to recognize the truth of what the impudent demon proclaimed. Mark Twain was not consciously prepared to repudiate the conception of literature represented by Emerson and Longfellow and Holmes; but he had a half-suppressed awareness that the role assigned to them by the official culture was false and sterile. It was the violent conflict between conscious and unconscious allegiances that made him—and also Howells—suffer so much over what Howells called the "hideous mistake" of his friend.

3

Emerson, Longfellow, and Holmes were too old and too secure to be very much concerned that American culture had shifted out from under them. But the newspaper-reading public was intensely interested in the crisis of values that the Whittier birthday dinner revealed. Mark Twain's speech was published in full (along with other speeches delivered at the dinner) not only in Boston but in Chicago and probably elsewhere. Within a day or two hostile criticism began to appear in the press—mainly, it should be noted, outside Boston: the geographical distribution of attacks on Mark Twain suggests that conventional assumptions had a stronger hold on what would now be called middlebrow readers in the hinterland than on Boston highbrows. The Worcester *Gazette* made up its mind at once. On 18 December this paper said in an editorial that has already been quoted in part:

Mark Twain made a speech at the Atlantic dinner, last night, which was in bad taste. We refer to it, because Mark's sense of propriety needs development, and it is not his first offence. He told a story in which Messrs. Longfellow, Emerson and Holmes were represented as crowding their society upon a California miner, guzzling his whiskey and cheating him at cards. It was, of course, meant to be a piece of incongruous absurdity, and although the idea was not at all original, it might have seemed funny in some circles, when told with Mark's drawl, but men who have attained the years and fame of Longfellow and Emerson are entitled to some degree of respect amongst a company of their friends. The offence is easier to feel than describe, but it is one which if repeated would cost Mark Twain his place among the contributors to the Atlantic Monthly, where indeed his appearance was in the beginning considered an innovation.

On the same day the Boston *Transcript* said that although there might be a difference of opinion concerning the good taste of the speech, "There was no mistaking the hearty fun elicited by the droll attitude in which these literary lights were represented. They appreciated the joke, as will the public who read, and laugh while they read." But by December 19 this paper had had second thoughts about the occasion, and reported: "The general verdict seems to be that Mark Twain's speech, though witty and well worked-up, was in bad taste and entirely out of place. As one critic puts it, 'if the three gentlemen named in his remarks had been entertained in New York, and a speaker had said what Twain did, Boston would have felt insulted.'"

Nevertheless, the Boston papers were not inclined to participate in the continuing criticism of the speech which some papers in other cities kept alive for a couple of weeks. The Boston *Post* on 20 December carried a benign pun: "It would have been hard to make a Whittier speech than that of Mark Twain's," and the *Globe* of 26 December reported with some detachment: "the Western papers have just begun to write up the Whittier dinner, and abuse Mark Twain with great unanimity. The Nevada journals have not yet spoken on the subject, but something racy may be looked for in that quarter." "Western" here clearly means Middle Western, and the *Globe* seems to look forward with pleasure to a Far Western counterattack. Unfortunately, the Nevada and California papers did not rise to the occasion. But the Middle West, like inland Massachusetts, did indeed take a stern view of Mark Twain's offense. The *Globe* reprinted by way of documentation a homily from the Cincinnati *Commercial*:

MARK TWAIN'S OFFENCE AGAINST GOOD TASTE

If amazement did not sit on each brow in that assemblage as Mr. Twain went on with his extraordinary narrative, it was because courtesy restrained its expression. It would have read queer enough as a humorous sketch, but delivered, as it was, in the august presence of the men in whose lives there is nothing to suggest such an adventure in the remotest manner, it must have excited far other than humorous emotions . . . Mr. Twain may have . . . thought that by bringing these poets and philosophers, whose lives have been passed amid books, in college cloisters, and in refined society, into intimate relations with whisky, cards, bowie-knives and larceny, he was doing an irresistibly funny thing, that would set the table into a roar and wrinkle a continent with laughter. It was a mistake, however. On the contrary, Mr. Twain has been scored for his exceedingly bad taste, and there is a disposition to deal anything but tenderly with him. It is assumed that he ought to have known better; that even with his innocent desire to enliven the proceedings with something humorously quaint, and mix it with quotations from the respective writings of the poets, the instincts of a gentleman would have forbidden its presentation in a character-sketch so coarse and absurd in every incident. It will require a good deal of ingenuity on the part of the humorist to extricate himself gracefully from the predicament in which he is involved, and soften away the painful sensations that followed his unique performance.

A correspondent of the Chicago *Tribune* wrote from Boston a few days after the speech that although it was "funny in its way," he was appalled at the thought of "making Mr. Emerson, even in travesty, stand for such a vulgar little scamp, and Holmes and Longfellow in such a guise." He could not believe they had enjoyed it even though "Of course they had to laugh." The speech, he admitted, was "very Mark-Twainish; but how he ever made up his face, as the children say, to stand up there and poke his fun at those beautiful, austere old men, is a mystery." On 26 December the *Tribune* implied its support of the hostile critics by reprinting on the editorial page a brief but supercilious article from an unidentified exchange. The reminder that Mark Twain was after all only a jester, and should know his place, must have been especially galling to the unfortunate speaker.

MARK TWAIN has been considered very clever at a *post-prandial* speech, and we recall one or two that were worthy of his reputation as a humorist. If it was his intention on this occasion to say something that would not really be humorous, but sensational, he succeeded, possibly beyond his own anticipation. The effect is not probably what he intended it should be. Boston does not take it kindly, and is as cold as its sharpest winter's day, because of the irreverence of the mad wag. Even a King's jester should know when it will do to shake his cap and bells in the royal presence.

The most rancorous criticism of the speech, however, came from the Springfield (Massachusetts) *Republican.* In a full report of the dinner on 19 December the *Republican,* after mentioning the remarks of Whittier and Longfellow, said: "Of the other speeches, Mark Twain's was the longest—too long if it had been good; and it was not good, it was vulgar." The *Republican* was displeased by other aspects of the program—it objected for example to Emerson's choice of "Ichabod," which as the "dirge of a great fame" might have led the audience to speculate concerning putative moral lapses of Whittier—but it returned relentlessly to the nuisance committed by Mark Twain:

What would we not have given to watch the Boston and Cambridge men, as they drank in the high-flavored Nevada delirium tremens of Mark Twain! How exquisitely adapted to the company was this fable of Longfellow and Emerson and Holmes, repeating their own and others' verses, with an accompaniment of hot whisky in a tipsy miner's cabin! It must have been very much as if the Nevada beverage itself had been slyly substituted in their glasses for the delicate wines that should have been there, and they had quaffed it unaware of the change.

On 24 December the paper was still insisting on the heinousness of the speech, which

has doubtless excited more attention than any other feature of the feast. People feel about it as they do about a fly in amber,—
> "The thing, we know, is neither rich nor rare,
> But wonder how the devil it got there."

And on 27 December the *Republican* delivered a long and explicit lecture to Mark Twain in an unsigned letter to the editor. The document throws so much light on the canons of taste and morals Mark Twain was felt to have violated that it warrants full quotation:

MARK TWAIN'S MISTAKE AT THE WHITTIER DINNER

To the Editor of The Republican:—
No one caring in the least for the "fitness of things" can read without a sense of pain the words of "Mark Twain" at the late Atlantic-Whittier dinner. Imagine the scene, the really brilliant company, bright in the best sense of that suggestive word—"shedding much light, opposed to dark," as Webster has it—gathered to celebrate with sober joy and good cheer the 70th

anniversary of a man of the most singular delicacy and refinement, combined with a strength, simplicity and sturdiness not always found with so much gentleness! Fit combination of events, the celebration of the progress of a life, which has had for its object the making of to-morrow better than today; and the speeding of an enterprise, which having passed its teens, looks forward to an earnest, ever broadening life. Gathered about the charming board with the gentle poet and the friend whose skill and enterprise enable them to sing to the whole round world, we see him who thinks that "life is not an empty dream," but that it holds high and holy, bright and gladsome things, of which he who has clean hands and a pure heart may taste. Beside him sits the philosopher who has dug deep and brought to light much that makes us think and hope, even if the mines *have* encroached on what are sometimes considered pre-empted claims. Then, also, if wit and fun were wanted, and keen thrusts at sham and pretense, accompanied with a sincere reverence for the beautiful and true, he who sits at the left is able and willing, and there are two others, who, were quiet, delicately delicious humor cared for, could bring it forth. Into this China shop bursts a wild Californian bull. True gentlemen bear insult in silence, and let such things dash on to their own destruction. But there is food for reflection in the incident. The songs, the literature, the wit and humor of a land tell tales, and when a bright, clever man, who does possess genuine humor, and has really discovered a new and curious vein, instead of fitting it to something that will amuse and relax the mind, without polluting it, finds his greatest glory in embellishing with his gift the low, poor, weak parts of our nature, and dressing in the garb of bar-room habitues the men who stand at the other end of life,—is it not well to inquire whether the popularity of this man ought not to have already reached a climax? Literary men in America, where so much is tolerated, ought to aim higher than the gutter, no matter what they have of talent, or even genius. American social life, upon which, by God's aid, must be built the mighty fabric of the future state, is in the formative period, and, jealous as we might have been of our political honor, a thousand times more jealous must we be of that most precious possession—reverence for that which is truly high. According to England's laureate, the good things of time are ours:—

> "To shape and use; arise and fly
> The reeling Faun, the sensual feast!
> Move upward, working out the beast,
> And let the ape and tiger die!"

Springfield, December 19, 1877.

4

This effusion contains a number of ideas—or more properly speaking, prejudices and stock responses—that deserve notice, for they belong to the system of values that had been dominant in American society for a half-century and more. The focus of the letter is the moralistic-didactic conception of literature fittingly indicated by allusions to "A Psalm of Life" and *In Memoriam*. Mark Twain has polluted the minds of his readers by "embellishing with his gift the low, poor, weak parts of our nature"—that is, the animal impulses in conflict with ideality. The specific offense seems to consist in linking revered men of letters with the coarse manners and customs of a Western mining camp. This shows that the humorist is deficient in "reverence for that which is truly high." Since the poets were guardians of the ideal, to belittle them was to weaken the only force that could subdue the beast in man.

Thus we are brought back to the necessity for reverence. As the reviews of *The Innocents Abroad* had demonstrated, conservative spokesmen considered this the central issue. Josiah G. Holland, for example, had written in 1861:

Nothing is more apparent in American character and American life than a growing lack of reverence . . . The parent may be loved, but he is much less revered than in the olden time . . . In politics, it is the habit to speak in light and disrespectful terms of those whose experience gives them the right to counsel and command . . . We nickname our Presidents; and "old Buck" and "old Abe" are spoken of as familiarly as if they were a pair of old oxen we were in the habit of driving . . . What we call "Young America" is made up of about equal parts of irreverence, conceit, and that popular moral quality familiarly known as "brass."

Holland's contribution to the Whittier dinner had dwelt on the same theme. Unable to come up from New York, where he was now editor of *Scribner's Monthly,* Holland sent a letter that Howells read aloud shortly before he introduced Mark Twain:

I wonder if these old poets of ours—Mr. Dana, Mr. Bryant, Mr. Emerson, Mr. Longfellow and Mr. Whittier—appreciate the benefit they confer upon their fellow citizens by simply consenting to live among them as old men? Do they know how they help to save the American nation from the total wreck and destruction of the sentiment of reverence? Why, if they will only live and move and have their being among us from seventy years of age to 100, and consent to be loved and venerated, and worshipped and petted, they will be the most useful men we have in the development of the better elements in the American character . . . The influence which these beloved and venerated poets exercise upon the public mind and character, simply by being lovely and venerable, is, in the highest and sweetest degree, salutary and salvatory. May heaven bless them and spare them all to us these many, many years.

Holland was saying substantially the same thing he had been saying sixteen years earlier; and Mark Twain's critics in general had not really changed their tune since the publication of *The Innocents Abroad*. Then they had been made uneasy by his treatment of historical monuments, especially those with biblical associations; now they were defending the ideal of the man of letters. The weakening of the underpinnings of religious orthodoxy had led defenders of tradition to exalt poets to the status of surrogate priests, commanding (in Howells' phrase) a "species of religious veneration," and to assign to literature the function of holding institutions in place.

As Howells had implied in his introduction of Mark Twain at the Whittier dinner, reverence was ordinarily taken to be incompatible with humor. Most people who prided themselves on having a cultivated taste considered vernacular humor to be vulgar, if indeed not actually immoral. James Russell Lowell, in the introduction to the second series of *Biglow Papers* (1867), was careful to explain that he had written in a comic dialect only for the sake of reaching a wider audience with antislavery and Union sentiments:

If I put on the cap and bells and made myself one of the court-fools of King Demos, it was less to make his majesty laugh than to win a passage to his royal ears for certain serious things which I had deeply at heart. I say this because there is no imputation that could be more galling to any man's self-respect than that of being a mere jester.

Edmund Clarence Stedman, writing to Bayard Taylor in 1873, blamed the *"horrible* degeneracy in public taste" in the United States on such humorists as John Hay (in his *Pike County Ballads*), Bret Harte, Josh Billings, and "the Danbury *News* Man." The tendency to look down on humorists was if anything even more pronounced in the South. A biographer of Johnson J. Hooper (creator of Simon Suggs) wrote in 1872:

His ambition had been . . . to enjoy the respect of men; but he had unfortunately obtained a reputation [that is, that of being a humorist] which cut off all such hopes. It was an evil day to his fortunes and to his happiness when he embarked in that class of literature, or otherwise became a *chronic* story-teller for his companions.

In 1888, when Matthew Arnold cited "the addiction to 'the funny man'" as one of the principal forces making against "distinction" in the United

States, and a prime illustration of the American lack of "the discipline of awe and respect," he was merely repeating what had been a conventional opinion in this country for decades.

5

By the 1870's the system of values implied in the cult of ideality was rapidly losing the authority it had exercised in the decades before the Civil War. The changes brought about by the rise of previously submerged segments of the population to political and economic power during the nineteenth century seemed to men like Holland and Stedman sheer barbarism. Looking back from the vantage point of the present, we can see that the disintegration of the traditional culture was part of a transition that would lead to the formation of a new system of values and a new literary mode in the twentieth century. Cultural history is a procession of such transitions, but only in retrospect do the outlines become clear. The articulate spokesmen for American culture, the writers and editors in control of the leading magazines and publishing houses, were unable to comprehend what was happening because they were committed to the preservation of a complex institutional structure and the body of assumptions supporting it. They thought of themselves as the garrison of a beleaguered citadel and, being on the defensive, tended to find all kinds of novelty threatening.

One can sympathize with their attitude because so much of the emergent popular culture was merely a vulgarization of the high culture of the past. The germs of a new system of values and a new literature were buried in the debris. It is difficult even now to discriminate between the vital crudity of fresh insights and the sterile crudity of traditional attitudes degraded into clichés and stereotypes. Nevertheless, Mark Twain's place in American cultural history cannot be properly understood unless we are prepared to make distinctions that could not be made by either his critics or his defenders in his own lifetime. Both the best and the worst of his work derived from the popular culture—the tastes and assumptions of the "average practical American public" which Howells said must be his final court of appeal. In an often-quoted letter to Andrew Lang protesting against British attacks on *A Connecticut Yankee in King Arthur's Court* Mark Twain claimed that he had never addressed himself to "the cultivated classes," "the thin top crust of humanity," but only to "the mighty mass of the uncultivated who are underneath." He deliberately placed his work among the kinds of art dear to the mass audience: "cheap terra cotta groups" like those of the sculptor John Rogers, gaudy chromolithographs, "the hurdy-gurdy and the villagers' singing-society," the poems of Riley and Kipling.

In the domain of prose—although Mark Twain interestingly enough mentions no examples of work he considers comparable to his own—such a list would include two quite different types of writing: on the one hand, native humor; on the other, theatrical melodramas and the "sensation fiction" purveyed by the weekly story papers that during the 1850's and 1860's attained the first mass circulations in American publishing history. To mention these genres is to demonstrate that the popular culture embraced violent contrasts. Sensation novels were a hybrid of sentimental and Gothic conventions. So far from challenging the cult of ideality, they carried refinement to the point of unconscious caricature. They were emptily grandiose imitations of the silver-fork manner of Disraeli and Bulwer-Lytton or the medieval glamour of Scott. As we have seen, Mark Twain enjoyed burlesquing this kind of thing. Representative examples are the Legend of Court Luigi in *The Innocents Abroad* and the chapter on *The Weekly Occidental* in *Roughing It*, which contains thumbnail burlesques of half a dozen types of the sensation novel. Yet at the same time he could use characters and situations from popular fiction and drama with perfect seriousness, and his experience in writing literary burlesques provided him with structural patterns for *Tom Sawyer, The Prince and the Pauper*, and later books, including *Huckleberry Finn*.

The mass audience itself had an ambiguous attitude toward boiler-plate drama and fiction. When Fred G. Maeder's play *Buffalo Bill, the King of Bordermen* (based on a serial by Ned Buntline in the *New York Weekly*) began its successful run at the Bowery Theater in New York in 1872, a burlesque was rushed into production as a matter of course at Hooley's Opera House in Brooklyn under the title *Bill Buffalo, with His Great Buffalo Bull*. The two plays were presumably aimed at an identical clientele. Straight melodrama and burlesque could appear side by side in the same work, as in James J. McCloskey's *Across the Continent* (1870), which held the boards for ten seasons. At the other end of the spectrum the taste for sensation fiction was not confined to the semiliterate. The story papers had at least a few cultivated readers. In the 1860's Edward Everett found members of his own social circle reading the *New York Ledger*, chief of the story papers; and Spencer Baird, the paleontologist of the

Smithsonian Institution, declared that *"Ledger* day" was "an epoch in his family." He added that although he received "over a hundred periodicals a week, the *Ledger* is the only one that would be really missed." For years during the 1860's Henry Ward Beecher conducted a regular column in the *Ledger;* and his novel *Norwood,* combining didactic conversations with a sensational plot, was serialized in the paper in 1867. (He received for it the enormous sum of $30,000.)

The significance of American humor was difficult for the critics to grasp because it seemed to appeal to exactly the same audience as sensation fiction and melodrama. During the 1860's and 1870's most of the story papers, following the lead of the *Ledger,* began to publish the work of humorists such as Josh Billings, and some carried a regular section devoted to humor. The bizarre consequences of this practice are illustrated by the fact that Mark Twain's anecdote about Mother Utterback was reprinted in the same issue of the San Francisco *Golden Era* that carried the first installment of a preposterously genteel novel by Mary Braddon, editor of the London magazine *Belgravia.*

A mass audience that responded to both Miss Braddon and Mark Twain must have been confused in its tastes. Its aspiration to rise in the social scale was apparently gratified by the exaggerated ideality of characters, settings, and style in sensation fiction. Yet it did not have a traditional commitment to the cult of gentility; most members of it had received only a few years of schooling and were still close to their nonliterate rural origins. They could therefore respond with pleasure, if a little guiltily, to the coarse but fresh and vigorous work of the humorists —which they took to be entirely distinct from literature. If this interpretation is correct, the growing taste for native humor can be seen as an intrusion of attitudes originating in remote rural areas into the prim middlebrow world of the story papers, which ostensibly derived its standards from the upper-class traditional culture.

In the absence of reliable historical knowledge about levels of literary taste in the United States, we must make inferences from fragmentary data. These indicate that a few writers and critics at the top of the scale of sophistication, such as Francis J. Child and Thomas Sergeant Perry, appreciated the vitality of native humor. Even Emerson, according to his daughter, had often asked to have read to him "certain passages of 'The Innocents Abroad,'" and Holmes, although he himself mildly deprecated the "broad farce" of the Whittier dinner speech, reported that two of his friends, "gentlemen of education and the highest social standing, were infinitely amused" by it and "stoutly defended it against the charge of impropriety." Although Howells was distressed over the personal affront offered to honored guests by this particular speech, he had from the beginning praised the "delicious impudence" of his friend's "colloquial drolling." But the bulk of Mark Twain's vast audience was in the conventional sense uncultivated. His primary appeal was to the tens and hundreds of thousands of readers who delighted in Artemus Ward and Petroleum V. Nasby and Bill Nye—readers of whom Lincoln is the best known representative. Somewhere between Lincoln and Child along this dimension of tastes must be placed the middlebrow readers and critics represented by Holland, Mrs. Fairbanks, and Mrs. Severance. Olivia Langdon belonged to this group when Mark Twain met her, and she never entirely graduated from it. The geographical pattern of newspaper attacks on the supposed irreverence of the Whittier dinner speech permits certain further inferences. Boston, more secure in its sophistication than the rest of the country, was freer from the rigidity of taste imposed by the cult of gentility. As the strength of the traditional culture declined, it was finding its last stronghold in the middlebrow provinces, the upcountry of New England and the Middle West.

6

The confusion of tastes and attitudes in nineteenth-century American culture made it impossible for Mark Twain to arrive at a workable idea of his vocation. If he hoped to be accepted as a serious writer, he was apparently obliged to conform to the priestly role of the man of letters. If he devoted himself to humor he must be content with the humble function of providing comic relief from higher concerns. The program of the Whittier dinner was virtually a pageant translating his problem into quasi-dramatic terms. He was invited to enact as if on a stage the role of harmless jester offered him by the dominant culture. But he had also been invited to write his own lines, and the assignment had stirred his imagination to an act of expression more revealing than either he or Howells, the director of the pageant, intended. Despite Howells' contention that his friend was free of the crudities of other humorists, Mark Twain's humor was basically irreverent. When he went beyond a perfunctory gesture of politeness his speech was bound to be shocking to his sponsor.

Lacking a satisfactory rationale of his position, Mark Twain suffered a succession of pendulum swings of emotion. Howells remembered that "not so very long" after the dinner Mark Twain had reacted from his depression, declaring "with all his fierceness, 'But I don't admit that [the speech] *was* a mistake.'" Within two or three weeks he was able to write with self-possession to Mrs. Fairbanks, who had called to his attention an item about his apology in the New York *Sun:*

> I am pretty dull in some things, & very likely the Atlantic speech was in ill taste; but that is the worst that can be said of it. I am sincerely sorry if it in any wise hurt those great poets' feelings—I never wanted to do that. But nobody has ever convinced me that that speech was not a good one—for me; above my average, considerably.

He went on to draw a dubious analogy ignoring the charge of personal affront to men who were present when the speech was delivered:

> I could as easily have substituted the names of Shakespeare, Beaumont & Ben Jonson, (since the absurd *situation* was where the humor . . . lay,) & all these critics would have discovered the merit of it, then. But my purpose was clean, my conscience clear, & I saw no need of it.

His final argument is more cogent, for the insecurity of the defenders of ideality had made them unable to bear any suggestion of varied perspectives regarding questions of value:

> Why anybody should think three poets insulted because three fantastic tramps choose to personate them & use their language, passes my comprehension. Nast says it is very much the best speech & the most humorous situation I have contrived.

Mark Twain's difficulty in discovering a role and an identity for himself condemned him to further changes of mind about the speech. In March of 1882, writing to Howells, he said that the news of Longfellow's death "had a peculiar effect upon me; for it brought back that infernal breakfast and made me feel like an unforgiven criminal." (He had by that time confused the Whittier dinner with a ceremonial breakfast honoring Holmes two years later in the same hotel.) Almost thirty years after the speech was delivered, a woman wrote him from New York to ask where she might find the text; she remembered enjoying it from a newspaper report in 1877. He caused the files of the Boston *Transcript* to be searched and the speech copied out for him. In his autobiographical musings, he talks of the Whittier dinner at length. Upon first rereading the speech in 1906 he found it admirable:

I have read it twice, and unless I am an idiot, it hasn't a single defect in it from the first word to the last. It is just as good as good can be. It is smart; it is saturated with humor. There isn't a suggestion of coarseness or vulgarity in it anywhere.

He could only conclude that on the fateful evening his technique had been uncertain because he had lost courage when he saw "those great men up there whom I was going to describe in such a strange fashion." With an impulse to secure vindication, he thought of delivering the speech before the Twentieth Century Club of Boston, or at a banquet of newspapermen in Washington to which he had been invited. But a few days later he told Twichell:

I have examined that speech a couple of times since, and have changed my notion about it—changed it entirely. I find it gross, coarse—well, I needn't go on with particulars. I didn't like any part of it, from the beginning to the end. I found it always offensive and detestable. How do I account for this change of view? I don't know. I can't account for it . . . I expect this latest verdict to remain.

Nevertheless, there was to be yet one more swing of the pendulum. On the typescript of this passage in the Autobiographical Dictation is a footnote in Mark Twain's hand:

May 25th. [1906.] It did remain—until day before yesterday; then I gave it a final and vigorous reading—*aloud*—and dropped straight back to my former admiration of it. M.T.

VI

A Sound Heart and a Deformed Conscience

MARK TWAIN worked on *Adventures of Huckleberry Finn* at intervals over a period of seven years, from 1876 to 1883. During this time he wrote two considerable books (*A Tramp Abroad* and *The Prince and the Pauper*), expanded "Old Times on the Mississippi" into *Life on the Mississippi,* and gathered various shorter pieces into three other volumes. But this is all essentially minor work. The main line of his development lies in the long preoccupation with the Matter of Hannibal and the Matter of the River that is recorded in "Old Times" and *The Adventures of Tom Sawyer* and reaches a climax in his book about "Tom Sawyer's Comrade. Scene: The Mississippi Valley. Time: Forty to Fifty Years Ago."

In writing *Huckleberry Finn* Mark Twain found a way to organize into a larger structure the insights that earlier humorists had recorded in their brief anecdotes. This technical accomplishment was of course inseparable from the process of discovering new meanings in his material. His development as a writer was a dialectic interplay in which the reach of his imagination imposed a constant strain on his technical resources, and innovations of method in turn opened up new vistas before his imagination.

The dialectic process is particularly striking in the gestation of *Huckleberry Finn*. The use of Huck as a narrative persona, with the consequent elimination of the author as an intruding presence in the story, resolved the difficulties about point of view and style that had been so conspicuous in the earlier books. But turning the story over to Huck brought into view previously unsuspected literary potentialities in the vernacular perspective, particularly the possibility of using vernacular speech for serious purposes

113

and of transforming the vernacular narrator from a mere persona into a character with human depth. Mark Twain's response to the challenge made *Huckleberry Finn* the greatest of his books and one of the two or three acknowledged masterpieces of American literature. Yet this triumph created a new technical problem to which there was no solution; for what had begun as a comic story developed incipiently tragic implications contradicting the premises of comedy.

Huckleberry Finn thus contains three main elements. The most conspicuous is the story of Huck's and Jim's adventures in their flight toward freedom. Jim is running away from actual slavery, Huck from the cruelty of his father, from the well-intentioned "sivilizing" efforts of Miss Watson and the Widow Douglas, from respectability and routine in general. The second element in the novel is social satire of the towns along the river. The satire is often transcendently funny, especially in episodes involving the rascally Duke and King, but it can also deal in appalling violence, as in the Grangerford-Shepherdson feud or Colonel Sherburn's murder of the helpless Boggs. The third major element in the book is the developing characterization of Huck.

All three elements must have been present to Mark Twain's mind in some sense from the beginning, for much of the book's greatness lies in its basic coherence, the complex interrelation of its parts. Nevertheless, the intensive study devoted to it in recent years, particularly Walter Blair's establishment of the chronology of its composition, has demonstrated that Mark Twain's search for a structure capable of doing justice to his conceptions of theme and character passed through several stages. He did not see clearly where he was going when he began to write, and we can observe him in the act of making discoveries both in meaning and in method as he goes along.

The narrative tends to increase in depth as it moves from the adventure story of the early chapters into the social satire of the long middle section, and thence to the ultimate psychological penetration of Huck's character in the moral crisis of Chapter 31. Since the crisis is brought on by the shock of the definitive failure of Huck's effort to help Jim, it marks the real end of the quest for freedom. The perplexing final sequence on the Phelps plantation is best regarded as a maneuver by which Mark Twain beats his way back from incipient tragedy to the comic resolution called for by the original conception of the story.

2

Huck's and Jim's flight from St. Petersburg obviously translates into action the theme of vernacular protest. The fact that they have no means of fighting back against the forces that threaten them but can only run away is accounted for in part by the conventions of backwoods humor, in which the inferior social status of the vernacular character placed him in an ostensibly weak position. But it also reflects Mark Twain's awareness of his own lack of firm ground to stand on in challenging the established system of values.

Huck's and Jim's defenselessness foreshadows the outcome of their efforts to escape. They cannot finally succeed. To be sure, in a superficial sense they do succeed; at the end of the book Jim is technically free and Huck still has the power to light out for the Territory. But Jim's freedom has been brought about by such an implausible device that we do not believe in it. Who can imagine the scene in which Miss Watson decides to liberate him? What were her motives? Mark Twain finesses the problem by placing this crucial event far offstage and telling us nothing about it beyond the bare fact he needs to resolve his plot. And the notion that a fourteen-year-old boy could make good his escape beyond the frontier is equally unconvincing. The writer himself did not take it seriously. In an unpublished sequel to *Huckleberry Finn* called "Huck Finn and Tom Sawyer among the Indians," which he began soon after he finished the novel, Aunt Sally takes the boys and Jim back to Hannibal and then to western Missouri for a visit "with some of her relations on a hemp farm out there." Here Tom revives the plan mentioned near the end of *Huckleberry Finn*: he "was dead set on having us run off, some night, and cut for the Injun country and go for adventures." Huck says, however, that he and Jim "kind of hung fire. Plenty to eat and nothing to do. We was very well satisfied." Only after an extended debate can Tom persuade them to set out with him. Their expedition falls into the stereotyped pattern of Wild West stories of travel out the Oregon Trail, makes a few gibes at Cooper's romanticized Indians, and breaks off.

The difficulty of imagining a successful outcome for Huck's and Jim's quest had troubled Mark Twain almost from the beginning of his work on the book. After writing the first section in 1876 he laid aside his manuscript near the end of Chapter 16. The narrative plan with which he had impulsively begun had run into difficulties. When Huck and Jim shove off from Jackson's Island on their section of a lumber raft (at the end of Chapter 11) they do so in haste, to escape the immediate danger of the slave hunters Huck has learned about from Mrs. Loftus. No long-range plan is mentioned until the beginning of Chapter 15, when Huck says that at Cairo they intended to "sell the raft and get on a steamboat and go way up the Ohio amongst the free states, and then be out of trouble." But they drift past Cairo in the fog, and a substitute plan of making their way back up to the mouth of the Ohio in their canoe is frustrated when the canoe disappears while they are sleeping: "we talked about what we better do, and found there warn't no way but just to go along down with the raft till we got a chance to buy a canoe to go back in." Drifting downstream with the current, however, could not be reconciled with the plan to free Jim by transporting him up the Ohio; hence the temporary abandonment of the story.

3

When Mark Twain took up his manuscript again in 1879, after an interval of three years, he had decided upon a different plan for the narrative. Instead of concentrating on the story of Huck's and Jim's escape, he now launched into a satiric description of the society of the prewar South. Huck was essential to this purpose, for Mark Twain meant to view his subject ironically through Huck's eyes. But Jim was more or less superfluous. During Chapters 17 and 18, devoted to the Grangerford household and the feud, Jim has disappeared from the story. Mark Twain had apparently not yet found a way to combine social satire with the narrative scheme of Huck's and Jim's journey on the raft.

While he was writing his chapter about the feud, however, he thought of a plausible device to keep Huck and Jim floating southward while he continued his panoramic survey of the towns along the river. The device was the introduction of the Duke and the King. In Chapter 19 they come aboard the raft, take charge at once, and hold Huck and Jim in virtual captivity. In this fashion the narrative can preserve the overall form of a journey down the river while providing ample opportunity for satire when Huck accompanies the two rascals on their forays ashore. But only the outward form of the journey is retained. Its meaning has changed, for Huck's and Jim's quest for freedom has in effect come to an end. Jim is physically present but he assumes an entirely passive role, and is hidden with the raft for considerable periods. Huck is also essentially passive; his function now is that of an observer. Mark Twain postpones acknowledging that the quest for freedom has failed, but the issue will have to be faced eventually.

The satire of the towns along the banks insists again and again that the dominant culture is decadent and perverted. Traditional values have gone to seed. The inhabitants can hardly be said to live a conscious life of their own; their actions, their thoughts, even their emotions are controlled by an outworn and debased Calvinism, and by a residue of the eighteenth-century cult of sensibility. With few exceptions they are mere bundles of tropisms, at the mercy of scoundrels like the Duke and the King who know how to exploit their prejudices and delusions.

The falseness of the prevalent values finds expression in an almost universal tendency of the townspeople to make spurious claims to status through self-dramatization. Mark Twain has been concerned with this topic from the beginning of the book. Chapter 1 deals with Tom Sawyer's plan to start a band of robbers which Huck will be allowed to join only if he will "go back to the widow and be respectable"; and we also hear about Miss Watson's mercenary conception of prayer. In Chapter 2 Jim interprets Tom's prank of hanging his hat on the limb of a tree while he is asleep as evidence that he has been bewitched. He "was most ruined for a servant, because he got stuck up on account of having seen the devil and been rode by witches." Presently we witness the ritual by which Pap Finn is to be redeemed from drunkenness. When his benefactor gives him a lecture on temperance, it will be recalled,

the old man cried, and said he'd been a fool, and fooled away his life; but now he was a-going to turn over a new leaf and be a man nobody wouldn't be ashamed of, and he hoped the judge would help him and not look down on him. The judge said he could hug him for them words; so *he* cried, and his wife she cried again; pap said he'd been a man that had always been misunderstood before, and the judge said he believed it. The old man said that what a man wanted that was down was sympathy, and the judge said it was so; so they cried again.

As comic relief for the feud that provides a way of life for the male Grangerfords Mark Twain dwells lovingly on Emmeline Grangerford's pretensions to culture—her paintings with the fetching titles and the ambitious "Ode to Stephen Dowling Bots, Dec'd.," its pathos hopelessly flawed by the crudities showing through like the chalk beneath the enameled surface of the artificial fruit in the parlor: "His spirit was gone for to sport aloft/In the realms of the good and great."

The Duke and the King personify the theme of fraudulent role-taking. These rogues are not even given names apart from the wildly improbable identities they assume in order to dominate Huck and Jim. The Duke's poses have a literary cast, perhaps because of the scraps of bombast he remembers from his experience as an actor. The illiterate King has "done considerable in the doctoring way," but when we see him at work it is mainly at preaching, "workin' camp-meetin's, and missionaryin' around." Pretended or misguided piety and other perversions of Christianity obviously head the list of counts in Mark Twain's indictment of the prewar South. And properly: for it is of course religion that stands at the center of the system of values in the society of this fictive world and by implication in all societies. His revulsion, expressed through Huck, reaches its highest pitch in the scene where the King delivers his masterpiece of "soul-butter and hogwash" for the benefit of the late Peter Wilks's fellow townsmen.

By and by the king he gets up and comes forward a little, and works himself up and slobbers out a speech, all full of tears and flapdoodle, about its being a sore trial for him and his poor brother to lose the diseased, and to miss seeing diseased alive after the long journey of four thousand mile, but it's a trial that's sweetened and sanctified to us by this dear sympathy and these holy tears, and so he thanks them out of his heart and out of his brother's heart, because out of their mouths they can't, words being too weak and cold, and all that kind of rot and slush, till it was just sickening; and then he blubbers out a pious goody-goody Amen, and turns himself loose and goes to crying fit to bust.

4

Huck is revolted by the King's hypocrisy: "I never see anything so disgusting." He has had a similar reaction to the brutality of the feud: "It made me so sick I most fell out of the tree." In describing such scenes he speaks as moral man viewing an immoral society, an observer who is himself free of the vices and even the weaknesses he describes. Mark Twain's satiric method requires that Huck be a mask for the writer, not a fully developed character. The method has great ironic force, and is in itself a technical landmark in the history of American fiction, but it prevents Mark Twain from doing full justice to Huck as a person in his own right, capable of mistakes in perception and judgment, troubled by doubts and conflicting impulses.

Even in the chapters written during the original burst of composition in 1876 the character of Huck is shown to have depths and complexities not relevant to the immediate context. Huck's and Jim's journey down the river begins simply as a flight from physical danger; and the first episodes of the voyage have little bearing on the novelistic possibilities in the strange comradeship between outcast boy and escaped slave. But in Chapter 15, when Huck plays a prank on Jim by persuading him that the separation in the fog was only a dream, Jim's dignified and moving rebuke suddenly opens up a new dimension in the relation. Huck's humble apology is striking evidence of growth in moral insight. It leads naturally to the next chapter in which Mark Twain causes Huck to face up for the first time to the fact that he is helping a slave to escape. It is as if the writer himself were discovering unsuspected meanings in what he had thought of as a story of picaresque adventure. The incipient contradiction between narrative plan and increasing depth in Huck's character must have been as disconcerting to Mark Twain as the difficulty of finding a way to account for Huck's and Jim's continuing southward past the mouth of the Ohio. It was doubtless the convergence of the two problems that led him to put aside the manuscript near the end of Chapter 16.

The introduction of the Duke and the King not only took care of the awkwardness in the plot but also allowed Mark Twain to postpone the exploration of Huck's moral dilemma. If Huck is not a free agent he is not responsible for what happens and is spared the agonies of choice. Throughout the long middle section, while he is primarily an observer, he is free of inner conflict because he is endowed by implication with Mark Twain's own unambiguous attitude toward the fraud and folly he witnesses.

In Chapter 31, however, Huck escapes from his captors and faces once again the responsibility for deciding on a course of action. His situation is much more desperate than it had been at the time of his first struggle with his conscience. The raft has borne Jim hundreds of miles downstream from the pathway of escape and the King has turned him over to Silas Phelps as a runaway slave. The quest for freedom has "all come to nothing, everything all busted up and ruined." Huck thinks of notifying Miss Watson where Jim is, since if he must be a slave he would be better off "at home where his family was." But then Huck realizes that Miss Watson would probably sell Jim down the river as a punishment for running away. Furthermore, Huck himself would be denounced by every-one for his part in the affair. In this fashion his mind comes back once again to the unparalleled wickedness of acting as accomplice in a slave's escape.

The account of Huck's mental struggle in the next two or three pages is the emotional climax of the story. It draws together the theme of flight from bondage and the social satire of the middle section, for Huck is trying to work himself clear of the perverted value system of St. Petersburg. Both adventure story and satire, however, are now subordinate to an exploration of Huck's psyche which is the ultimate achievement of the book. The issue is identical with that of the first moral crisis, but the later passage is much more intense and richer in implication. The differences appear clearly if the two crises are compared in detail.

In Chapter 16 Huck is startled into a realization of his predicament when he hears Jim, on the lookout for Cairo at the mouth of the Ohio, declare that "he'd be a free man the minute he seen it, but if he missed it he'd be in a slave country again and no more show for freedom." Huck says: "I begun to get it through my head that he *was* most free—and who was to blame for it? Why, *me*. I couldn't get that out of my conscience, no how nor no way." He dramatizes his inner debate by quoting the words in which his conscience denounces him: "What had poor Miss Watson done to you that you could see her nigger go off right under your eyes and never say one single word? What did that poor old woman do to you that you could treat her so mean? Why, she tried to learn you your book, she tried to learn you your manners, she tried to be good to you every way she knowed how. *That's* what she done." The counterargument is provided by Jim, who seems to guess what is passing through Huck's mind and does what he can to invoke the force of friendship and grati-tude: "Pooty soon I'll be a-shout'n' for joy, en I'll say, it's all on accounts o' Huck; I's a free man, en I couldn't ever ben free ef it hadn' ben for Huck; Huck done it. Jim won't ever forgit you, Huck; you's de bes' fren' Jim's ever had; en you's de *only* fren' ole Jim's got now." Huck neverthe-less sets out for the shore in the canoe "all in a sweat to tell on" Jim, but when he is intercepted by the two slave hunters in a skiff he suddenly contrives a cunning device to ward them off. We are given no details about how his inner conflict was resolved.

In the later crisis Huck provides a much more circumstantial account of what passes through his mind. He is now quite alone; the outcome of the debate is not affected by any stimulus from the outside. It is the memory of Jim's kindness and goodness rather than Jim's actual voice that impels Huck to defy his conscience: "I see Jim before me all the time: in the day and in the night-time, sometimes moonlight, sometimes storms, and we a-floating along, talking and singing and laughing." The most striking feature of this later crisis is the fact that Huck's conscience, which formerly had employed only secular arguments, now deals heavily in religious cant:

> At last, when it hit me all of a sudden that here was the plain hand of Providence slapping me in the face and letting me know my wickedness was being watched all the time from up there in heaven, whilst I was stealing a poor old woman's nigger that hadn't ever done me no harm, and now was showing me there's One that's always on the lookout, and ain't a-going to allow no such miserable doings to go only just so fur and no further, I most dropped in my tracks I was so scared.

In the earlier debate the voice of Huck's conscience is quoted directly, but the bulk of the later exhortation is reported in indirect discourse. This apparently simple change in method has remarkable consequences. According to the conventions of first-person narrative, the narrator functions as a neutral medium in reporting dialogue. He remembers the speeches of other characters but they pass through his mind without affecting him. When Huck's conscience speaks within quotation marks it is in effect a character in the story, and he is not responsible for what it says. But when he paraphrases the admonitions of his conscience they are incorporated into his own discourse. Thus although Huck is obviously remembering the bits of theological jargon from sermons justifying slavery, they have become a part of his vocabulary.

The device of having Huck paraphrase rather than quote the voice of conscience may have been suggested to Mark Twain by a discovery he made in revising Huck's report of the King's address to the mourners in the Wilks parlor (Chapter 25). The manuscript version of the passage shows that the King's remarks were composed as a direct quotation, but in the published text they have been put, with a minimum of verbal change, into indirect discourse. The removal of the barrier of quotation marks brings Huck into much more intimate contact with the King's "rot and slush" despite the fact that the paraphrase quivers with disapproval. The voice of conscience speaks in the precise accents of the King but

Huck is now completely uncritical. He does not question its moral authority; it is morality personified. The greater subtlety of the later passage illustrates the difference between the necessarily shallow characterization of Huck while he was being used merely as a narrative persona, and the profound insight which Mark Twain eventually brought to bear on his protagonist.

The recognition of complexity in Huck's character enabled Mark Twain to do full justice to the conflict between vernacular values and the dominant culture. By situating in a single consciousness both the perverted moral code of a society built on slavery and the vernacular commitment to freedom and spontaneity, he was able to represent the opposed perspectives as alternative modes of experience for the same character. In this way he gets rid of the confusions surrounding the pronoun "I" in the earlier books, where it sometimes designates the author speaking in his own person, sometimes an entirely distinct fictional character. Furthermore, the insight that enabled him to recognize the conflict between accepted values and vernacular protest as a struggle within a single mind does justice to its moral depth, whereas the device he had used earlier—in *The Innocents Abroad,* for example—of identifying the two perspectives with separate characters had flattened the issue out into melodrama. The satire of a decadent slaveholding society gains immensely in force when Mark Twain demonstrates that even the outcast Huck has been in part perverted by it. Huck's conscience is simply the attitudes he has taken over from his environment. What is still sound in him is an impulse from the deepest level of his personality that struggles against the overlay of prejudice and false valuation imposed on all members of the society in the name of religion, morality, law, and refinement.

Finally, it should be pointed out that the conflict in Huck between generous impulse and false belief is depicted by means of a contrast between colloquial and exalted styles. In moments of crisis his conscience addresses him in the language of the dominant culture, a tawdry and faded effort at a high style that is the rhetorical equivalent of the ornaments in the Grangerford parlor. Yet speaking in dialect does not in itself imply moral authority. By every external criterion the King is as much a vernacular character as Huck. The conflict in which Huck is involved is not that of a lower against an upper class or of an alienated fringe of outcasts against a cultivated elite. It is not the issue of frontier West versus genteel East, or of backwoods versus metropolis, but of fidelity to the uncoerced self versus the blurring of attitudes caused by social conformity, by the effort to achieve status or power through exhibiting the approved forms of sensibility.

The exploration of Huck's personality carried Mark Twain beyond satire and even beyond his statement of a vernacular protest against the dominant culture into essentially novelistic modes of writing. Some of the passages he composed when he got out beyond his polemic framework challenge comparison with the greatest achievements in the world's fiction.

The most obvious of Mark Twain's discoveries on the deeper levels of Huck's psyche is the boy's capacity for love. The quality of the emotion is defined in action by his decision to sacrifice himself for Jim, just as Jim attains an impressive dignity when he refuses to escape at the cost of deserting the wounded Tom. Projected into the natural setting, the love of the protagonists for each other becomes the unforgettable beauty of the river when they are allowed to be alone together. It is always summer, and the forces of nature cherish them. From the refuge of the cave on Jackson's Island the thunderstorm is an exhilarating spectacle; Huck's description of it is only less poetic than his description of the dawn which he and Jim witness as they sit half-submerged on the sandy bottom.

Yet if Mark Twain had allowed these passages to stand without qualification as a symbolic account of Huck's emotions he would have undercut the complexity of characterization implied in his recognition of Huck's inner conflict of loyalties. Instead, he uses the natural setting to render a wide range of feelings and motives. The fog that separates the boy from Jim for a time is an externalization of his impulse to deceive Jim by a Tom Sawyerish practical joke. Similarly Jim's snake bite, the only injury suffered by either of the companions from a natural source, is the result of another prank played by Huck before he has learned what friends owe one another.

Still darker aspects of Huck's inner life are projected into the natural setting in the form of ghosts, omens, portents of disaster—the body of superstition that is so conspicuous in Huck's and Jim's world. At the end of Chapter 1 Huck is sitting alone at night by his open window in the Widow Douglas' house:

I felt so lonesome I most wished I was dead. The stars was shining, and the leaves rustled in the woods ever so mournful; and I heard an owl, away off, who-whooing about somebody that was dead, and a whippowill and a dog crying about somebody that was going to die; and the wind was trying to whisper something to me, and I couldn't make out what it was, and so it made the cold shivers run over me. Then away out in the woods I heard that kind of a sound that a ghost makes when it wants to tell about something that's on its mind and can't make itself understood, and so can't rest easy in its grave, and has to go about that way every night grieving. I got so downhearted and scared I did wish I had some company.

The whimpering ghost with something incommunicable on its mind and Huck's cold shivers suggest a burden of guilt and anxiety that is perhaps the punishment he inflicts on himself for defying the mores of St. Petersburg. Whatever the source of these sinister images, they develop the characterization of Huck beyond the needs of the plot. The narrator whose stream of consciousness is recorded here is much more than the innocent protagonist of the pastoral idyl of the raft, more than an ignorant boy who resists being civilized. The vernacular persona is an essentially comic figure; the character we glimpse in Huck's meditation is potentially tragic. Mark Twain's discoveries in the buried strata of Huck's mind point in the same direction as does his intuitive recognition that Huck's and Jim's quest for freedom must end in failure.

A melancholy if not exactly tragic strain in Huck is revealed also by the fictitious autobiographies with which he so often gets himself out of tight places. Like the protocols of a thematic apperception test, they are improvisations on the basis of minimal clues. Huck's inventions are necessary to account for his anomalous situation as a fourteen-year-old boy alone on the river with a Negro man, but they are often carried beyond the demands of utility for sheer love of fable-making. Their luxuriant detail, and the fact that Huck's hearers are usually (although not always) taken in, lend a comic coloring to these inventions, which are authentically in the tradition of the tall tale. But their total effect is somber. When Huck plans his escape from Pap in Chapter 7, he does so by imagining his own death and planting clues which convince everyone in St. Petersburg, including Tom Sawyer, that he has been murdered. In the crisis of Chapter 16 his heightened emotion leads him to produce for the benefit of the slave hunters a harrowing tale to the effect that his father and mother and sister are suffering smallpox on a raft adrift in mid-river, and he is unable to tow the raft ashore. The slave hunters are so touched by the story that they give him forty dollars and careful instructions about how to seek help—farther downstream. Huck tells the Grangerfords "how pap and me and all the family was living on a little farm down at the bottom of Arkansaw, and my sister Mary Ann run off and got married and never was heard of no more, and Bill went to hunt them and he warn't heard of no more, and Tom and Mort died, and then there warn't nobody but just me and pap left, and he was just trimmed down to nothing, on account of his troubles; so when he died I took what there was left, because the farm didn't belong to us, and started up the river, deck passage, and fell overboard."

5

A number of characters besides Huck are presented in greater depth than is necessary either for purposes of satire or for telling the story of his and Jim's quest for freedom. Perhaps the most striking of these is Pap Finn. Like most of the book, Pap comes straight out of Mark Twain's boyhood memories. We have had a glimpse of him as the drunkard sleeping in the shade of a pile of skids on the levee in the opening scene of "Old Times on the Mississippi." His function in the plot, although definite, is limited. He helps to characterize Huck by making vivid the conditions of Huck's childhood. He has transmitted to his son a casual attitude toward chickens and watermelons, a fund of superstitions, a picaresque ability to look out for himself, and even the gift of language. Pap takes Huck away from the comfort and elegance of the Widow's house to the squalor of the deserted cabin across the river, and then by his sadistic beatings forces the boy to escape to Jackson's Island, where the main action of the flight with Jim begins. After the three chapters which Pap dominates (5–7) we do not see him again except as a corpse in the house floating down the river, but Huck refers to him several times later, invoking Pap's testimony to authenticate the aristocratic status of the Widow Douglas, and to support the family philosophy of "borrowing."

In the sociological scheme of the novel Pap provides a matchless specimen of the lowest stratum of whites who are fiercely jealous of their superiority to all Negroes. His monologue on the "govment" in Chapter 6, provoked by the spectacle of the well-dressed free Negro professor from Ohio, seizes in a few lines the essence of Southern race prejudice. Huck shrewdly calls attention to his father's economic code. When the flooded river brings down part of a log raft, he says: "Anybody but pap would 'a' waited and seen the day through, so as to catch more stuff; but that warn't pap's style. Nine logs was enough for one time; he must shove right over to town and sell," mainly in order to buy whiskey.

But these documentary data supply only a minor part of the image of Pap in *Huckleberry Finn*. He provides some of the most mordant comedy in the book. The fashion in which he gives himself away in the monologue on "govment" is worthy of Jonson or Molière:

> It was 'lection day, and I was just about to go and vote myself if I warn't too drunk to get there; but when they told me there was a state in this country where they'd let that nigger vote, I drawed out. I says I'll never vote ag'in. Them's the very words I said; they all heard me; and the country may rot for all me—I'll never vote ag'in as long as I live. And to see the cool way of that nigger—why, he wouldn't 'a' give me the road if I hadn't shoved him out o' the way.

Even when the comedy verges on slapstick it retains its function as characterization. Pap is so completely absorbed in his diatribe that he barks his shins on the pork barrel:

> He hopped around the cabin considerable, first on one leg and then on the other, holding first one shin and then the other one, and at last he let out with his left foot all of a sudden and fetched the tub a rattling kick. But it warn't good judgment, because that was the boot that had a couple of his toes leaking out of the front end of it; so now he raised a howl that fairly made a body's hair raise, and down he went in the dirt, and rolled there, and held his toes; and the cussing he done then laid over anything he had ever done previous. He said so his own self afterwards. He had heard old Sowberry Hagan in his best days, and he said it laid over him, too; but I reckon that was sort of piling it on, maybe.

Pap's detached evaluation of his own accomplishment in swearing gives to his character an almost medieval flavor. In all his degradation he conceives of himself as enacting a role which is less a personal destiny than part of an integral natural-social reality—a reality so stable that he can contemplate it as if it were external to him. On election day he was drunk as a matter of course; it was an objective question, like an effort to predict the weather, whether he might be too drunk to get to the polls. When he settles down for a domestic evening in the cabin, he "took the jug, and said he had enough whiskey there for two drunks and one delirium tremens."

But when the delirium comes, it belies the coolness of his offhand calculation. Huck's description of the drunkard's agony is a nightmare of neurotic suffering that blots out the last vestige of comedy in Pap's image and relates itself in Huck's mind to the ominous sounds he had heard from his window in the Widow's house:

[Pap] rolled over and over wonderful fast, kicking things every which way, and striking and grabbing at the air with his hands, and screaming and saying there was devils a-hold of him . . . Then he laid stiller, and didn't make a sound. I could hear the owls and the wolves away off in the woods, and it seemed terrible still . . . By and by he raised up part way and listened, with his head to one side. He says, very low:
"Tramp—tramp—tramp; that's the dead; tramp—tramp—tramp; they're coming after me; but I won't go. Oh, they're here! don't touch me—don't! hands off—they're cold; let go. Oh, let a poor devil alone!"
Then he went down on all fours and crawled off, begging them to let him alone, and he rolled himself up in his blanket and wallowed in under the old pine table, still a-begging; and then he went to crying. I could hear him through the blanket.

Pap's hallucinations externalize inner suffering in images of ghosts and portents. Presently he sees in Huck the Angel of Death and chases him around the cabin with a knife "saying he would kill me, and then I couldn't come for him no more." In fact, the mystery of Pap's anguished psyche has had a supernatural aura all along. He is in a sense a ghost the first time we see him, for his faceless corpse has been found floating in the river; and immediately before his dramatic appearance in Huck's room Jim's hair-ball oracle has announced, "Dey's two angels hoverin' roun' 'bout him. One uv 'em is white en shiny, en t'other one is black. De white one gits him to go right a little while, den de black one sail in en bust it all up. A body can't tell yit which one gwyne to fetch him at de las'." Coming early in the story, at a time when Mark Twain had apparently not yet worked out the details of the plot, this sounds as if he had in mind the possibility of involving Pap more elaborately in the course of events. But aside from the relatively minor incidents that have been mentioned, what the angels might have led Pap to do is never revealed.

He does, however, have an important thematic function. He serves as a forceful reminder that to be a vernacular outcast does not necessarily bring one into contact with the benign forces of nature. Physical withdrawal

127

from society may be plain loafing, without moral significance. Huck's life with Pap in the cabin foreshadows his life with Jim on the raft, but lacks the suggestion of harmony with the natural setting:

> It was kind of lazy and jolly, laying off comfortable all day, smoking and fishing, and no books nor study. Two months or more run along, and my clothes got to be all rags and dirt, and I didn't see how I'd ever got to like it so well at the widow's, where you had to wash, and eat on a plate, and comb up, and go to bed and get up regular, and be forever bothering over a book, and have old Miss Watson pecking at you all the time. I didn't want to go back no more . . . It was pretty good times up in the woods there, take it all around.

More explicitly, Pap's denunciation of Huck for the civilized habits the Widow and Miss Watson have imposed on him is a grotesque version of vernacular hostility toward the conventions of refined society:

> Starchy clothes—very. You think you're a good deal of a big-bug, *don't* you? . . . You're educated, too, they say—can read and write. You think you're better'n your father, now, don't you, because he can't? . . . you drop that school, you hear? I'll learn people to bring up a boy to put on airs over his own father and let on to be better'n what *he* is . . . First you know you'll get religion, too. I never see such a son.

This adds another nuance to the book by suggesting that civilized values have something to be said for them after all.

The extent to which Mark Twain's imagination was released in *Huckleberry Finn* to explore multiple perspectives upon the Matter of Hannibal and the Matter of the River can be realized if one compares Pap with the sociologically similar backwoodsmen observed from the steamboat in "Old Times." These "jeans-clad, chills-racked, yellow-faced miserables" are merely comic animals. Pap is even more degraded than they are, lazier, more miserable, but he is not an object of scorn. The fullness with which his degradation and his misery are presented confers on him not so much a human dignity—although it is also that—as the impersonal dignity of art.

In relation to the whole of *Huckleberry Finn*, Pap serves to solidify the image of Huck's and Jim's vernacular paradise by demonstrating that Mark Twain is aware of the darker possibilities confronting them when they escape from the shore to the river. The mass of superstitions with which Pap is so vividly connected (we recall the cross of nails in his boot heel to ward off the devil), standing in contrast to the intimations of blissful harmony with nature in the passages devoted to Huck and Jim alone on the raft, keeps that lyrical vision from seeming mere pathetic fallacy. And the appalling glimpse of Pap's inner life beneath the stereotype of the town drunkard makes him into what might be called a note of tragic relief in a predominantly comic story.

6

It has become a commonplace of criticism that the drastic shift in tone in the last section of *Huckleberry Finn,* from Chapter 31 to the end, poses a problem of interpretation. The drifting raft has reached Arkansas, and the King and the Duke have delivered Jim back into captivity. They make their exit early in the sequence, tarred and feathered as punishment for one more effort to work the "Royal Nonesuch" trick. Tom Sawyer reappears by an implausible coincidence and takes charge of the action, which thereafter centers about his schemes to liberate Jim from confinement in a cabin on the plantation of Tom's Uncle Silas Phelps.

These events have for their prelude a vivid description of Huck's first approach to the Phelps place:

> When I got there it was all still and Sunday-like, and hot and sunshiny; the hands was gone to the fields; and there was them kind of faint dronings of bugs and flies in the air that makes it seem so lonesome and like everybody's dead and gone; and if a breeze fans along and quivers the leaves it makes you feel mournful, because you feel like it's spirits whispering—spirits that's been dead ever so many years—and you always think they're talking about *you.* As a general thing it makes a body wish *he* was dead, too, and done with it all.

And a few lines later:

> I went around and clumb over the back stile by the ash-hopper, and started for the kitchen. When I got a little ways I heard the dim hum of a spinning-wheel wailing along up and sinking along down again; and then I knowed for certain I wished I was dead—for that *is* the lonesomest sound in the whole world.

This passage has much in common with Huck's meditation before his open window in Chapter 1. They are the two most vivid expressions of

129

his belief in ghosts, and in both cases the ghosts are associated in his mind with a deep depression not fully accounted for by the context of the story.

It would be reasonable to suppose that the cause of Huck's depression is the failure of his long effort to help Jim toward freedom. The reader knows that even if Huck could manage to rescue Jim from the Phelpses, they face insuperable difficulties in trying to make their way back up the Mississippi to free territory. Yet oddly enough, Huck does not share this estimate of the situation. He is confident he can find a way out of the impasse: "I went right along, not fixing up any particular plan, but just trusting to Providence to put the right words in my mouth when the time come; for I'd noticed that Providence always did put the right words in my mouth if I left it alone." Somewhat later, Huck points out to Tom that they can easily get Jim out of the log cabin by stealing the key, and "shove off down the river on the raft with Jim, hiding daytimes and running nights, the way me and Jim used to do before. Wouldn't that plan work?" Tom agrees: "Why, cert'nly it would work, like rats a-fighting. But it's too blame' simple; there ain't nothing *to* it. What's the good of a plan that ain't no more trouble than that?"

The tone as much as the substance of the references to the problem of rescuing Jim makes it plain that Huck's view of his predicament cannot account for his depression as he approaches the Phelps plantation. The emotion is the author's rather than Huck's, and it is derived from sources outside the story. In order to determine what these were we must consult Mark Twain's autobiographical reminiscences. The Phelps place as he describes it in the novel has powerful associations for him because it is patterned on the farm of his Uncle John A. Quarles where he spent summers as a boy. "I can see the farm yet, with perfect clearness," he wrote in his *Autobiography*.

I can see all its belongings, all its details; the family room of the house, with a "trundle" bed in one corner and a spinning-wheel in another—a wheel whose rising and falling wail, heard from a distance, was the mournfulest of all sounds to me, and made me homesick and low spirited, and filled my atmosphere with the wandering spirits of the dead.

Additional associations with the Quarles farm are recorded in Mark Twain's "The Private History of a Campaign That Failed," written a few months after the publication of *Huckleberry Finn*. This bit of fictionalized autobiography describes his experiences as second lieutenant of the Marion

Rangers, a rather informal volunteer militia unit organized in Hannibal in the early months of the Civil War. The Quarles farm is here assigned to a man named Mason:

We stayed several days at Mason's; and after all these years the memory of the dullness, and stillness, and lifelessness of that slumberous farm-house still oppresses my spirit as with a sense of the presence of death and mourning. There was nothing to do, nothing to think about; there was no interest in life. The male part of the household were away in the fields all day, the women were busy and out of our sight; there was no sound but the plaintive wailing of a spinning-wheel, forever moaning out from some distant room—the most lonesome sound in nature, a sound steeped and sodden with homesickness and the emptiness of life.

The emotional overtones of the memories recorded in "The Private History" are made more explicit in a letter Mark Twain wrote in 1890:

I was a *soldier* two weeks once in the beginning of the war, and was hunted like a rat the whole time . . . My splendid Kipling himself hasn't a more burnt-in, hard-baked and unforgettable familiarity with that death-on-the-pale-horse-with-hell-following-after which is a raw soldier's first fortnight in the field—and which, without any doubt, is the most tremendous fortnight and the vividest he is ever going to see.

But while there are references to fear of the enemy in "The Private History," they are mainly comic, and the dullness and lifelessness that afflict the neophyte soldiers at the Mason farm do not suggest the feeling of being hunted like a rat. More significant, perhaps, is an incident Mark Twain places a few pages later in "The Private History." Albert B. Paine says it was invented; and it does have the air of fiction. But it reveals the emotional coloring of the author's recollections. He relates that he fired in the dark at a man approaching on horseback, who was killed. Although five other shots were fired at the same moment, and he did not at bottom believe his shot had struck its mark, still his "diseased imagination" convinced him he was guilty. "The thought shot through me that I was a murderer; that I had killed a man—a man who had never done me any harm. That was the coldest sensation that ever went through my marrow."

Huck also experiences a strong and not easily explicable feeling of guilt a few pages after his arrival at the Phelpses'. When he sees the Duke and the King ridden out of the nearby town on a rail, surrounded by a howling mob, he says:

It was a dreadful thing to see. Human beings *can* be awful cruel to one another . . . So we poked along back home, and I warn't feeling so brash as I was before, but kind of ornery, and humble, and to blame, somehow—though *I* hadn't done nothing. But that's always the way; it don't make no difference whether you do right or wrong, a person's conscience ain't got no sense, and just goes for him *anyway*. If I had a yaller dog that didn't know no more than a person's conscience does I would pison him.

The close linkage of the Phelps and Mason farms with Mark Twain's memory of the Quarles place strongly suggests that Huck's depression is caused by a sense of guilt whose sources were buried in the writer's child-hood. It is well known that Mark Twain was tormented all his life by such feelings. A fable written in 1876, "The Facts Concerning the Recent Carnival of Crime in Connecticut," makes comedy of his sufferings; but they were serious and chronic. In his twenties, because of an imaginary error in administering an opiate, he had insisted he was to blame for the death of his brother from injuries received in the explosion of a steamboat. Later he accused himself of murdering his son Langdon when he neglected to keep him covered during a carriage ride in cold weather, and the child died of diphtheria.

But why was Mark Twain's latent feeling of guilt drawn up into con- sciousness at a specific moment in the writing of *Huckleberry Finn*? The most probable explanation is that at this point he was obliged to admit finally to himself that Huck's and Jim's journey down the river could not be imagined as leading to freedom for either of them. Because of the symbolic meaning the journey had taken on for him, the recognition was more than a perception of difficulty in contriving a plausible ending for the book. He had found a solution to the technical problem that satisfied him, if one is to judge from his evident zest in the complicated pranks of Tom Sawyer that occupy the last ten chapters. But in order to write these chapters he had to abandon the compelling image of the happiness of Huck and Jim on the raft and thus to acknowledge that the vernacular values embodied in his story were mere figments of the imagination, not capable of being reconciled with social reality. To be sure, he had been half-aware from the beginning that the quest of his protagonists was doomed. Huck had repeatedly appeared in the role of a Tiresias power-less to prevent the deceptions and brutalities he was compelled to witness. Yet Providence had always put the right words in his mouth when the time came, and by innocent guile he had extricated himself and Jim from danger after danger. Now the drifting had come to an end.

At an earlier impasse in the plot Mark Twain had shattered the raft under the paddle wheel of a steamboat. He now destroys it again, symbolically, by revealing that Huck's and Jim's journey, with all its anxieties, has been pointless. Tom Sawyer is bearer of the news that Jim has been freed in Miss Watson's will. Tom withholds the information, however, in order to trick Huck and Jim into the meaningless game of an Evasion that makes the word (borrowed from Dumas) into a devastating pun. Tom takes control and Huck becomes once again a subordinate carrying out orders. As if to signal the change of perspective and the shift in his own identification, Mark Twain gives Huck Tom's name through an improbable mistake on the part of Aunt Sally Phelps. We can hardly fail to perceive the weight of the author's feeling in Huck's statement on this occasion: "it was like being born again, I was so glad to find out who I was." Mark Twain has found out who he must be in order to end his book: he must be Tom.

In more abstract terms, he must withdraw from his imaginative participation in Huck's and Jim's quest for freedom. If the story was to be stripped of its tragic implications, Tom's perspective was the logical one to adopt because his intensely conventional sense of values made him impervious to the moral significance of the journey on the raft. Huck can hardly believe that Tom would collaborate in the crime of helping a runaway slave, and Huck is right. Tom merely devises charades involving a man who is already in a technical sense free. The consequences of the shift in point of view are strikingly evident in the treatment of Jim, who is subjected to farcical indignities. This is disturbing to the reader who has seen Jim take on moral and emotional stature, but it is necessary if everything is to be forced back into the framework of comedy. Mark Twain's portrayal of Huck and Jim as complex characters has carried him beyond the limits of his original plan: we must not forget that the literary ancestry of the book is to be found in backwoods humor. As Huck approaches the Phelps plantation the writer has on his hands a hybrid—a comic story in which the protagonists have acquired something like tragic depth.

In deciding to end the book with the description of Tom's unnecessary contrivances for rescuing Jim, Mark Twain was certain to produce an anticlimax. But he was a great comic writer, able to score local triumphs in the most unlikely circumstances. The last chapters have a number of brilliant touches—the slave who carries the witch pie to Jim, Aunt Sally's trouble in counting her spoons, Uncle Silas and the ratholes, the unforgettable Sister Hotchkiss. Even Tom's horseplay would be amusing if it were not spun out to such length and if we were not asked to accept it as the conclusion of *Huckleberry Finn*. Although Jim is reduced to the level of farce, Tom is a comic figure in the classical sense of being a victim of delusion. He is not aware of being cruel to Jim because he does not perceive him as a human being. For Tom, Jim is the hero of a historical romance, a peer of the Man in the Iron Mask or the Count of Monte Cristo. Mark Twain is consciously imitating *Don Quixote,* and there are moments not unworthy of the model, as when Tom admits that "we got to dig him out with the picks, and *let on* it's case-knives."

But Tom has no tragic dimension whatever. There is not even any force of common sense in him to struggle against his perverted imagination as Huck's innate loyalty and generosity struggle against his deformed conscience. Although Mark Twain is indulgent toward Tom, he adds him to the list of characters who employ the soul-butter style of false pathos. The inscriptions Tom composes for Jim to "scrabble onto the wall" of the cabin might have been composed by the Duke:

1. Here a captive heart busted.
2. Here a poor prisoner, forsook by the world and friends, fretted his sorrowful life.
3. Here a lonely heart broke, and a worn spirit went to its rest, after thirty-seven years of solitary captivity.
4. Here, homeless and friendless, after thirty-seven years of bitter captivity, perished a noble stranger, natural son of Louis XIV.

While he was reading these noble sentiments aloud, "Tom's voice trembled . . . and he most broke down."

7

Mark Twain's partial shift of identification from Huck to Tom in the final sequence was one response to his recognition that Huck's and Jim's quest for freedom was only a dream: he attempted to cover with a veil of parody and farce the harsh facts that condemned it to failure. The brief episode involving Colonel Sherburn embodies yet another response to his disillusionment. The extraordinary vividness of the scenes in which Sherburn figures—only a half-dozen pages all told—is emphasized by their air of being an intrusion into the story. Of course, in the episodic structure of *Huckleberry Finn* many characters appear for a moment and disappear. Even so, the Sherburn episode seems unusually isolated. None of the principal characters is involved in or affected by it: Jim, the Duke, and the King are offstage, and Huck is a spectator whom even the author hardly notices. We are told nothing about his reaction except that he did not want to stay around. He goes abruptly off to the circus and does not refer to Sherburn again.

Like Huck's depression as he nears the Phelps plantation, the Sherburn episode is linked with Mark Twain's own experience. The shooting of Boggs follows closely the murder of "Uncle Sam" Smarr by a merchant named Owsley in Hannibal in 1845, when Sam Clemens was nine years old. Although it is not clear that he actually witnessed it, he mentioned the incident at least four times at intervals during his later life, including one retelling as late as 1898, when he said he had often dreamed about it. Mark Twain prepares for the shooting in *Huckleberry Finn* by careful attention to the brutality of the loafers in front of the stores in Bricksville. "There couldn't anything wake them up all over, and make them happy all over, like a dog-fight—unless it might be putting turpentine on a stray dog and setting fire to him, or tying a tin pan to his tail and see him run himself to death." The prurient curiosity of the townspeople who shove and pull to catch a glimpse of Boggs as he lies dying in the drugstore with a heavy Bible on his chest, and their pleasure in the re-enactment of the shooting by the man in the big white fur stovepipe hat, also help to make Bricksville an appropriate setting for Sherburn's crime.

The shooting is in Chapter 21, and the scene in which Sherburn scatters the mob by his contemptuous speech is in the following chapter. There is evidence that Mark Twain put aside the manuscript for a time near the end of Chapter 21. If there was such an interruption in his work on the novel, it might account for a marked change in tone. In Chapter 21 Sherburn is an unsympathetic character. His killing of Boggs is motivated solely by arrogance, and the introduction of Boggs's daughter is an invitation to the reader to consider Sherburn an inhuman monster. In Chapter 22, on the other hand, the Colonel appears in an oddly favorable light. The townspeople have now become a mob; there are several touches that suggest Mark Twain was recalling the descriptions of mobs in Carlyle's

French Revolution and other works of history and fiction. He considered mobs to be subhuman aggregates generating psychological pressures that destroyed individual freedom of choice. In a passage written for *Life on the Mississippi* but omitted from the book Mark Twain makes scathing generalizations about the cowardice of mobs, especially in the South but also in other regions, that closely parallel Sherburn's speech.

In other words, however hostile may be the depiction of Sherburn in Chapter 21, in Chapter 22 we have yet another instance of Mark Twain's identifying himself, at least partially, with a character in the novel other than Huck. The image of Sherburn standing on the roof of the porch in front of his house with the shotgun that is the only weapon in sight has an emblematic quality. He is a solitary figure, not identified with the townspeople, and because they are violently hostile to him, an outcast. But he is not weaker than they, he is stronger. He stands above the mob, looking down on it. He is "a heap the best dressed man in that town," and he is more intelligent than his neighbors. The scornful courage with which he defies the mob redeems him from the taint of cowardice implied in his shooting of an unarmed man who was trying to escape. Many members of the mob he faces are presumably armed; the shotgun he holds is not the source of his power but merely a symbol of the personal force with which he dominates the community.

The Colonel's repeated references to one Buck Harkness, the leader of the mob, whom he acknowledges to be "half-a-man," suggest that the scene represents a contest between two potential leaders in Bricksville. Harkness is the strongest man with whom the townspeople can identify themselves. In his pride Sherburn chooses isolation, but he demonstrates that he is stronger than Harkness, for the mob, including Harkness, obeys his command to *"leave*—and take your half-a-man with you."

Sherburn belongs to the series of characters in Mark Twain's later work that have been called "transcendent figures." Other examples are Hank Morgan in *A Connecticut Yankee;* Pudd'nhead Wilson; and Satan in *The Mysterious Stranger*. They exhibit certain common traits, more fully developed with the passage of time. They are isolated by their intellectual superiority to the community; they are contemptuous of mankind in general; and they have more than ordinary power. Satan, the culmination of the series, is omnipotent. Significantly, he is without a moral sense— that is, a conscience, a sense of guilt. He is not torn by the kind of inner struggle that Huck experiences. But he is also without Huck's sound heart. The price of power is the surrender of all human warmth.

Colonel Sherburn's cold-blooded murder of Boggs, his failure to experience remorse after the act, and his withering scorn of the townspeople are disquieting portents for the future. Mark Twain, like Huck, was sickened by the brutality he had witnessed in the society along the river. But he had an adult aggressiveness foreign to Huck's character. At a certain point he could no longer endure the anguish of being a passive observer. His imagination sought refuge in the image of an alternative persona who was protected against suffering by being devoid of pity or guilt, yet could denounce the human race for its cowardice and cruelty, and perhaps even take action against it. The appearance of Sherburn in *Huckleberry Finn* is ominous because a writer who shares his attitude toward human beings is in danger of abandoning imaginative insight for moralistic invective. The slogan of "the damned human race" that later became Mark Twain's proverb spelled the sacrifice of art to ideology. Colonel Sherburn would prove to be Mark Twain's dark angel. His part in the novel, and that of Tom Sawyer, are flaws in a work that otherwise approaches perfection as an embodiment of American experience in a radically new and appropriate literary mode.

VII

An Object Lesson in Democracy

HOWELLS considered *A Connecticut Yankee in King Arthur's Court* to be Mark Twain's masterpiece. It is undoubtedly his most ambitious undertaking, brilliant in conception and sometimes outrageously funny. The basic fable is so captivating that it has been used twice in musical comedies and three times in films. But under critical analysis the book now seems on the whole a failure. As V. L. Parrington said, it is "a curious medley, half philippic and half farce"—a burlesque of Malory's *Morte d'Arthur* into which has been poured a passionate invective against "thirteen centuries of reputed Christian civilization that under pretense of serving God has enslaved and despoiled the children of God." The mixture of farce and social criticism is further confused by impulses of doubt and despair from some obscure level of the writer's mind that contradict his original intention. In fact, the conflict between manifest and latent meanings in the novel denotes a crisis in Mark Twain's career. He was subjecting the vernacular perspective developed so variously in his earlier work to a test that destroyed it. He tried not merely to transform the vernacular value system into a political ideology, but to make it the conceptual framework for a novel embodying his philosophy of history and using this philosophy to interpret nineteenth-century civilization. Although the fantasy of transporting the superintendent of the Colt arms factory in Hartford to sixth-century Britain was a promising device for contrasting a preindustrial society with modern industrial civilization, the comic fable proved too fragile to sustain the burden of thought and emotion Mark Twain imposed on it.

As the book took form in his mind over a period of three or four years

he became more and more deeply entangled in the paradoxes of his subject. These were summed up in the character of Hank Morgan, the Connecticut Yankee. The plan of the story involved conferring a mastery of
machine technology on a hero conceived in the tradition of rural and backwoods humor. It was an imaginative version of the central issue in American culture of the 1880's and the following decades—the need to adapt an
agrarian system of values to an industrial order that was felt by thinkers
as diverse as Henry George, Edward Bellamy, Frederick Jackson Turner,
and especially Henry Adams, whose great *History of the United States
during the Administrations of Jefferson and Madison* was also published
in 1889. Mark Twain's inability to make Hank Morgan a consistent character parallels Turner's and Adams' failure to find a basis for democracy
in a world dominated by technology.

In analyzing *A Connecticut Yankee* it will be convenient to distinguish
the original comic fable from three clusters of ideas Mark Twain incorporated in it: a political ideology that his contemporaries called "the
spirit of democracy"; a philosophy of history centering about the idea of
progress; and a doctrine of determinism that provides a rationale at first
for optimistic and later for extremely pessimistic views of political reform.

2

The idea of adding to Malory's cast of characters an American vernacular hero in "fifteen-dollar slop-shops" clothing has genuine, if limited,
comic possibilities. It recalls the burlesque of *Hamlet* Mark Twain had
prepared in 1880 by inserting a subscription book agent into the play. The
notebook entry containing the germ of *A Connecticut Yankee* would
have delighted his readers of the 1860's in Virginia City and San Francisco:

> Dream of being a knight errant in armor in the middle ages. Have the
> notions & habits of thought of the present day mixed with the necessities of
> that. No pockets in the armor. Can't scratch. Cold in the head—can't blow—
> can't get a handkerchief, can't use iron sleeve. Iron gets red hot in the sun
> —leaks in the rain, gets white with frost & freezes me solid in winter. Make
> disagreeable clatter when I enter church. Can't dress or undress myself. Always
> getting struck by lightning. Fall down & can't get up.

The exploitation of physical discomfort was a standard practice in native
American humor. Mark Twain had often used such material, although

he usually lessened the crudity of it, as he does here, by making himself the comic butt. One can perhaps find some satire of the Middle Ages in the demonstration that plate armor was awkward for daily wear. But the ridiculous figure trying to blow his nose on an iron sleeve is a very different thing from the culture-hero eventually depicted in the novel, who brings all the technology and enlightenment of the nineteenth century to bear on the backwardness and ignorance of Arthur's Britain.

Many aspects of Hank Morgan's role are reminiscent of Mark Twain's earlier work. For example, he resembles the Vandal of the *Quaker City* excursion in being an American irreverently confronting the European past. His conversations with the Demoiselle Alisaunde la Corteloise, or Sandy, sometimes recall the dialogue between Scotty Briggs and the parson who cannot understand his slang. On other occasions Sandy's interminable irrelevancies—patterned on Mark Twain's exasperated impression of Malory's style—make Hank a victim somewhat as the narrator of *Roughing It* is "sold" by Jim Blaine's story about his grandfather's old ram. Although the Yankee belongs to this general vernacular tradition instead of being a direct literary descendant of Huck Finn, Mark Twain takes over from Huck a number of touches in Morgan's characterization —for example, the proposal that he and the King "borrow" some horses in order to escape their pursuers, his devices for throwing the pursuers off the scent, his skill at talking himself out of tight places, and his complaint about the nuisance of having a conscience, which has no apparent relation to the plot of *A Connecticut Yankee*. One is tempted to see a further reminiscence of Huck in Morgan's passivity through long sequences of chapters when he is traveling about incognito. This feature of the plot may be simply the result of Mark Twain's need to find a means for surveying a society, but it is nevertheless true that both Huck and the Yankee are compelled to witness outrages they can do nothing to prevent.

The best illustration of the comic use of the Yankee as a vernacular persona is the episode of the enchanted pigsty. Here his role is again similar to Huck's, for he grudgingly humors Sandy's delusion just as Huck suppresses his common-sense objections and serves as Tom Sawyer's assistant in the Evasion. The fact that the pigsty incident is imitated from Cervantes also recalls the Cervantesque raid of Tom's gang of robbers on the Sunday-school picnic. In all these situations the narrator is essentially passive; he surrenders direction of affairs to a companion who is acting on the basis of fantasies like those recorded in romances of chivalry.

The Yankee finds himself obliged to go with Sandy to the rescue of forty-five noble ladies imprisoned in an ogre's castle. Through what she recognizes as a dire enchantment, he perceives the castle as a pigsty and the ladies as swine; but he performs his duty by buying the animals from their keepers and thus delivering them from captivity: "when I know that an ostensible hog is a lady," he tells her, "that is enough for me, I know how to treat her." He continues:

We had to drive those hogs home—ten miles; and no ladies were ever more fickle-minded or contrary. They would stay in no road, no path; they broke out through the brush on all sides, and flowed away in all directions, over rocks, and hills, and the roughest places they could find. And they must not be struck, or roughly accosted; Sandy could not bear to see them treated in ways unbecoming their rank. The troublesomest old sow of the lot had to be called my Lady, and your Highness, like the rest. It is annoying and difficult to scour around after hogs, in armor.

Mark Twain warms to his topic with malicious zest:

There was one small countess, with an iron ring in her snout and hardly any hair on her back, that was the devil for perversity. She gave me a race of an hour, over all sorts of country, and then we were right where we had started from, having made not a rod of real progress. I seized her at last by the tail, and brought her along squealing. When I overtook Sandy she was horrified, and said it was in the last degree indelicate to drag a countess by her train.

3

The episode of the pigsty illustrates the satiric possibilities in Mark Twain's original plan for *A Connecticut Yankee*. Although the comparison of princesses to hogs gives vent to his hatred of aristocracy, the brutality of the attack is mitigated by his comic verve and by his great inventiveness. Surely no American writer of the nineteenth century ever conceived a more imaginative repudiation of the sentimental ideal of womanhood than the Yankee's deadpan allusion to a small countess "with an iron ring in her snout and hardly any hair on her back." Given the oversimplified thesis that the nobility of Europe is wholly corrupt, Mark Twain exemplifies here the power that Satan would ascribe to humor in a memorable passage of *The Mysterious Stranger*:

You have a mongrel perception of humor, nothing more; a multitude of you possess that. This multitude see the comic side of a thousand low-grade and trivial things—broad incongruities, mainly; grotesqueries, absurdities, evokers of the horse-laugh. The ten thousand high-grade comicalities which exist in the world are sealed from their dull vision. Will a day come when the race will detect the funniness of these juvenilities and laugh at them—and by laughing at them destroy them? For your race, in its poverty, has unquestionably one really effective weapon—laughter. Power, money, persuasion, supplication, persecution—these can lift at a colossal humbug—push it a little—weaken it a little, century by century; but only laughter can blow it to rags and atoms at a blast. Against the assault of laughter nothing can stand.

Unfortunately, Mark Twain's growing rage against titled and royal oppressors could not be confined within the limits of humor and imaginative satire; it burst out again and again in passages of invective attributed to Hank Morgan but actually expressing the author's own opinions. Mark Twain's concern with social and political issues rose to a peak of intensity during the later eighties. As late as November 1886, almost a year after he had outlined to Howells the idea of a story about a "Hartford man waking up in King Arthur's time," he told Mrs. Fairbanks that "The story isn't a satire peculiarly, it is more especially a *contrast*. It merely exhibits under high lights, the daily life of the time & that of to-day." And he added: "Of course in my story I shall leave unsmirched & unbelittled the great & beautiful *characters* drawn by the master hand of old Malory." But by the summer of 1887, when the pigsty episode was written, he had begun to see strong political implications in his materials. In August of that year he wrote to Howells:

How stunning are the changes which age makes in a man while he sleeps. When I finished Carlyle's French Revolution in 1871, I was a Girondin; every time I have read it since, I have read it differently—being influenced & changed, little by little, by life & environment (& Taine, & St. Simon): & now I lay the book down once more, & recognize that I am a Sansculotte!—And not a pale, characterless Sansculotte, but a Marat. Carlyle teaches no such gospel: so the change is in *me*—in my vision of the evidences.

The immediate American environment must have played a part in Mark Twain's increasing concern with social and political issues. The later 1880's were a turbulent period. The manifold discontents that would find expression in the Populist movement were already much in evidence: the press was filled with the varied and contradictory demands of an unprecedented number of dissident groups—for regulation or even government ownership of the railroads, for expansion of the currency, for a single tax on the unearned increment in the value of land, for curbs on the power of Wall Street, for the destruction of monopolies, for a hundred measures declared necessary to save the Republic from ruin. The Knights of Labor had emerged during the decade as the first national organization of workers in all types of industry. The hysteria over the Haymarket Riot in Chicago in 1886, leading to the execution of four anarchists falsely accused of murder, revealed the depth of conservative anxieties over radical influences in the labor movement. It was a period of utopian novels (Edward Bellamy's *Looking Backward* was published in 1888) and of grim apocalypses such as Ignatius Donnelly's *Caesar's Column,* published in 1890, which revels in the carnage resulting from a revolt of the American people against their tyrannical oppressors.

Although Mark Twain was not strongly attracted toward any of the radical programs, he had joined the Mugwump seceders from the Republican Party in 1884, and he ascribed to the Yankee Mugwump doctrines about tariff and civil-service reform. More importantly, he was responsive to the general sense of outrage with which many popular spokesmen dwelt on the dislocations caused by the consolidation of power in the hands of industrialists and financiers after the Civil War. Yet with a curious displacement that must bespeak some kind of inhibition, he chose to dramatize the issues in historical rather than contemporary terms, and to pour out his wrath ostensibly upon British rather than American targets.

When he does mount an attack, the force of his indignation leads him into moralizing that destroys the fictive world of the story. The Yankee's purchase of the hogs, for example, reminds Mark Twain that he is out to demolish the Established Church as well as the nobility, and he stops the action in order to insert a bit of polemic embroidery:

I was just in time; for the Church, the lord of the manor, and the rest of the tax-gatherers would have been along next day and swept off pretty much all the stock, leaving the swineherds very short of hogs and Sandy out of princesses. But now the tax people could be paid in cash, and there would be a stake left besides. One of the men had ten children; and he said that last year when a priest came and of his ten pigs took the fattest one for tithes, the wife burst out upon him, and offered him a child and said:
"Thou beast without bowels of mercy, why leave me my child, yet rob me of the wherewithal to feed it?"
How curious. The same thing had happened in the Wales of my day, under this same old Established Church, which was supposed by many to have changed its nature when it changed its disguise.

When Hank Morgan speaks in this fashion he has ceased being the protagonist of a comic burlesque and has become a mouthpiece for the author. His language retains some colloquial color (in such phrases as "pretty much all the stock" and "leaving . . . Sandy out of princesses") but is for the most part Mark Twain's own workmanlike prose: "supposed by many to have changed its nature when it changed its disguise" is not colloquial in either diction or syntax. The identification of author with narrator destroys the kind of fictional integrity Mark Twain had been able to confer on Huck Finn and thus rules out the kind of ironic effect that is so powerful in the earlier novel. In the Yankee's harangues addressed directly to the reader he resembles instead the narrator of the second part of *Life on the Mississippi,* who is not identified, as Huck is, with the society being criticized, but enters it as an observer from a distance endowed with absolute moral authority.

The basis of Hank Morgan's authority is a simplified but passionate commitment to the cause of the common people against the nobles, the monarchy, and the Established Church. The image of the French Revolution is constantly in Mark Twain's mind when he approaches this theme. The Yankee refers to it as "the ever memorable and blessed Revolution, which swept a thousand years of . . . villainy away in one swift tidal wave of blood—one: a settlement of that hoary debt in the proportion of half a drop of blood for each hogshead of it that had been pressed by slow tortures out of that people in the weary stretch of ten centuries of wrong and shame and misery the like of which was not to be mated but in hell." This is the language of political pamphleteering. It presupposes a Manichean universe in which one of two contending forces represents absolute right and the other absolute wrong. The rhetoric lunges out straight from the shoulder; it eliminates the possibility of viewing the target from a variety of perspectives. The tone is shrill and one can hear the orator raising his voice to the climax. The crudity of the thought and feeling finds appropriate expression in clichés: "a thousand years of villainy," "hoary debt," "slow tortures," "not to be mated but in hell."

Something like this happens to Mark Twain's style almost invariably when he assumes the stance of righteous indignation. Hank Morgan provides many examples:

It is enough to make a body ashamed of his race to think of the sort of froth that has always occupied its thrones without shadow of right or reason, and the seventh-rate people that have always figured as its aristocracies.

"Without shadow of right or reason" is unworthy of Mark Twain and not characteristic of the Hartford mechanic. Hank goes on in a similar vein of trite but passionate invective:

The truth was, the nation as a body was in the world for one object, and one only: to grovel before king and Church and noble; to slave for them, sweat blood for them, starve that they might be fed, work that they might play, drink misery to the dregs that they might be happy, go naked that they might wear silks and jewels, pay taxes that they might be spared from paying them, be familiar all their lives with the degrading language and postures of adulation that they might walk in pride and think themselves the gods of this world.

Translated into fictional terms, the ideas and the emotion that govern this kind of rhetoric become melodrama. Many pages of *A Connecticut Yankee* are given over to incidents that have no relation to comedy or to the vernacular perspective, but are simply exempla illustrating the injustices and cruelties visited on the common people by the kind of despotism Mark Twain imagines to have existed in the Middle Ages. The language and the visual effects of the popular stage abound, as in the sudden entrance of the grandmother of the page Queen Morgan le Fay has stabbed in a fit of pique—"an old and bent and white-haired lady, leaning upon a crutch-stick," who points the stick toward the Queen and invokes the curse of God upon her. A fragrance of grease-paint is also perceptible in the description of the "native young giant of thirty or thereabouts" stretched on the rack in le Fay's dungeon who is determined to accept death by torture rather than leave his wife and child destitute by confessing to his crime. When the Yankee is describing such scenes he ceases for long stretches to have an identity apart from the author's; the style becomes indistinguishable from that, say, of *The Prince and the Pauper:*

The queen's guards fell into line, and she and they marched away, with their torch-bearers, and woke the echoes of the cavernous tunnels with the measured beat of their retreating footfalls. I had the prisoner taken from the rack and placed upon his bed, and medicaments applied to his hurts, and wine given him to drink.

The element of comedy that has vanished from the dungeon sequence lingers in Mark Twain's mind to reappear inappropriately in a macabre sequel. One of the knights employed as a traveling salesman plays a practical joke on a colleague by sending him on a three-hour jaunt across country to sell toothwash to five toothless patriarchs whom the Yankee has just released from prison.

4

Mark Twain's abandonment of a comic and ironic perspective under the influence of political ideology was of little moment for his contemporary readers. They placed so high a value on what they took to be the doctrine of *A Connecticut Yankee* that they paid no attention to its technical confusions. While Howells was reading proof sheets in advance of publication, he wrote: "It's a mighty great book, and it makes my heart burn and melt. It seems that God didn't forget to put a soul into you; he shabs most literary men off with a brain merely." His review in the Editor's Study of *Harper's* called the novel "an object-lesson in democracy," and emphasized its bearing on contemporary society:

It makes us glad of our republic and our epoch; but it does not flatter us into a fond content with them; there are passages in which we see that the noble of Arthur's day, who battened on the blood and sweat of his bondmen, is one in essence with the capitalist of Mr. Harrison's day who grows rich on the labor of his underpaid wagemen.

With few exceptions, Howells' opinion was shared by all American critics. Edmund C. Stedman, the Wall Street broker who was also a poet and editor of the *Library of American Literature* being published by Charles L. Webster & Co., wrote to Mark Twain:

My belief is, on the whole, that you have written a great book: in some respect[s] your most original, most imaginative,—certainly the most effective and sustained . . . You are going at the *still existing* radical principles or fallacies which made "chivalry" possible once, & servilities & flunkeyism & tyranny possible now.

The labor press greeted the book with equal enthusiasm. Chapter 33 ("Sixth Century Political Economy," in which the Yankee expounds the evils of a protective tariff and predicts that organizations of workers will attain great power in the nineteenth century) was reprinted in trade-union papers. And Dan Beard, an enthusiastic socialist, wrote Mark Twain that he was honored by being asked to draw the illustrations for the story. He considered it "a great missionary work to bring Americans back to the safe honest and manly position, intended for them to occupy, by their ancestors when they signed the declaration of independence."

Object Lesson in Democracy

As some reviewers noticed, Beard's illustrations were considerably more explicit than the text in applying the lessons of Mark Twain's fantasy to contemporary America. One of the drawings, for example, entitled "Decorations of Sixth Century Aristocracy," depicts a row of medals on whose ribbons are inscribed titles and slogans appropriate for the Arthurian nobility: "Slave Driver & K. of Catfish"; "Robber of Unarmed Savages"; "Robber of Orphans"; "Oppressor of Slaves"; "Prince of Gluttons"; "Land Grabber"; "Absorber of Unearned Increment"; "Arson Is Only Arson for Common People." The phrase "unearned increment," slogan of Henry George's single-tax movement, does not appear in the novel; nor is any character accused of land-grabbing, or of arson for profit. An unsigned review in the New York *Standard,* Henry George's paper, accurately states the relation of the pictures to the text:

Though but little is said in the book about specific social or political reforms, it is impossible to read these extracts [in the review] without seeing that the great American humorist has been moved by the spirit of democracy. Human equality, natural rights, unjust laws, class snobbery, the power of the rich and the dependence and oppression of the poor, are subjects of frequent allusion in the text; and whatever of definiteness the text may lack in pointing out the fundamental cause and radical cure for wrongs, is admirably supplied by Dan Beard in the illustrations.

Beard is, in fact, "not only an excellent artist but an intelligent single-tax man as well."

It should be added that Mark Twain was enraptured by Beard's illustrations. "Hold me under permanent obligations," he wrote to the artist. "What luck it was to find you! There are hundreds of artists who could illustrate any other book of mine, but there was only one who could illustrate this one. Yes, it was a fortunate hour that I went netting for lightning-bugs and caught a meteor. Live forever!" Howells agreed that the pictures were "extraordinarily sympathetic and interpretative."

Members of the Nationalist movement that had grown out of Bellamy's *Looking Backward* were also delighted with *A Connecticut Yankee.* Sylvester Baxter, a friend of Bellamy and of Howells, declared in a four-column review in the Boston *Sunday Herald:*

The sources of the claims of aristocratic privileges and royal prerogatives that yet linger in the world are so exposed to the full glare of the sun of 19th century common sense, are shown in so ridiculous an aspect, that the work can hardly fail to do yeoman service in destroying the still existing remnants

147

of respect for such pretensions. Through the book there is a steady flowing current of earnest purpose, and the pages are eloquent with a true American love of freedom, a sympathy with the rights of the common people, and an indignant hatred of the oppression of the poor, the lowly and the weak, by the rich, the powerful and the proud.

Baxter characterizes the book as "another and very instructive sort of 'Looking Backward.'" Declaring that Beard's illustrations are "graceful, picturesque and thoroughly characteristic of the spirit of the book," he reproduces six drawings and describes others:

Many of them embody instructive allegories, as, for instance, in a cut of Justice, with her scales, one containing the heavy hammer of "Labor" and the other the baubles of "Aristocracy," but the latter made to outweigh the former by means of the string of "Self-interest," artfully attached to the toe of "Law," who stands by . . . Another illustrates the remark of the king concerning a peasant: "Brother! to dirt like this?" by depicting the three phases of oppression of man by man, first by violence under the sword of royal power, then by the book of the "law," making man subject to the slave driver's lash, and last, the subjection of the workingman to the millions of the monopolist. A strong and spirited picture of an arrogant slave driver shows in its face the unmistakable portrait of a celebrated American billionaire and stock gambler.

The portrait is of Jay Gould; Baxter agrees with Beard that modern counterparts of medieval oppressors can be found in the United States. But his reference to "a true American love of freedom" implies that the enemies of the working class are mainly foreign. Jingoism, directed principally against England (which was regarded by free-silver agitators, for example, as the bulwark of the gold standard), provided in these years an odd link between American populists and a small intellectual elite "representing, in general, the same type that had once been Mugwumps, whose spokesmen were such solid and respectable gentlemen as Henry and Brooks Adams, Theodore Roosevelt, Henry Cabot Lodge, John Hay, and Albert J. Beveridge." Thus it is not so surprising as it might seem offhand that the conservative Stedman approved the attack on "flunkeyism & tyranny" in *A Connecticut Yankee*.

Left-wing critics endorsed Mark Twain's attack on British institutions in almost the same breath with their denunciations of capitalists and monopolists. A reviewer for the *Plumas National* (of Quincy, California), who saw the book as "one long satire on modern England and Englishmen," gave expression to the blend of jingoism and pro-labor sentiment characteristic of much grass-roots radicalism: "Mark Twain has come up from the people. He is American to the backbone, and the assumption of natural superiority by titled English aristocrats and the terrible wrongs inflicted on the working people, evidently galled him beyond endurance." The critic's tone recalls *The Innocents Abroad:* "He has no more reverence for the beautiful legends which Tennyson has embalmed in his 'Idyles [*sic*] of the King' than Bob Ingersoll has for St. Peter's or the best works of some of the old masters." Beard, incidentally, shared the general populist hostility to England. Among the celebrities whose features he gave to various Arthurian aristocats were Tennyson (depicted as Merlin) and the Prince of Wales.

Beard also frequently uses stereotyped images of fat, vulgar, debauched members of the clergy—a residue of the Know-Nothing hostility to the Roman Catholic Church that was prominent in populist agitation (and also conspicuous in *A Connecticut Yankee:* Mark Twain even repeats the ancient anti-Catholic slander that involves a foundling asylum near the monastery and nunnery in the Valley of Holiness). Beard enjoys portraying tonsured clerics ogling girls, a bishop kicking a king in the rump, and a repulsive monk being blown in the air by an explosion, with the derisive caption "High Church." The caption is Beard's invention, but the picture is based on an incident in the story (in Chapter 42) and the tone is not unlike Mark Twain's. Both Nationalist and single-tax reviewers noted as a matter of course that the Established Church was the ally of king and aristocracy in oppressing the common people in Arthur's Britain, with the implication that the evil had lasted into modern times. Howells took cognizance of the violence of Mark Twain's treatment of the Church, which he deprecated, by pointing out in his review that the hostile depiction of the clergy is relieved by examples of true Christian charity like that of the priest who promises to care for the child of the young mother hanged for theft (Chapter 35).

The reviewers were right about Mark Twain's manifest intention in *A Connecticut Yankee.* He not only praised Beard's illustrations, but was so pleased with Baxter's review in the *Herald* that he invited Baxter and Bellamy to visit him in Hartford, and read *Looking Backward,* which he found to be "the latest and best of all the Bibles." In that simpler day, radical political and economic theory had not been subjected to the scholastic discipline of the twentieth-century debate over Marxism; left-wing groups of quite varied persuasions could unite under the vague slogans of democracy and sympathy for the common people. Mark Twain did not have a clearly thought-out position, despite the passion with which he could express his attitudes toward specific issues. Yet at the very peak of his political enthusiasm in the late 1880's he remained appreciably farther to the right than the Nationalists or the single-taxers or even Howells, who had been much more disturbed than Clemens by the execution of the Haymarket anarchists and had already embraced a kind of Christian socialism under the influence of Tolstoy. The spirit of democracy in *A Connecticut Yankee* is on the whole rather conservative. It might appropriately be called an ideology of republicanism. Morgan never mentions any proposals for creating an economic system different from that of the United States; he is a laissez-faire capitalist not disposed to favor even the mild types of governmental regulation of business advocated by the populists. The novel is a kind of inverse utopia; it implies an endorsement of the political and economic structure of the United States in the 1880's without basic changes.

In a note accompanying selections from the book published in *Century* magazine in November 1889, Mark Twain says that the Yankee "has privately set himself the task of introducing the great and beneficent civilization of the nineteenth century, and of peacefully replacing the twin despotisms of royalty and aristocratic privilege with a 'Republic on the American plan' when Arthur shall have passed to his rest." Even when Mark Twain defends the bloodshed of the French Revolution, he does so on the assumption that the revolution was the overthrow of feudalism by middle-class capitalism, not the overthrow of capitalism by the proletariat. The significant class conflict presupposed in *A Connecticut Yankee* is that between the aristocracy and "the mass of the nation," and the aristocracy is taken quite literally to mean holders of hereditary titles. Once or twice, as in his prediction about labor unions, the Yankee recognizes a possible clash of interests between workers and employers, but this notion cannot find expression in the plot because the only industrial capitalist in the cast of characters is Hank Morgan himself, and his interest is assumed to be identical with that of the oppressed peasants, serfs, and slaves.

5

One of the principal components of the Yankee's character is the widely current image of the self-made man—an image that influenced Mark

Twain's view of himself. Hank Morgan is the son of a rural blacksmith, and he had tried his hand at horse-doctoring before becoming a workman in the Colt factory. By the time of his translation to sixth-century Britain he has risen to the position of head superintendent with a couple of thousand men under him; and in the course of the story he becomes executive head of a vast industrial system. His career resembles that of many industrial giants such as Carnegie and Rockefeller who were in the public eye in the 1880's. Mark Twain sees in careers of this kind a confirmation of the idea that "The master minds of all nations, in all ages, have sprung in affluent multitude from the mass of the nation, and from the mass of the nation only—not from its privileged classes."

The self-made man is without the aristocratic graces conferred by a college education; he belongs to the American type Mark Twain had celebrated in *The Innocents Abroad*. In introducing himself at the beginning of the narrative, Hank Morgan says: "I am a Yankee of the Yankees—and practical; yes, and nearly barren of sentiment, I suppose—or poetry, in other words." "Practical" was a word with two equally important clusters of meanings. It referred to the Yankee's mechanical skill and inventiveness ("Why, I could make anything a body wanted—anything in the world, it didn't make any difference what"), and at the same time to his lack of culture in the conventional sense—here identified with sentiment and poetry. The composite image is precisely the one Frederick Jackson Turner would present in 1893 as the basic American character shaped by frontier experience:

That coarseness and strength combined with acuteness and inquisitiveness; that practical, inventive turn of mind, quick to find expedients; that masterful grasp of material things, lacking in the artistic but powerful to effect great ends; that dominant individualism, working for good and for evil, and withal that buoyancy and exuberance that comes with freedom—these are traits of the frontier, or traits called out elsewhere because of the existence of the frontier.

Both Turner and Mark Twain were describing their versions of the generic image of the American Adam that had been current in the United States for more than a century.

Mark Twain's irritation over Matthew Arnold's lofty disdain for the American "glorification of 'the average man'" strengthened his determination to depict a hero in whom philistine indifference to the fine arts was actually a merit. He told Beard: "this Yankee of mine has neither the

refinement nor the weakness of a college education; he is a perfect ignoramus; he is boss of a machine shop; he can build a locomotive or a
Colt's revolver, he can put up and run a telegraph line, but he's an ignoramus nevertheless." In accordance with this conception, Mark Twain
gives Hank Morgan a passion for bad art: "in our house in East Hartford,
all unpretending as it was, you couldn't go into a room but you would
find an insurance-chromo, or at least a three-color God-Bless-Our-Home
over the door; and in the parlor we had nine." On the other hand Hank
criticizes the tapestries in Arthur's palace—"battle pieces, they were, with
horses shaped like those which children cut out of paper or create in
gingerbread; with men on them in scale armor whose scales are represented by round holes—so that the man's coat looks as if it had been
done with a biscuit-punch."

When Mark Twain calls the Yankee an ignoramus he means that he
has had no formal training in the fine arts or literature. Morgan has read
widely if unsystematically in European history, and he is familiar with
the doctrines of free-trade theorists. This erudition may be—like his
passing reference to the indecency of the conversation in *Tom Jones* and
Roderick Random—merely an inadvertent consequence of the author's
failure to keep his protagonist distinct from himself. It was a populist
assumption that the common sense of the average man was a better guide
in politics and economics than the bookish theories of professors, who
were generally regarded as conservative apologists. Mark Twain's in-
sistence that the Yankee is practical reflects the familiar American suspicion of theory which has survived in our day, with a curious reversal
of positions, as the popular belief that the universities are hotbeds of
subversive ideas. *A Connecticut Yankee* embodies some of the anti-
intellectualism which has always been implicit in the vernacular point of
view.

It is nevertheless true that Hank Morgan's principal role in the action
of the book is defined by a clearly articulated philosophy of history derived
from W. E. H. Lecky, Lord Acton, and other British historians, as well as
from the Jeffersonian tradition in American thought. In an unpublished
essay of the 1880's Mark Twain summarized the theory as the "law of
human progress, human betterment, otherwise called civilization." The
marks of progress were for him legal and political rather than economic:
the destruction of serfdom and slavery, the separation of church and state,
the introduction of representative government with unlimited suffrage, the

elimination of special privileges of the nobility. He believed that these changes, partially effected in Europe but brought to fulfillment only in America, had been caused by the advance of technology, by mechanical inventions applied to practical ends in industry.

Although Mark Twain devotes much space to Hank Morgan's denunciation of feudal tyranny, it is of less moment than his positive function in bringing to bear on sixth-century Britain the accumulated technology of the nineteenth century. He is a Prometheus who undertakes to bring the light of freedom to the common people by first giving them control over the forces of nature. He intends to transform Arthur's kingdom into a republic by means of an industrial revolution. Here lies what Mark Twain considered the primary allegorical relevance of the story to the society of his own day. He meant to announce in it the imminent rise to power of workers trained in the school of experience by their operation of the machines that had created modern civilization.

The ideas represented in the Promethean atributes of the Yankee are set forth in a paper entitled "The New Dynasty" which Mark Twain read before the Monday Evening Club in Hartford in March 1886. This essay grew out of an experience he had had in January of that year when he went to Washington to testify before a joint Congressional Committee in favor of a proposed treaty with Britain establishing international copyright. He had been deeply impressed by the able performance of another witness, James Welsh, spokesman for the Philadelphia typographical unions. Mark Twain said that when this "foreman of a printing office, clad in unpretending gray" appeared before the committee as the representative of five million workers (presumably the Knights of Labor, who claimed such a membership), "This was the first time in this world, perhaps, that ever a nation did actually and in its own person, not by proxy, speak. And by grace of fortune I was there to hear and see." Presently, by implication, Welsh becomes the representative of "the banded voters among a laboring kinship of 45,000,000 of persons," who are collectively "the rightful sovereign of this world." Mark Twain maintains that the new king has earned his power to rule by virtue of his education:

He is the most stupendous product of the highest civilization the world has ever seen—and the worthiest and the best; and in no age but this, no land but this, and no lower civilization than this, could he ever have been brought forth. The average of his genuine, practical, valuable knowledge—and knowledge is the truest right divine to power—is an education contrasted with which the education possessed by the kings and nobles who ruled him for a hundred centuries is the untaught twaddle of a nursery, and beneath contempt. The *sum* of his education, as represented in the ten thousand utterly new and delicate and exact handicrafts, and divisions and subdivisions of handicrafts, exercised by his infinite brain and multitudinous members, is a sum of knowledge compared to which the sum of human knowledge in any and all ages of the world previous to the birth-year of the eldest person here present in this room, was as a lake compared to the ocean, the foot-hills compared to the Alps . . . Without his education, he had continued what he was, a slave; with it, he is what he is, a sovereign.

Hank Morgan's command of technology embraces the knowledge possessed by experts in all the separate industries, and in Mark Twain's fable it makes him The Boss.

6

At the outset of his career in Arthur's Britain the Yankee views the realm as a frontier of untouched resources awaiting development: "Look at the opportunities here for a man of knowledge, brains, pluck, and enterprise to sail in and grow up with the country." He sets to work at once. Within a short time,

in various quiet nooks and corners I had the beginnings of all sorts of industries under way—nuclei of future vast factories, the iron and steel missionaries of my future civilization. In these were gathered together the brightest young minds I could find, and I kept agents out raking the country for more, all the time. I was training a crowd of ignorant folk into experts—experts in every sort of handiwork and scientific calling.

After seven years,

slavery was dead and gone; all men were equal before the law; taxation had been equalized. The telegraph, the telephone, the phonograph, the typewriter, the sewing-machine, and all the thousand willing and handy servants of steam and electricity were working their way into favor. We had a steamboat or two on the Thames, we had steam war-ships, and the beginnings of a steam commercial marine; I was getting ready to send out an expedition to discover America.

This thumbnail sketch of modern history presupposes a typology consisting of three stages: a primitive preindustrial mode of existence, the transforming force of technology, and the state of affairs resulting from the transformation. The doctrine of progress held that the sequence led to a vast increase not only in comfort and material well-being, but also in human freedom and the moral condition of mankind. Mark Twain's contrast between the sixth century and the nineteenth was intended to illustrate this course of events.

Nevertheless, the book also contains suggestions of a dark view of history, calling in question the beneficent effect of industrialism and implying that nineteenth-century civilization has threatened rather than fulfilled human happiness. The towns of sixth-century Britain, with their similarity to Bricksville, seem to justify almost any measures Hank Morgan might take to transform them into places like Quincy, Illinois, as Mark Twain had described it in *Life on the Mississippi*. But the countryside of Arthur's kingdom has a singular freshness and charm. It seems to belong to a different world altogether. When the Yankee sets out with Sandy on his knightly adventures, he describes the landscape with delight:

We crossed broad natural lawns sparkling with dew, and we moved like spirits, the cushioned turf giving out no sound of footfall; we dreamed along through glades in a mist of green light that got its tint from the sun-drenched roof of leaves overhead, and by our feet the clearest and coldest of runlets went frisking and gossiping over its reefs and making a sort of whispering music, comfortable to hear; and at times we left the world behind and entered into the solemn great deeps and rich gloom of the forest, where furtive wild things whisked and scurried by and were gone before you could even get your eye on the place where the noise was; and where only the earliest birds were turning out and getting to business with a song here and a quarrel yonder and a mysterious far-off hammering and drumming for worms on a tree-trunk away somewhere in the impenetrable remotenesses of the woods. And by and by out we would swing again into the glare.

This pastoral landscape might have been presented merely to make the towns seem more sordid by contrast. But there are other hints that after the Yankee's return to the modern world he feels a nostalgia for Arthur's Britain quite at variance with his belief that it is a panorama of tyranny and backwardness. After the introduction recounting how Mark Twain meets a "curious stranger" in Warwick Castle in 1886 and listens to the beginning of his strange story of having been transported thirteen centuries backward in time, the stranger, who proves to be Hank Morgan, turns over to the author a bulky manuscript written mostly on sheets of parchment. The remainder of *A Connecticut Yankee* purports to be a transcription of this manuscript, which bears the significant title, "The Tale of the Lost Land." And as the Yankee lies dying next morning, in his delirium he pleads with his wife Sandy to protect him against the hideous dream that he has been brought back to the nineteenth century, "set down, a stranger and forlorn in that strange England, with an abyss of thirteen centuries yawning between me and you! between me and my home and my friends! between me and all that is dear to me, all that could make life worth the living!"

Morgan's yearning for a preindustrial Arcadia was not a touch added to the story at the last moment. An entry in Mark Twain's notebook made not later than January 1886, at a time when the book was only begun, reads as follows: "He mourns his lost land—has come to England & revisited it, but it is all changed & become old, so old!—& it was so fresh & new, so virgin before . . . Has lost all interest in life—is found dead next morning—suicide." Furthermore, the Yankee's description of the Arthurian landscape closely resembles nostalgic passages in Mark Twain's *Autobiography* about the Quarles Farm. Just beyond the stables and the tobacco-curing house, he recalled in 1897–98, was "a limpid brook which sang along over its gravelly bed and curved and frisked in and out here and there and yonder in the deep shade of overhanging foliage and vines." Another passage describes the woods on the Quarles place: "I can call back the solemn twilight and mystery of the deep woods, the earthy smells, the faint odors of the wild flowers, the sheen of rain-washed foliage, the rattling clatter of drops when the wind shook the trees, the far-off hammering of woodpeckers and the muffled drumming of wood pheasants in the remoteness of the forest, the snapshot glimpses of disturbed wild creatures scurrying through the grass."

In addition to these verbal echoes, the Yankee's descriptions of the countryside are linked with Mark Twain's reminiscences of his childhood by their dreamlike quality. In the passage just quoted from *A Connecticut Yankee* the narrator says, "we dreamed along through glades in a mist of green light"; earlier he had described the countryside near Camelot as "a soft, reposeful summer landscape, as lovely as a dream, and as lonesome as Sunday." ("Lonesome as Sunday," of course, recalls the description of the Phelps farm in *Huckleberry Finn,* but the emphasis here is on the beauty of the scene rather than on the sense of loneliness.) The evocation of the Quarles place in the *Autobiography* is a reverie, almost an incantation: "I can call it all back and make it as real as it ever was, and as blessed . . . I can see the woods . . . I can feel the thumping rain, upon my head . . . I can remember."

Both Mark Twain's personal past and the historical past were frequently associated in his mind with dreams and sleep. Both existed only in memory, and both therefore belonged to a subjective realm which most American writers of the earlier nineteenth century equated with the domain of ideality. The contrast in *Life on the Mississippi* between the dreaming South and the wide-awake, energetic North becomes a basic theme in *A Connecticut Yankee,* where everything connected with Arthur's Britain is dreamlike. When the author first meets Hank Morgan he says that the stranger's conversation "gradually wove such a spell about me that I seemed to move among the specters and shadows and dust and mold of a gray antiquity, holding speech with a relic of it!" Reading the *Morte d'Arthur* that evening in his inn, the writer is "steeped in a dream of the olden time" when the stranger enters and begins to tell his story. Camelot, in his narrative, is "a far-away town sleeping in a valley by a winding river"; even as the stranger speaks he almost dozes off; and when he hands his manuscript to the author he is "steeped in drowsiness."

The sleepy indolence that characterizes both the American South and Arthur's Britain has for Mark Twain two contrasting kinds of associations. On one hand it connotes intellectual apathy, ignorance, and credulity; on the other it connotes the dreamlike peace and happiness of childhood. A corresponding ambiguity appears in his attitude toward Hank Morgan, who is the force transforming Arthur's Britain. The Yankee's sudden intrusion into the sixth century has an effect like that of the irreverent steam locomotive in *The Innocents Abroad* disturbing the "solemn mysteries" of Pompeii. The machine is theoretically good but emotionally disturbing. Like most of his countrymen, Mark Twain oscillated between enthusiasm for the brave new world of science and technology, and nostalgia for the simple agrarian world that the industrial revolution was destroying before his eyes. *A Connecticut Yankee* expresses his emotions about the shattering transformation and is on this account, for all its confusions (indeed, because of them), a central document in American intellectual history. As Leo Marx has pointed out, "Our literature, virtually from the beginning, has embodied the experience of a people crossing the line which sets off the era of machine production from the rest of human history." Such early nineteenth-century spokesmen as Daniel Webster and Edward Everett "enthusiastically endorsed the new machine power," yet in the very essays and speeches which ostensibly praised the advent of technology they often employed figures of speech that "associate machines with the destructive and the repulsive," and thus "communicate an unmistakable sense of anxiety and menace." A similar conflict between overt acceptance and covert fear of the machine appears in the writings of Cooper, Thoreau, Hawthorne, and Melville.

Since Hank Morgan is the protagonist of an industrial revolution, he awakens in Mark Twain some of the latent anxiety that other Americans experienced when they contemplated the impact of machine technology on society. The author's mixed emotions are apparent in the Yankee's summary of what he had accomplished within four years after his introduction to Arthur's kingdom. The principal metaphors have exactly contradictory overtones: "Unsuspected by this dark land, I had the civilization of the nineteenth century booming under its very nose! It was fenced away from the public view, but there it was, a gigantic and unassailable fact—and to be heard from, yet, if I lived and had luck." The first image, drawing upon Mark Twain's perennial fascination with volcanoes, foreshadows the catastrophic Battle of the Sand Belt: "There it was, as sure a fact and as substantial a fact as any serene volcano, standing innocent with its smokeless summit in the blue sky and giving no sign of the rising hell in its bowels." But this is immediately followed by an image embodying the familiar association between progress and enlightenment: "My schools and churches were children four years before; they were grown up now; my shops of that day were vast factories now; where I had a dozen trained men then, I had a thousand now; where I had one brilliant expert then, I had fifty now. I stood with my hand on the cock, so to speak, ready to turn it on and flood the midnight world with light at any moment."

Hank Morgan's actions cast doubt upon the outcome of his transformation of Britain in yet another way by suggesting that his development of machine manufacturing leads to shady transactions on the stock exchange. The key incident concerns the hermit who lives on top of a sixty-foot pillar in the Valley of Holiness:

He was now doing [says the Yankee] what he had been doing every day for twenty years up there—bowing his body ceaselessly and rapidly almost to his feet. It was his way of praying. I timed him with a stop-watch, and he made twelve hundred and forty-four revolutions in twenty-four minutes and forty-six seconds. It seemed a pity to have all this power going to waste. It was one of the most useful motions in mechanics, the pedal movement; so I made a note in my memorandum-book, purposing some day to apply a system of elastic cords to him and run a sewing-machine with it.

The plan worked. The Yankee manufactured eighteen thousand tow-linen shirts that "sold like smoke to pilgrims . . . as a perfect protection against sin." "But about that time I noticed that the motive power had taken to standing on one leg, and I found that there was something the matter with the other one; so I stocked the business and unloaded, taking Sir Bors de Ganis into camp financially along with certain of his friends; for the works stopped within a year, and the good saint got him to his rest."

This passage deflates medieval religion as ruthlessly as the episode of the enchanted pigsty deflates the notion of hereditary aristocracy. The quantitative engineering attitude toward pious exercises and the diversion of energy previously wasted into a commercially profitable channel exactly express the Yankee's skeptical attitude toward the ascetic ideal. But the trickery involved in selling a property he knows will soon become worthless raises a serious question about his motives. Can he be both a missionary of enlightenment and justice, and a fraudulent businessman?

British reviewers, annoyed by the anglophobia that runs through the book, were able to perceive here an ambiguity that escaped American critics. The *Scots Observer* characterized *A Connecticut Yankee* as "a 'lecture' in dispraise of monarchical institutions and religious establishments as the roots of all evil, and in praise of Yankee 'cuteness and Wall Street chicanery as compared to the simple fidelity and devotion of the knightly ideal." The London *Daily Telegraph* emphasized the taint of dishonesty and cynical self-interest in the economic life of the United States:

The Republic is a "land of liberty," yet its commerce, its railways, and its manufactures are in the hands of a few cliques of almost irresponsible capitalists, who control tariffs, markets, and politics in order that they may be enriched, to the disadvantage of the masses. Which, then, is to be most admired—the supremacy of a knight or the success of a financier? Under which King will the Americans serve—the ideal or the real? Will they own allegiance to King ARTHUR or JAY GOULD?

The Victorian stuffiness of these critics, for whom the Tennysonian image of Arthur's court gave some color of ethical nobility even to nineteenth-century Britain as against the United States, does not render invalid their contention that the civilization represented by the Yankee could hardly serve as a model. They were less confused about the book than were the single-taxers and Nationalists who in one breath proclaimed the admirable Americanism of Hank Morgan and in the next breath denounced American monopolists for grinding the faces of the poor.

The imagery employed by the Yankee supports the notion that he is more of a businessman and speculator than a master technician. He makes few references to technical processes; his richest source of allusion and metaphor is the world of business—buying and selling, advertising, bookkeeping, and especially transactions in stocks and staple commodities. If an eclipse of the moon "had been booked for only a month away," says Morgan, "I could have sold it short." "Merlin's stock was flat." "The boys all took a flier at the Holy Grail now and then." Knights who surrender to him are assets that he has acquired. Morgan le Fay's prisoners are also "assets, inherited, along with the throne, from the former firm." The Yankee reduces the expense of the gift of money made to each person touched for the King's evil by debasing the currency. "As a rule," he comments, "I do not approve of watering stock, but I consider it square enough in this case, for it was just a gift, anyway." In a similar vein of ethical severity, he observes:

Knight-errantry is a most chuckle-headed trade, and it is tedious hard work, too, but I begin to see that there *is* money in it, after all, if you have luck. Not that I would ever engage in it as a business; for I wouldn't. No sound and legitimate business can be established on a basis of speculation. A successful whirl in the knight-errantry line—now what is it when you blow away the nonsense and come down to the cold facts? It's just a corner in pork, that's all, and you can't make anything else out of it. You're rich —yes—suddenly rich—for about a day, maybe a week; then somebody corners the market on *you,* and down goes your bucketshop.

Often, as in the passage just quoted, the commercial imagery is deliberately used for comic purposes: Hank Morgan's technical terms bewilder Sandy in the pattern of Scotty Briggs's interview with the parson. But the effect, both here and in the incident of the hermit on the pillar, is to overshadow the vernacular coloring of the Yankee's character, and at the same time to undermine his status as a source of valid moral judgments on Arthur's society. It is significant that speculation on the stock market is a principal cause of the civil war leading to the collapse of his program of reform. In the end, Mark Twain's uncertainty concerning the effects of the industrial revolution undercuts the ideology of progress.

7

Just as the Yankee's Promethean mission results in an unforeseen disaster, his authority as a spokesman for republican principles is compromised by his growing estrangement from the mass of the people in whose behalf he has instigated his revolution. At the outset, of course, he is convinced that they are the only creative force in history. When he encounters a group of peasants gathered for forced labor on a road, he states his opinion with emphasis:

> By a sarcasm of law and phrase they were freemen. Seven-tenths of the free population of the country were of just their class and degree: small "independent" farmers, artisans, etc.; which is to say, they were the nation, the actual Nation; they were about all of it that was useful, or worth saving, or really respectworthy, and to subtract them would have been to subtract the Nation and leave behind some dregs, some refuse, in the shape of a king, nobility and gentry, idle, unproductive, acquainted mainly with the arts of wasting and destroying, and of no sort of use or value in any rationally constructed world.

Even after Morgan has suffered the disillusionment of seeing the peasants of Abblasoure turn out in pursuit of their unjustly imprisoned fellows who set fire to the manor house, he can take heart when a charcoal burner rejoices that the lord has been burned to death: "A man *is* a man, at bottom. Whole ages of abuse and oppression cannot crush the manhood clear out of him. Whoever thinks it a mistake is himself mistaken. Yes, there is plenty good enough material for a republic in the most degraded people that ever existed."

Yet the Yankee finds it increasingly difficult to sustain this democratic faith. He begins to realize that the basic manhood of the mass of the nation can be corrupted by vicious institutions. The common people are subjected by their environment to conditioning or "training" that implants in them from infancy a social heritage of wrong attitudes and beliefs. A few pages later he is disgusted when this same charcoal burner shows himself to be a consummate snob by his carefully discriminated attitudes toward various people they meet on the way: he is reverent toward a monk, abject in the presence of a gentleman, freely cordial to men of his own degree, contemptuous of a slave. "Well," remarks Morgan, "there are times when one would like to hang the whole human race and finish the farce." He notes the similarity between the behavior of the peasants of Abblasoure and that of the Southern poor whites who fought in defense of the slavery system. It is merely another illustration of the power of inherited ideas, of "old habit of mind," to coerce men into accepting any set of institutions, no matter how absurd or iniquitous.

The Yankee had intended to transform feudal society by substituting good training for bad—in promising individual cases by sending people to his Man Factories for a technical education; on a broader scale by founding free public schools and newspapers and by the pervasive influence of industrialization. Almost to the end he hopes for the success of his program. But at the outbreak of civil war among the knights, when the Church seizes the opportunity to impose an interdict on the nation, the superstitious dread of authority ingrained in the people proves stronger than the Yankee's training. His proclamation of a republic has no effect, and he grows bitter about their cowardice and bondage to the established order of things:

Ah, what a donkey I was! Toward the end of the week I began to get this large and disenchanting fact through my head: that the mass of the nation had swung their caps and shouted for the republic for about one day, and there an end! The Church, the nobles, and the gentry then turned one grand, all-disapproving frown upon them and shriveled them into sheep! From that moment the sheep had begun to gather to the fold—that is to say, the camps—and offer their valueless lives and their valuable wool to the "righteous cause." Why, even the very men who had lately been slaves were in the "righteous cause," and glorifying it, praying for it, sentimentally slabbering over it, just like all the other commoners. Imagine such human muck as this; conceive of this folly!

Morgan now shares the contempt of the nobles for the commoners. In calling the people "human muck" he echoes the remark of King Arthur that Beard chose for ironic illustration: "Brother!—to dirt like that?"

8

Hank Morgan's disillusionment, and the dreadful slaughter of the Battle of the Sand Belt that follows, convey to the twentieth-century reader an impression of bleak despair. The book seems to end up as a declaration that democracy is a naïve delusion and technology a force which merely multiplies man's power of destruction. Even more significant is the fact that the Yankee's denunciation of the mass of the nation as "human muck" is the climax of a series of episodes revealing in him a deep-seated although unacknowledged contempt for mankind in general. The attitude first appears near the beginning of the story, in the scene which shows him attaining dictatorial powers by convincing everyone he is able to produce an eclipse of the sun. It appears again in his destruction of Merlin's tower, in the ceremony he builds around his restoration of the well in the Valley of Holiness, and in his triumph over Sir Sagramor le Desirous and other knights in the tournament. The exploits reveal Morgan's extravagant delight in creating theatrical effects. In all these situations he stands alone in the presence of a vast multitude; they are "strong" scenes, of a sort familiar on the nineteenth-century stage, but magnified in the novel to a scale beyond the resources of even the biggest and best equipped theater. Morgan inspires fear in his audiences that merges into awe and ends in wild applause, which he covets despite his contempt for the masses that give it to him. The crowd experiences a shared emotion deliberately aroused by the solitary magician, and he derives an immense pleasure from demonstrating his power over it.

Since the obliteration of individual freedom by group pressure is the prime obstacle the Yankee faces in his efforts to reform sixth-century Britain, his passion for spectacular effects runs profoundly counter to the goal set for him by his ideology. It is noteworthy, further, that all his effects, even in the single instance—the restoration of the well—when his "miracle" is an act of construction rather than destruction, are achieved by fraudulent methods. This is what he means when he says, "You can't throw too much style into a miracle."

The "cute tricks" of Yankee peddlers had long been comic material in American folkore, as Hank Morgan himself points out in an allusion to "the ingenious way in which the aldermen of London raised the money that built the Mansion House" by imposing a heavy fine on anyone who should refuse to be a candidate for sheriff, and then electing wealthy Dissenters who could not qualify for candidacy because their religious principles prevented them from taking communion according to the Anglican rite. The aldermen, says Morgan, "without any question were Yankees in disguise." His own deceptions are in the tradition but it is not clear whether Mark Twain views them ironically as part of the characterization of a fictional persona or is too closely identified with his protagonist to recognize them as dishonest.

The fraud involved in the Yankee's first miracle, that of the eclipse in Chapter 6, consists in his pretending to have power to blot out the sun. The convention of the fanciful tale excuses the improbability of his happening to recall that a total eclipse of the sun had occurred on 21 June, A.D. 528, beginning at 12:03 P.M.; and the need to find some means of saving himself from being burned at the stake provides a considerably sounder justification for his bluff than some of his later miracles have. One should also keep in mind that in these early chapters Mark Twain's projection of the Yankee as a distinct persona lends an irony to the narrator's explanations of his own motives which is less apparent later on. Nevertheless, even from the beginning Hank Morgan's arrogance is incongruous with the vernacular character as it had been developed in earlier books. "If everybody about here was so honestly and sincerely afraid of Merlin's pretended magic," he says, "certainly a superior man like me ought to be shrewd enough to contrive some way to take advantage of such a state of things." When he has worked out his plan, he remarks: "I was even impatient for to-morrow [the day set for his execution] to come, I so wanted to gather in that great triumph and be the center of all the nation's wonder and reverence. Besides, in a business way it would be the making of me; I knew that."

When the time for burning the Yankee at the stake arrives, he is led into a courtyard of the palace and finds himself in the presence of four thousand people. The audience is frozen with fear because of his claim to magical powers: "there was not a movement perceptible in those masses of humanity; they were as rigid as stone images, and as pale; and dread sat upon every countenance." As the eclipse begins, "With a common impulse the multitude rose slowly up and stared into the sky." The narrator continues: "I knew that this gaze would be turned upon me, next. When it was, I was ready. I was in one of the most grand attitudes I ever struck, with my arm stretched up pointing to the sun. It was a noble effect. You could *see* the shudder sweep the mass like a wave." He exploits this success by forbidding the audience to leave, and reports with exultation: "The multitude sank meekly into their seats, and I was just expecting they would." Later, when he has extorted the concessions he desires from the King and the sun begins to reappear, "the assemblage broke loose with a vast shout and came pouring down like a deluge to smother me with blessings and gratitude."

In the scene of the destruction of Merlin's tower, in the next chapter, Morgan's hubris is even more conspicuous. He says that the glare of the explosion revealed "a thousand acres of human beings grovelling on the ground in a general collapse of consternation," and he refers sardonically to "a good many thousand tracks in the mud the next morning . . . all outward bound." The note of derision is evident again in his attitude toward the crowd that gathers to witness the miracle of the well: "It was immense—that effect! Lots of people shrieked, women curled up and quit in every direction, foundlings collapsed by platoons," and "One mighty groan of terror started up from the massed people."

Since *A Connecticut Yankee* presents an almost continual conflict between manifest and latent meanings, and has in constantly shifting degree the "unconscious depth" that T. S. Eliot found in Mark Twain's fiction, one hesitates to draw conclusions from any single passage. The term "mass," so frequently applied to the Yankee's audiences, is particularly ambiguous. At first it may refer merely to the physical image of a crowd so large and so densely packed that individuals can hardly be distinguished. But in later passages the word carries the implication that the members of the multitude have surrendered their identity to a larger, more powerful, yet subhuman organism. This semantic development is paralleled by the Yankee's contemptuous references to the people of the kingdom as "worms," "pygmies" ("Here I was, a giant among pygmies, a man among children, a master intelligence among intellectual moles"), "clams," "spaniels," and of course at the end, "sheep" and "human muck." Sheer visual effect, again, justifies the comparisons between crowds and waves—an image, incidentally, that is conspicuous in the description of the mob confronted by Sherburn in *Huckleberry Finn* and in accounts of the French Revolution that Mark Twain had read—but the repetition of the image strengthens the impression of particles swept along by an irresistible force. And the presence of such implications in the scenes involving vast multitudes of spectators is thematically continuous with the vivid representation of mobs engaged in lynchings in later chapters. Since so much else in *A Connecticut Yankee* points forward to *The Mysterious Stranger*, it is relevant in this connection that the later book emphasizes the power of mob spirit to coerce individuals into cruelties they inwardly strive to avoid.

Hank Morgan's miracles are intended to demonstrate the superiority of science to superstition: "every time the magic of fol-de-rol tried conclusions with the magic of science, the magic of fol-de-rol got left." For purposes of fiction it is convenient to personify the meaningless rigama-role of prescientific spells and incantations in Merlin, and to bring him into direct collision with the hero. Morgan makes some amusing witti-cisms at his rival's expense: "Merlin is a very good magician in a small way, and has quite a neat provincial reputation. He is struggling along, doing the best he can, and it would not be etiquette for me to take his job until he himself abandons it." But as the contest becomes more and more intense, the Yankee begins to exhibit an unpleasant arrogance, al-most a megalomania, that seems to be related to his naïve enjoyment of the applause when he wins each successive round from his antagonist. After he has succeeded where Merlin failed in restoring the well in the Valley of Holiness, he reports that "the populace uncovered and fell back reverently to make a wide way for me, as if I had been some kind of a superior being—and I was. I was aware of that." In the Yankee's account of his combat with Sir Sagramor le Desirous, who is assisted by Merlin's charms, the reader can hardly fail to notice an egotism that Mark Twain does not seem to be aware of. The contest is described as "a duel between two mighty magicians; a duel not of muscle but of mind, not of human skill but of superhuman art and craft; a final struggle for supremacy be-tween the two master enchanters of the age," indeed a "mysterious and awful battle of the gods." The phrasing suggests that the metaphorical collision between superstition and modern technology has become a rather juvenile fantasy of triumph over dastardly foes.

To be sure, the Yankee says that "there was a vast matter at stake here . . . *the life of knight-errantry* . . . I was the champion of hard unsenti-mental common sense and reason." But the allegorical overtones are not perceptible in the actual incident; they are a moral tacked on to a narra-tive which mingles burlesque with dime-novel bloodthirstiness. The Yan-kee chooses to wear clothing fully expressive of what Mark Twain later called his "circus side": "the simplest and comfortablest of gymnast cos-tumes—flesh-colored tights from neck to heel, with blue silk puffings about my loins." And who but a Ned Buntline hero could be mounted so ad-mirably? "My horse was not above medium size, but he was alert, slender-limbed, muscled with watch-springs, and just a greyhound to go. He was a beauty, glossy as silk, and naked as he was when he was born, except for bridle and ranger-saddle." Morgan's first weapon, a cowboy's lasso, is not an appropriate symbol of scientific technology, and his attitude to-ward the contest is that of a showman. He carefully reports the volume of applause when he dodges the ponderous charges of the heavily armored Sir Sagramor. He analyzes his triumph as if he were a theatrical manager: "Unquestionably, the popular thing in this world is novelty. These people had never seen anything of that cowboy business before, and it carried them clear off their feet with delight. From all around and everywhere, the shout went up: 'Encore! encore!'"

The incident follows the time-tested pattern of popular drama. At a moment when the Yankee, "drunk with glory," is resting from his first triumphs, Merlin steals the lasso, but the hero pulls out two revolvers and challenges all the knights at once. Just as he spends the last of his twelve bullets, the attack crumbles.

The episode affects the plot in that the Yankee's triumph over knight-errantry enables him to reveal his hidden schools, mines, and factories to the world. Yet this circus performance has an energy of its own, not related to the mission of bringing nineteenth-century civilization to the sixth century. Even though Morgan's playing the role of cowboy in the costume of a circus acrobat ridicules the genteel pretensions of belted knights, the scene belongs to popular fiction and to show-business; it has little to do either with the ideology of progress or with the vernacular mode represented by the story of Huck and Jim on the raft.

The tone of the Yankee's challenge ("I name none, I challenge all! Here I stand, and dare the chivalry of England to come against me—not by individuals, but in mass!") and his later reference to the time "When I broke the back of knight-errantry" seem to make his victory somehow personal. It was proverbial that Cervantes had destroyed Spain's chivalry with a book; was not Mark Twain beginning to conceive of himself as duplicating the feat? The rancorous comments about Matthew Arnold in his notebook during the period when he was writing *A Connecticut Yankee* lend color to the supposition, for he regarded Arnold as a representative of aristocratic Britain criticizing the plebeian society of the United States. The prospectus for the book issued by Mark Twain's publishing company—which he must have edited, even if he did not actually write the copy—contains the following passage. "The book answers the Godly slurs that have been cast at us for generations by the titled gentry of England. It is a gird at Nobility and Royalty, and makes the most irreverent fun of these sacred things . . . Without knowing it the Yankee is constantly answering modern English criticism of America, and pointing out the weakness and injustice of government by a privileged class." On the next page is a display advertisement, apparently intended as a model to be followed by agents in local advertising, which reads in part: "A keen and powerful satire on English Nobility and Royalty. A book that appeals to all true Americans. It will be to English Nobility and Royalty what Don Quixote was to Ancient Chivalry."

Speculation about the emotional life of a man long dead is risky, but the violence of the catastrophic ending of *A Connecticut Yankee* is so disturbing that one is tempted to seek a psychological explanation for it. Morgan's callous pleasure in the slaughter of knights appears not only in the tournament scene but earlier, when he throws a dynamite bomb at the armored horsemen charging the disguised King: "Yes, it was a neat thing, very neat and pretty to see. It resembled a steamboat explosion on the Mississippi; and during the next fifteen minutes we stood under a steady drizzle of microscopic fragments of knights and hardware and horse-flesh." Blowing enemies to bits with explosives receives comic treatment again in the final sequence. Clarence reports to the Boss that he has prepared a defensive belt of sand covering "glass-cylinder dynamite torpedoes"—"the prettiest garden that was ever planted"—and that a Church committee coming to demand the surrender of Morgan's forces has tested it. Morgan asks:

"Did the committee make a report?"
"Yes, they made one. You could have heard it a mile."
"Unanimous?"
"That was the nature of it."

But this is a trifle compared to the final massacre of the knights. After the buried mines have reduced an uncounted number of the enemy to "homogeneous protoplasm, with alloys of iron and buttons," the Yankee issues a Napoleonic proclamation congratulating his little garrison:

SOLDIERS, CHAMPIONS OF HUMAN LIBERTY AND EQUALITY: Your General congratulates you! In the pride of his strength and the vanity of his renown, an arrogant enemy came against you. You were ready. The conflict was brief; on your side, glorious. This mighty victory, having been achieved utterly without loss, stands without example in history. So long as the planets shall continue to move in their orbits, the BATTLE OF THE SAND-BELT will not perish out of the memories of men.   THE BOSS.

There is a degree of irony in Mark Twain's attitude toward this document. Morgan comments: "I read it well, and the applause I got was very gratifying to me," and his further remarks to the beleaguered garrison are followed by a note enclosed within square brackets—"[Loud and long-continued applause.]"—recalling passages from earlier books in which Mark Twain undercuts his own flights of rhetoric. It is difficult, however, to believe that the author is not to some degree identified with the narrator here, if only because the rhetoric so closely resembles that of other pronouncements by Morgan evidently meant to be taken seriously. And Mark Twain unmistakably shares the exultation of the Yankee's comments on the last charge, which results in the destruction of the entire attacking force: "I shot the current through all the fences and struck the whole host dead in their tracks! *There* was a groan you could *hear!* It voiced the death-pang of eleven thousand men. It swelled out on the night with awful pathos." Finally: "Within ten short minutes after we had opened fire [with Gatling guns], armed resistance was totally annihilated, the campaign was ended, we fifty-four were masters of England! Twenty-five thousand men lay dead around us."

9

Howells, usually so sensitive to violence, was delighted with the Battle of the Sand Belt. "Last night," he wrote, "I read your last chapter. As Stedman says of the whole book, it's Titanic." Yet comparing *A Connecticut Yankee* with *Don Quixote* in his published review, he said Mark Twain's book showed "the kindlier and truer heart of our time." And when he "re-re-read" it twenty years later he still found it "the most delightful, truest, most humane, sweetest fancy that ever was."

The reader of the book today can account for these judgments only by ascribing to Howells an invincible innocence. The raw aggression expressed in Mark Twain's description of the slaughter of the knights reveals a massive disillusionment and frustration. He had identified himself with Hank Morgan more and more fully in the course of the story, and there is much autobiographical significance in the fact that the hero who set out to transform society ends up by being transformed himself. Merlin's magic, understood as the force of bigotry and superstition, defeats him by destroying his belief that the common people can be made worthy of governing themselves. In the story Merlin's victory is achieved by means of a spell that puts the Yankee to sleep and awakens him again in the nineteenth century to a life of hopeless longing for the dream world of the past. In testimony to his alienation from the modern world, he dies as soon as he has handed his manuscript to the narrator. Roger B. Salomon's analysis is convincing: *A Connecticut Yankee* might be called "The Fall of Prometheus." In adopting the ideology of progress Mark Twain had staked all his hopes on history. He had planned a fable illustrating how the advance of technology fosters the moral improvement of mankind. But when he put his belief to the test by attempting to realize it in fiction, the oracle of his imagination, his intuition, the unconsciously formulated conclusions based on his observation and reading, his childhood heritage of Calvinism, at any rate some force other than his conscious intention convinced him that his belief in progress and human perfectibility was groundless.

The exact causes of this loss of faith are irrecoverable, but the evidence that it occurred is plain to be seen in the book itself. What had seemed the inevitable salvation of man by the course of history now seemed man's inevitable damnation by the same power, operating as the training that perverted every member of society. Mark Twain's response to this shattering realization had been anticipated in the conception of Colonel Sherburn. He sought to escape from the nightmare of history by creating transcendent figures with whom he could identify himself. His later work returns again and again to the themes of the degradation of man in society and the immunity of the detached observer. Whatever may be the merits of these themes as an interpretation of the human condition, they made it impossible for Mark Twain to regain contact with the vernacular affirmations that had sustained his development toward the climax of his achievement in *Huckleberry Finn*.

VIII

This Pathetic Drift between the Eternities

CHAPTER 18 of *A Connecticut Yankee* contains a paragraph curiously out of tone with the immediate context and with the book as a whole. In the castle of Queen Morgan le Fay the Yankee has just had his first encounter with outright physical brutality toward the common people. He has seen the Queen stab a page who by accident "fell lightly against her knee," and in the dungeons he has found the young husband being tortured on the rack. He has invoked his authority as Boss to free the prisoner, but the Queen cannot accept the idea that killing the page was a crime. "Crime, forsooth!" she exclaims. "Man, I am going to *pay* for him!" Her retort elicits from the Yankee a long address to the reader:

Oh, it was no use to waste sense on her. Training—training is everything; training is all there is *to* a person. We speak of nature; it is folly; there is no such thing as nature; what we call by that misleading name is merely heredity and training. We have no thoughts of our own, no opinions of our own; they are transmitted to us, trained into us. All that is original in us, and therefore fairly creditable or discreditable to us, can be covered up and hidden by the point of a cambric needle, all the rest being atoms contributed by, and inherited from, a procession of ancestors that stretches back a billion years to the Adam-clam or grasshopper or monkey from whom our race has been so tediously and ostentatiously and unprofitably developed.

Although Hank Morgan has earlier referred to the common people of Arthur's realm as "these innumerable clams," this discourse on heredity and training is not really his but the author's. It contains the gist of Mark Twain's "gospel," the philosophical treatise called *What Is Man?* he had been gestating for years. The last sentence of the paragraph sets forth

ideas especially inappropriate for the Yankee: "And as for me, all that
I think about in this plodding sad pilgrimage, this pathetic drift between
the eternities, is to look out and humbly live a pure and high and blame-
less life, and save that one microscopic atom in me that is truly *me:* the
rest may land in Sheol and welcome for all I care."

On the next page the Yankee passes on to the subject of slavery ("A
master might kill his slave for nothing: for mere spite, malice, or to pass
the time") and then, by a rather arbitrary transition, to the bother of having a conscience ("I have noticed my conscience for many years, and I
know it is more trouble and bother to me than anything else I started
with"). The topics in his meditation do not seem to be logically connected,
but they have a significant relation to one another; for they are the themes
that would dominate *Pudd'nhead Wilson* (1894), "The Man That Corrupted Hadleyburg" (1899), and *The Mysterious Stranger* (published
posthumously in 1916).

The themes are all connected with the notion of training—the shaping
of the personality by society, a process that for Mark Twain embraced
the cumulative social pressure he called heredity. Training constantly
threatens and often annihilates personal identity, the ultimate *me,* especially by implanting in the individual the sense of guilt, or moral sense,
or conscience. These ideas find expression in two recurrent metaphors:
the institution of slavery, which Mark Twain considered the most striking illustration of how society perverts its members; and dreams, which
bear on the theme of identity because, as he explains in "My Platonic
Sweetheart" (written in 1898), the self that enjoyed or suffered such vivid
experiences in his dreams seemed to him an alter ego, somehow distinct
from his waking self. It may or may not be a coincidence that shortly
after the Yankee's meditation about Morgan le Fay, when he comes upon
a wretched woman imprisoned alone in an underground cell for nine
years, he speaks of "the meaningless dull dream that was become her
life." In other contexts, particularly in *The Mysterious Stranger,* Mark
Twain relates the imagery of dreaming to the idea of escape from an in-
tolerable reality.

2

The defeat of Hank Morgan that is foreshadowed in the description
of life as a "pathetic drift between the eternities" was for Mark Twain's
imagination final. No later character sets out with the Yankee's élan to

reform society. Yet the central theme of *Pudd'nhead Wilson* is still the corrupt state of the official culture of Dawson's Landing—that is, Hannibal—and the plot of the novel is focused around two acts which, in quite different ways, call attention to evils beneath the apparently placid surface of it. The first act, the slave Roxana's desperate effort to free her son by exchanging him with her master's son in the cradle, is frustrated by the second, which consists in Wilson's detection of Roxy's stratagem more than twenty years later.

In Mark Twain's unusually full account of the gestation of *Pudd'nhead Wilson* he says the three central characters, "a stranger named Pudd'nhead Wilson . . . a woman named Roxana" and "a young fellow named Tom Driscoll," made their unexpected appearance while he was trying to write a farce about "a youthful Italian 'freak'—or 'freaks'—which was—or which were—on exhibition in our cities—a combination consisting of two heads and four arms joined to a single body and a single pair of legs." The fragments of the farce published separately as "Those Extraordinary Twins" show that it was, as Mark Twain says, "an extravagantly fantastic little story," developed at the level of slapstick comedy. A Negro maid drops a tray of dishes when she first sees the twins; they cooperate at table in helping one another eat; one of them, a teetotaler, gets drunk from the liquor consumed by his brother; they sing different and discordant songs at the same time; and Wilson defends them against a charge of assault by challenging the prosecution to prove which of them willed the act of kicking Tom Driscoll. Mark Twain was evidently attracted to this material because the monstrosity posed in so vivid a fashion the problem of identity. Were the twins one person, or two? If two, could either be considered truly his own master? And was not this sideshow freak an emblem of Mark Twain's own frequent impression that two distinct and conflicting personalities were housed in his body?

One of the twins, the blond Angelo, is a prim young fellow who chooses *The Whole Duty of Man* for his bedtime reading. The other, Luigi, a brunet, is a rowdy type who when he is in control of the common pair of legs insists on keeping late hours for dissipation, and reads *The Age of Reason*. Even in this farce, Mark Twain is dramatizing the conflict between propriety and nonconformity that had served him so often before as comic material. The playful fantasy, however, touched off deeper responses—hence the appearance of the three characters who figure in *Pudd'nhead Wilson*. Roxy's son, known as Tom Driscoll during most of the story, is the psychological equivalent of the twins. He is two persons in one: a Negro (according to the definition operative in Dawson's Landing —he "has one thirty-second Negro blood") who appears "white" and is reared as the adopted son of the great man of the town. He is by law a slave but apparently free. The duality of white and Negro introduces the theme of false appearance and hidden reality, which is repeated in Tom's activities as a burglar in the disguise of a woman while he is ostensibly leading the life of the idle young heir to the town's largest fortune.

The material drawn up thus into consciousness is not comic, but intensely serious. When Mark Twain has conceived of Tom Driscoll he is launched upon a fable involving the tragic theme of slavery, with all it implies of hereditary but constantly renewed guilt and of perverted social conventions distorting human fact. For what but a morass of arbitrary assumptions makes Tom originally "black" and enslaved, later "white" and free, then converts him back into a Negro and a slave when the "truth" is revealed? The society of Dawson's Landing imposes upon slaves and masters alike the fictions which sustain the institution of slavery. The training corrupts both: the slave by destroying his human dignity, by educating him to consider himself inferior, by building up in him a ferocious hatred of himself as well as of his rulers; the master by encouraging cruelty toward the human beings he is taught to regard as animals, and thus by blunting his sensibilities and fostering an unwarranted pride of place.

Tom's mixed biological heritage points to the further fact that slavery debases sexual relations. To be sure, Mark Twain handles this topic with marked reticence. From the standpoint of imaginative coherence Judge York Leicester Driscoll is the father of Tom just as clearly as Roxy is his mother. But Mark Twain places the unmentionable fact of sexual intercourse between master and slave at two removes from the actual story— first by making Roxy, Tom's mother, the slave of a shadowy brother of Judge Driscoll at the time of Tom's birth; and then by the further precaution of creating an even more shadowy figure, Colonel Cecil Burleigh Essex, to be his biological father.

3

Half of Tom's heritage is that of the town's aristocracy. Judge Driscoll embodies the official culture. He is the "chief citizen," immensely proud of his descent from the First Families of Virginia. He is also a conspicuous exponent of the chivalric *code duello* which is the most explicit formulation of the ideal values inherent in the culture—cherished both by the gentlemen whom it obligates and by the townspeople in general, who consider themselves exalted by the presence of a ruling caste defined in this fashion. The characterization of the Judge is filled out by three close variants. His younger brother, Percy Northumberland Driscoll, Tom's supposed father, reveals the economic base of the aristocracy: he was "a prosperous man, with a good head for speculations [in land], and his fortune was growing." Judge Driscoll inherits his brother's fortune; and he himself is engaged in counting money and going over business records on the evening when Tom stabs him. Further details are added to the portrait of the complete Dawson's Landing gentleman by the military title of Colonel Essex and his sexual interest in handsome slave women. The fourth member of the dominant clique, Pembroke Howard, is the leading local authority on the etiquette of dueling. The names borrowed from Tudor nobility that are given to Judge Driscoll and his congeners, and to Tom (who was christened Thomas à Becket Driscoll), establish an ironic link between the rather paltry elite of Dawson's Landing and the English aristocracy Hank Morgan had annihilated at the end of *A Connecticut Yankee.*

The problem of tone is often difficult in *Pudd'nhead Wilson,* but Mark Twain's earlier ridicule of Southern aristocratic pretensions in *Life on the Mississippi* and elsewhere strengthens one's suspicion that he intends to caricature Judge Driscoll's pride of ancestry and his equation of honor with readiness to send or accept a challenge. The Judge is unmistakably an object of satire in Chapter 7, when he shows the newly arrived Italian counts the sights of the town—including the slaughter house and the volunteer fire company—and naïvely tells them "all about his several dignities, and how he had held this and that and the other place of honor or profit, and had once been to the legislature." There is some ambiguity in the treatment of the Judge's duel with Luigi; Mark Twain admired physical courage, and the reader is expected to feel contempt for Tom because he is too cowardly to challenge the Count. Yet the duel in *Pudd'nhead Wilson* replaces a farcical encounter in "Those Extraordinary Twins" in which Angelo, physically joined to Luigi and therefore exposed to the Judge's fire against his will, dodges about so violently that he frustrates the efforts of both combatants, and finally assumes control of the twins' common pair of legs to run away. And the bit of slapstick that gives rise to the duel in "Those Extraordinary Twins" is retained in the novel. When Tom directs a sneering jest at Luigi from the platform of an anti-prohibition meeting, Luigi "took a couple of strides and halted behind the unsuspecting joker. Then he drew back and delivered a kick of such titanic vigor that it lifted Tom clear over the footlights and landed him on the heads of the front row of the Sons of Liberty."

Mark Twain's ironic attitude toward the Judge's sense of honor is also indicated by the sequel to the duel. Tom rationalizes his refusal to fight Luigi by declaring that the Count is an assassin. Without asking for particulars, the Judge instantly accepts the explanation, and declares: "That this assassin should have put the affront upon me of letting me meet him on the field of honor as if he were a gentleman is a matter which I will presently settle—but not now. I will not shoot him until after the election [for town officers]. I see a way to ruin them both before; I will attend to that first." The Judge waits until the eve of the election and then, still without any effort to verify Tom's slander, repeats it in a campaign speech. The coup brings about Luigi's defeat.

This incident would be more significant than it is if Judge Driscoll were a fully rounded character. But he is not. Mark Twain is not really interested in him as a person; he merely represents the aristocratic part of Tom Driscoll's heritage, which the writer means to satirize in the composite figure of the four descendants of the First Families of Virginia. Yet there is one odd obscurity of outline in the portrait. Pembroke Howard, the Judge's closest friend, is "a devoted Presbyterian" whereas the Judge is a freethinker. The theological difference is of no consequence in the plot. The Judge's unorthodoxy, like his pride in his Virginian ancestry, seems to be a reminiscence of Samuel Clemens' father, John Marshall Clemens. The parallel is a fleeting reminder that as the story of *Pudd'nhead Wilson* emerged from the farce about the Italian twins it drew into itself buried memories of Mark Twain's childhood—not always to the advantage of the novel.

4

The other half of Tom's heritage is that of his mother, Roxy the slave. The two parts of it are at war with each other. When Tom is but an infant Percy Northumberland Driscoll, Roxy's master, threatens to sell some of his slaves down the river. Although he relents and sells them in the town, Roxy suddenly realizes he has the power to carry out his threat:

"Her child could grow up and be sold down the river! The thought crazed her with horror." She says to the sleeping infant: "I hates yo' pappy; he hain't got no heart—for niggers he hain't, anyways. I hates him, en I could kill him!" She is the only articulate enemy of the aristocracy of Dawson's Landing. Just as in some not negligible sense Judge Driscoll takes over the function of the Arthurian aristocracy in representing the values of a society stained by tyranny and cruelty, Roxy takes over Hank Morgan's role as adversary of the dominant class. In doing so, she becomes a successor to the vernacular protagonists of earlier stories.

Of course, there are important differences. Because she is a Negro (however "white" in appearance) and a woman, Mark Twain cannot identify himself with her as he identifies himself with Hank Morgan. And her aggression against the established order is not motivated by a program of reform. Mark Twain has accepted the demonstration in *A Connecticut Yankee* that society cannot be redeemed. Yet in *Pudd'nhead Wilson* he continues his preoccupation with the question of values, stripping down the fictive world of the Matter of Hannibal to the only vestige of affirmation he can find in it: the warmth, the passion of love and of hate, the sheer personal force in this representative of the submerged slave caste.

Roxy thus represents the last trace of unhandseled nature that has survived the perverted training of society in Dawson's Landing. But with a beautiful irony Mark Twain shows that she has adopted many of the values of the white aristocrats: their pride of ancestry, their code of honor, even their contempt for Negroes. Her denunciation of Tom, setting forth Judge Driscoll's sentiments in her heavy dialect, is one of the great passages in this uneven but often powerful book:

En you refuse' to fight a man dat kicked you, 'stid o' jumpin' at de chance! En you ain't got no mo' feelin' den to come en tell me, dat fetched sich a po' low-down ornery rabbit into de worl'! Pah! it makes me sick! It's de nigger in you, dat's what it is. Thirty-one parts o' you is white, en on'y one part nigger, en dat po' little one part is yo' *soul*. 'Tain't wuth savin'; 'tain't wuth totin' out on a shovel en throwin' in de gutter. You has disgraced yo' birth. What would yo' pa think o' you? It's enough to make him turn in his grave.

Roxy herself has stood in range of bullets from the duel in order to watch it, and a ricochet shot has tipped her nose. When Tom asks her, "Weren't you afraid?" she invokes in unconscious parody of Judge Driscoll the absurd pedigree she has invented for herself. She believes that "My great-great-great-gran'father en yo' great-great-great-great-gran'father was Ole Cap'n John Smith, de highest blood dat Ole Virginny ever turned out, en *his* great-great-gran'mother or somers along back dah, was Pocahontas de Injun queen, en her husbun' was a nigger king outen Africa." It is a sufficient explanation of her behavior that "De Smith-Pocahontases ain't 'fraid o' nothin', let alone bullets."

Except when she is momentarily under the influence of her "strong and sincere" piety, Roxy is indifferent toward property rights; she offers as a matter of course to help Tom in his burglaries when he needs money to pay his gambling debts. But on the crucial occasion of the theft of money that led her master to sell the guilty slaves, she had overcome temptation herself because she had "got religion" a fortnight before at a revival. Mark Twain is at his comic-ironic best in this scene, culminating in Roxy's exclamation, "Dad blame dat revival, I wisht it had 'a' be'n put off till tomorrow!" Roxy is nevertheless free of the heaviest burden that slavery has imposed on the whites: the sense of guilt. She is not torn by inner conflict, and she conveys the suggestion of subliminal energy, of darkness and mystery, that is attached to women and Negroes in American culture. The aggressiveness of the Judge is controlled by traditional forms, and even on the dueling ground he merely wounds his adversary. But when Roxy, without reference to code or etiquette, conceives the idea of killing her master, or herself and her child, the reader is convinced she is capable of these actions.

There is a haughty grandeur in her character that shines through the degraded speech and manners of a slave, and confers on her an intimation of tragic dignity: "She was of majestic form and stature, her attitudes were imposing and statuesque, and her gestures and movements distinguished by a noble and stately grace." We have seen with what assurance she has imagined an Indian queen and an African king among her ancestors. Mark Twain never conceived a more effective passage than the scene, at once tragic and comic, in which she determines to exchange her son with the Driscoll heir, and justifies the action to herself by a process of reasoning both humble (for she takes for granted the inferiority of the Negro—" 'Tain't no sin—*white* folks has done it!") and arrogant, because she compares herself with royalty and even usurps the divine prerogative of arbitrarily conferring free grace on her child:

Now I's got it; now I 'member. It was dat old nigger preacher dat tole it, de time he come over here fum Illinois en preached in de nigger church. He said dey ain't nobody kin save his own self—can't do it by faith, can't do it by works, can't do it no way at all. Free grace is de *on'y* way, en dat don't come fum nobody but jis' de Lord; en *he* kin give it to anybody he please, saint or sinner—*he* don't kyer. He do jis' as he's a mineter. He s'lect out anybody dat suit him, en put another one in his place, en make de fust one happy forever en leave t'other one to burn wid Satan. De preacher said it was jist like dey done in Englan' one time, long time ago. De queen she lef' her baby layin' aroun' one day, en went out callin'; en one o' de niggers roun' 'bout de place dat was 'mos' white, she come in en see de chile layin' aroun', en tuck en put her own chile's clo'es on de queen's chile, en put de queen's chile's clo'es on her own chile, en den lef' her own chile layin' aroun' en tuck en toted de queen's chile home to de nigger-quarter, en nobody ever foun' it out, en her chile was de king bimeby, en sole de queen's chile down de river one time when dey had to settle up de estate.

Roxy's subversive threat to the dominant culture is the only aspect of the material of *Pudd'nhead Wilson* that stirs Mark Twain's imagination. As a result, she is the only fully developed character, in the novelistic sense, in the book. She has a different order of fictional reality from the figures of fable with which she is surrounded. She resembles a portrait in full color set in a black-and-white background.

5

Although Tom Driscoll is evidently the key figure in the imaginative logic of *Pudd'nhead Wilson,* he is, like Judge Driscoll, not so much a character as a complex of themes. He incarnates both the tortured paradox of uncertain identity and the perversions resulting from generations of the bad training imposed by slavery. He exhibits the worst traits ascribed to both races in this fictive world—the lax morals and cowardice of the Negro, together with the hatred of the master that is putatively expressed in his murder of Judge Driscoll; the indolence and affectation of white aristocrats (he is sent to Yale and returns with mannerisms of dress that are offensive to the community); the cruelty toward slaves that Mark Twain's latent respect for the ideal of the Southern gentleman, related to his feeling for John Marshall Clemens, prevents him from attributing directly to Judge Driscoll. The brutality inculcated in Tom by the attitudes current in the community is exhibited in his behavior as a boy toward his body servant Chambers (actually, of course, the rightful Thomas à Becket Driscoll) and reaches a climax in the scene of his wanton cuffing and kicking of Chambers when the slave enters to ask an audience for Roxy. In a passage deleted from the final version Mark Twain carefully explained that the incident was an illustration of training rather than of native disposition:

> At this distance of time it seems nearly incredible that such a performance as the above would have furnished to a stranger no sure indication of Tom's character—for the reason that such conduct was not confined to young men of harsh nature. Humane young men were quite capable of it, good-hearted young fellows who would protect with their brave lives a dog that was being treated so. Slavery was to blame, not innate nature. It placed the slave below the brute, without the white man's realizing it.

Tom's most atrocious act, his betrayal of Roxy by selling her down the river after she has helped him pay his debts by allowing herself to be sold back into slavery, comes after he is aware that he is a Negro and himself legally a slave. It is not an expression of aristocratic arrogance but of the unmotivated melodramatic villainy that Mark Twain ascribes to Tom along with his sociologically determined traits. While this deed is not inconsistent with Tom's character, it does not belong to the imaginative fabric of the novel or even to its ideological structure; it represents the infection by stereotypes from popular fiction and the theater to which Mark Twain was always exposed when he lost control of his materials.

6

The third of the three characters who Mark Twain said "got to intruding themselves" into his farce about the Italian twins "and taking up more and more room with their talk and their affairs" was Pudd'nhead Wilson. Comments in Mark Twain's letters make it clear that Wilson remained a minor character through the first drastic revision of the original farce into a "tragedy." Not until later, when Francis Galton's *Finger Prints* (published in 1892) provided a sound scientific method for establishing the identities of Tom and Chambers and for proving Tom guilty of the murder of Judge Driscoll, did Mark Twain undertake the revision that made Wilson the "chiefest" figure. This version of the novel, incidentally, has survived in manuscript. Still another revision would be necessary to dissect out the Siamese-twins motive.

Even when Wilson was given a crucial role in the plot, Mark Twain did not undertake to characterize him fully. A letter to Livy in 1894 contains a revealing comment on his intention. A lecturer in New York, he reported, had said that "Pudd'nhead was clearly & powerfully drawn & would live & take his place as one of the great creations of American fiction." Mark Twain continued: "Isn't that pleasant—& unexpected! For I have never thought of Pudd'nhead as a *character,* but only as a piece of machinery—a button or a crank or a lever, with a useful function to perform in a machine, but with no dignity above that." Wilson is incarnate analytical intelligence, the personification of science. Mark Twain liked to embody the notion of rational analysis, either farcically or seriously, in a figure borrowed from the newspapers and from popular fiction: the detective. In the later 1870's he had experimented with a novel and a play called "Cap'n Simon Wheeler, the Amateur Detective," traces of which survive in *Tom Sawyer, Detective* (1896); and he makes much of allegedly scientific methods of investigation in *The Stolen White Elephant* (1878) and *A Double Barrelled Detective Story* (1901, containing a burlesque of Sherlock Holmes). Closely tied to the solving of crimes is the sensational effect of the detective's courtroom revelation of the identity of the criminal —a motive that links Wilson retrospectively with Tom Sawyer and proleptically with Wilhelm Meidling, or rather with Satan in the guise of Meidling, in *The Mysterious Stranger.*

These affiliations of Wilson suggest that he has some qualities of transcendence. He does not have the omniscience of the fully transcendent figure: he is deceived by Tom's disguises and is temporarily convinced by Tom's argument that the twins never possessed the valuable dagger they say has been stolen from them. We are also asked to believe that Wilson suffers from his twenty years' isolation and wishes to be accepted as a member of the community, even to the point of being gratified by his popularity after his triumph in the trial scene. But his transcendent traits are unmistakable. He is much better educated and more intelligent than anyone else in the village; he is an outsider who arrives from a great distance and is therefore free from the guilt of slavery that the Virginia gentlemen have brought with them to Dawson's Landing; his mastery of the science of reading palms, like his discovery of the principle of identification through fingerprints, strikes the townspeople as almost miraculous; and he feels no warmth for any human being.

When Wilson reveals in the courtroom that the supposed Tom Driscoll is a bastard, a thief, a murderer, and worst of all a Negro, he demonstrates that the official culture, with its vaunted ideals of honor and chivalry and ancient lineage, is merely a façade for deceit, avarice, and illegitimacy. He also defeats Roxy by frustrating her plan to free her son: Tom suffers precisely the fate of being sold down the river that she had tried to save him from.

The insight of the transcendent figure thus destroys both elements of the long-established pattern of dominant culture versus vernacular protest. For Mark Twain's conception of truth has undergone a drastic change. From the time when he had claimed in the preface to *The Innocents Abroad* to have written "honestly," his standard of truth had been the spontaneous judgments of a vernacular character revealing the falsity of accepted values. This truth was moral rather than metaphysical; it expressed the intuitive good sense of the common man, which was assumed to be valid because it had not been perverted by upper-class affectations and stereotypes. In the course of *A Connecticut Yankee,* however, Mark Twain had reached the conclusion that the intuitions of the common people as well as of the aristocracy were hopelessly debauched by training; both lacked the power to free themselves from the incubus of tyrannical institutions. This growing conviction had led him to ascribe to Hank Morgan some of the contempt for man in general that is characteristic of the transcendent figure.

In *Pudd'nhead Wilson* the disintegration of the vernacular persona has proceeded further. Many of the traits with which Morgan had been endowed at the beginning of *A Connecticut Yankee* are assigned to Roxy: she has the vernacular humor and vitality and emotional wholeness, and she seizes the only means at her disposal to subvert the depraved social system. The transcendent attitudes Morgan eventually acquired are embodied in Wilson, particularly the power of perceiving the truth. Roxy tries to conceal the truth that her son is a slave, whereas Wilson's function is to reveal it. The grim social reality reasserted through his agency has no place for the vernacular values that Roxy represents. At the end of the book she is in effect dead: "the spirit in her eyes was quenched, her martial bearing departed with it, and the voice of her laughter ceased in the land. In her church and its affairs she found her only solace."

The chapter headings from "Pudd'nhead Wilson's Calendar," clearly expressing the attitudes of Mark Twain himself, provide a choral commentary on the universe of which Dawson's Landing is a microcosm:

"Why is it that we rejoice at a birth and grieve at a funeral? It is because we are not the person involved." "Whoever has lived long enough to find out what life is, knows how deep a debt of gratitude we owe to Adam, the first great benefactor of our race. He brought death into the world." The red-letter days of this calendar are April 1, which reminds us that we are fools, and October 12, Columbus Day, which suggests that "It would have been wonderful to find America, but it would have been more wonderful to miss it."

7

"The Man That Corrupted Hadleyburg," a shorter, simpler fable, treats the theme of human bondage in an almost algebraic fashion. The central character is Richards, cashier of the bank in a small town faintly reminiscent of Hannibal even though the local color has been almost entirely sweated out of it. There is no reference to Negro slavery—the time is late nineteenth century—but Richards calls himself a "slave" to the bank president Pinkerton, and all the leading citizens, including Pinkerton, are enslaved by greed. Their love of money contrasts ironically with the town's self-righteous pride in its reputation for honesty, that is, "commercial incorruptibility." The story concentrates on the hollowness of this outward show of rectitude, bringing together once again the themes of training and of the contrast between appearance and reality.

The demonstration that the elite of Hadleyburg is not honest, but basically corrupt, is undertaken by an outsider who is fleetingly assimilated to the group of Mark Twain's literary sleuths: on the only occasion when his appearance is described he resembles "an amateur detective gotten up like an impossible English earl." Like Pudd'nhead Wilson, although by a different method, he reveals the truth beneath the façade of the town's respectability. His motive is vengeance for some undisclosed offense against him by a resident of Hadleyburg—a motive that, together with his aura of mystery, causes him to resemble the Deity in Mark Twain's later thought. In order to demonstrate that greed is universal in "poor, tempted, and mistrained" humanity, he leaves in the village a bag supposed to contain a fortune in gold coins. At the same time he sends anonymous letters to nineteen prominent citizens saying the money is to be given to an unknown benefactor who can identify himself by recalling what he said when he gave money on a certain occasion to a stranger in distress. The cynical device works: in nineteen households the same

183

process of rationalization begins, the same conversations take place between husband and wife, and an effect of sardonic comedy is achieved by the choreographic automatism. Through close attention to Richards and his wife Mark Twain reveals in scathing detail the methods by which human beings conceal their motives from themselves.

A boisterous town meeting makes public eighteen identical efforts to get the money by means of fabricated evidence. Richards, however, is spared for a worse torment. The minister Burgess protects him by suppressing the fraudulent note that Richards, along with the other men tempted by the stranger, has submitted in support of his claim to the money. Richards succumbs again to the more grievous temptation of being publicly acclaimed for his integrity, receives a fortune together with the praise of the community, and dies from the pangs of guilt and shame. It is hard to conceive of a more tightly mathematical demonstration of human depravity.

A faint suggestion that the humble ones of this earth may be free of the compulsions binding the upper class is provided by Jack Halliday, "the loafing, good-natured, no-account irreverent fisherman, hunter, boys' friend, stray-dogs' friend" who mocks the leading citizens. But Mark Twain has so little interest in Halliday that he forgets the vernacular precedents in his own work and calls him the "typical 'Sam Lawson' of the town"—invoking as a model a character in Mrs. Stowe's *Oldtown Folks* who is portrayed from the patronizing viewpoint of local-color writing.

Hadleyburg is Dawson's Landing without either the intimations of evil radiating from the character of Tom Driscoll or the vivid thrust of Roxy's passion. It is not tragic, even potentially, but merely smug and hypocritical. The story nevertheless attains a considerable distinction by its tightness of construction, its evenness of tone, and its hard, spare prose. Mark Twain's mastery of a style based on oral speech but fined down to an instrument of precision survived the collapse of his power to create full-bodied characters or complex fictive worlds.

8

Both *Pudd'nhead Wilson* and "The Man That Corrupted Hadleyburg" belong to the decade of the 1890's, during which Mark Twain suffered a series of personal disasters: the bankruptcy of his publishing company, the failure of his nine-year struggle to get the Paige typesetter on the market, and as a final blow the death of his most cherished daughter, Susy. The other published work of the period is decidedly inferior. Near the end of his life Mark Twain declared that *Personal Recollections of Joan of Arc* (1896) was "the best" of his books, but this tribute to a "stainlessly pure" child is little more than an outpouring of dated sentimentality. *Following the Equator* (1897), written during the months of anguish following the death of Susy, is merely the travel diary of his lecture tour through the Southern hemisphere in 1895 doggedly made into a book under financial pressure. In 1906–07 Mark Twain published twenty-five installments of what he called his *Autobiography* in the *North American Review*. The title is somewhat misleading: the material might better be described as table talk, random comments on whatever happened to occur to him, dictated to a secretary. Although like everything he wrote it contains interesting passages, it is so incoherent that his editors have been content to mine it for publishable fragments.

In addition to published work during these years Mark Twain began dozens of manuscripts he was unable to finish. Bernard De Voto's memorable essay entitled "The Symbols of Despair" interprets this body of unpublished material as a series of efforts by Mark Twain to free himself from responsibility for the misfortunes he believed he had brought upon his family. De Voto regarded *The Mysterious Stranger,* the most important of the unfinished manuscripts, as "a minor masterpiece," largely because he saw in it an act of self-healing. He found the meaning of the book in the fact that it gathers all the unbearable scenes of man's meanness and cowardice and cruelty, the whole bloodstained panorama of history, into a single vision which then is declared to be but a dream. Placed at such a psychological distance, the spectacle that had previously been too painful to be mastered by the artist's imagination became tolerable; even the torment of his own guilt was assuaged by the pronouncement of young Satan that "there is no God, no universe, no human race, no earthly life, no heaven, no hell. It is all a dream—a grotesque and foolish dream. Nothing exists but you. And you are but a *thought,*—a vagrant thought, a useless thought, a homeless thought, wandering forlorn among the empty eternities!"

This speech of Satan comes in the last chapter, which Paine discovered separately in Mark Twain's papers after the writer's death and added to one among several incomplete versions of the story in order to make the book he published as *The Mysterious Stranger*. The ending does not unequivocally belong with the version Paine chose: in the manuscript of the chapter as he found it Satan is called by the curious name "44" borne by a cognate figure in a quite different version of the story. The question is however not crucial, for in all the versions Mark Twain clearly intends to adopt the perspective of a transcendent observer in order to depict human experience as meaningless.

Such a procedure does provide an imaginative escape from his sense of guilt. But it has a significantly close relation to ideas and themes that appear not only in *Pudd'nhead Wilson* and "The Man That Corrupted Hadleyburg" but in *A Connecticut Yankee,* which was written before any of the misfortunes mentioned by De Voto. The despair expressed in Mark Twain's late work had its origins in an intellectual crisis antedating the period of his personal misfortunes.

Mark Twain declared to Howells that in *The Mysterious Stranger* he intended to "tell what I think of Man, & how he is constructed, & what a shabby poor ridiculous thing he is." When Satan says that mankind is "dull and ignorant and trivial and conceited, and . . . a shabby, poor, worthless lot all around" he is voicing the author's disillusionment with the glittering promise for man's continuous moral improvement held out by the doctrine of progress. Just as Mark Twain had poured all the capital he could muster into the typesetter, he had invested all his political enthusiasm, his humanitarian emotion, and his hope for the future of his country in the idea that the common man was the prime creative force in history. Hank Morgan's conclusion that the mass of the nation in Arthur's Britain was only "human muck," which was of course a judgment on the mass of the American nation in the 1880's, proclaimed the bankruptcy of the writer's idealisms. The outcome had been in sight since the moment when Mark Twain confronted the fact that Huck's and Jim's quest for freedom was doomed to failure. For these protagonists had become the bearers of the vernacular system of values that had sustained his writing career. Hank Morgan's doctrinaire republicanism in *A Connecticut Yankee* translated into ideological terms the broader, deeper, subtler affirmations that had been frustrated in *Huckleberry Finn.* Since Mark Twain was trying to sustain by force of will a belief that had already lost its intuitive solidity, the outcome of the story was latent in it from the beginning.

The most significant trait of Satan in *The Mysterious Stranger* is his lack of a moral sense and of sympathy for mere human beings. The pressures that finally drove Mark Twain to conceive of an observer thus protected against suffering are neatly expressed in a scene that recalls the traumatic spectacle of the young husband on the rack in Morgan le Fay's dungeon. Satan miraculously transports himself and Theodor, the boy who tells the story, to the interior of a prison.

We were in the torture-chamber, Satan said. The rack was there, and the other instruments, and there was a smoky lantern or two hanging on the walls and helping to make the place look dim and dreadful. There were people there—the executioners—but as they took no notice of us, it meant that we were invisible. A young man lay bound, and Satan said he was suspected of being a heretic, and the executioners were about to inquire into it. They asked the man to confess to the charge, and he said he could not, for it was not true. Then they drove splinter after splinter under his nails, and he shrieked with the pain. Satan was not disturbed, but I could not endure it, and had to be whisked out of there.

Satan explains that the spectacle illustrates the moral sense, which causes man to inflict pain for the pleasure of it. Theodor is next shown a French factory in which the workers, "little children and all," are forced to work fourteen hours a day, with a four-mile walk to and from "the pigsties they inhabit." The torture undergone by these unfortunates, Satan declares, is worse than that of the young man in the prison, for his agony lasted but a few hours, whereas the agony of the workers lasts through years and decades. "It is the Moral Sense," he adds, "which teaches the factory proprietors the difference between right and wrong—you perceive the result."

Given this image of human society, a rational observer could have but one wish—to carry out Hank Morgan's impulse by hanging the race and ending the farce. Satan performs such an act in an early chapter of *The Mysterious Stranger*. He has created little men and women of clay and brought them to life for the amusement of Theodor and his friends. Two of the men quarrel and begin to fight one another. "Satan reached out his hand and crushed the life out of them with his fingers, threw them away, wiped the red from his fingers on his handkerchief, and went on talking where he had left off." When the wives of the dead men find the bodies of their husbands and fall to weeping a crowd collects about them, and the noise attracts Satan's attention; "then he reached out and took the heavy board seat out of our swing and brought it down and mashed

187

all those people into the earth just as if they had been flies, and went on talking just the same."

Satan's destruction of the mimic world he has created is the symbolic gesture of a writer who can no longer find any meaning in man or society. Mark Twain's only refuge is to identify himself with a supernatural spectator for whom mankind is but a race of vermin, hardly worth even contempt. And this marks the end of his career as a writer, for there was nothing more to say.

NOTES
INDEX

Autobiography	*Mark Twain's Autobiography,* ed. Albert B. Paine, 2 vols., New York, 1924.
Letters	*Mark Twain's Letters,* ed. Albert B. Paine, 2 vols., New York, 1917.
Love Letters	*The Love Letters of Mark Twain,* ed. Dixon Wecter, New York, 1949.
MTP	Mark Twain Papers, University of California Library, Berkeley.
Mark Twain–Howells Letters	*Mark Twain–Howells Letters,* ed. Henry N. Smith and William M. Gibson, 2 vols., Cambridge, 1960.
Mark Twain in Eruption	*Mark Twain in Eruption. Hitherto Unpublished Pages about Men and Events,* ed. Bernard DeVoto, New York, 1940.
Mark Twain to Mrs. Fairbanks	*Mark Twain to Mrs. Fairbanks,* ed. Dixon Wecter, San Marino, California, 1949.
My Mark Twain	William D. Howells, *My Mark Twain. Reminiscences and Criticism,* New York, 1910.
Notebook	*Mark Twain's Notebook,* ed. Albert B. Paine, New York, 1935.
Paine, *Biography*	Albert B. Paine, *Mark Twain. A Biography,* 4 vols., New York, 1912.
Writings	*The Writings of Mark Twain,* Definitive Edition, ed. Albert B. Paine, 37 vols., New York, 1922–25.

NOTES

The notes that follow are keyed to page and line of text; thus, "1.17" refers to page 1, line 17.

1.17   Virginia City (Nevada) *Territorial Enterprise,* 28 January 1866, reprinted in *Mark Twain: San Francisco Correspondent,* ed. Henry N. Smith and Frederick Anderson, San Francisco, 1957, pp. 98–99. Further interruptions come from the cries of street vendors of brooms, newspapers, and potatoes.

2.12   "The Young American" (A Lecture Read to the Mercantile Library Association, in Boston, February 7, 1844), in *Nature, Addresses, and Lectures,* Boston, 1849, p. 351.

2.21   *Winds of Doctrine: Studies in Contemporary Opinion,* London, 1913, pp. 187–188.

2.35   *Winds of Doctrine,* p. 201.

3.10   The phenomenon is described by Richard Bridgman in his unpublished dissertation, "The Stylization of Vernacular Elements in American Fiction, 1880–1925," University of California, Berkeley, 1960.

4.2   The best general account of American humor is Walter Blair's introduction to his anthology, *Native American Humor (1800–1900),* New York, 1937. Further details are provided by Norris W. Yates, *William T. Porter and The Spirit of the Times,* Baton Rouge, 1957. The social and political implications of native humor are explored in Kenneth S. Lynn, *Mark Twain and Southwestern Humor,* Boston, 1959.

5.16   Harriette M. Plunkett, *Josiah Gilbert Holland,* New York, 1894, p. 72.

5.20   *Emily Dickinson's Letters to Dr. and Mrs. J. G. Holland,* ed. Theodora V. W. Ward, Cambridge, 1951, p. 61. Holland's great popularity in the Middle West is noted by a recent biographer, who attributes it to the fact that the Corn Belt was "a much more naïve region than the Atlantic Coast" (Harry M. Peckham, *Josiah Gilbert Holland in Relation to His Times,* Philadelphia, 1940, pp. 55–56). In an editorial in *Scribner's Monthly* ("Triflers on the Platform," February 1872, p. 489) Holland attacked humorous lecturers as "literary mountebanks" and "triflers and buffoons." Mark Twain, believing the attack was directed principally at him, wrote a reply (not published) in which he called Holland "our great & good Tupper," referred to his "oracular complacency, in dealing with aged platitudes," and declared that "he moves through the lecture field a remorseless intellectual cholera" because he is "the very incarnation of the commonplace" (quoted by permission of the Mark Twain Estate and the Berg Collection, New York Public Library). Reviewing Holland's *Plain Talks on Familiar Subjects,* William Dean Howells said that "he rehearses his common-

NOTES

places with a dignified carefulness and a swelling port of self-satisfaction inexpressibly amusing" (*Nation,* 23 November 1865, p. 659).

5.27   Plunkett, *Holland,* p. 194.

6.25   *Lessons in Life. A Series of Familiar Essays. By Timothy Titcomb,* New York, 1861, pp. 306–307.

8.16   Letter to the *Territorial Enterprise* dated San Francisco, 13 September 1863, reprinted in *Mark Twain of the "Enterprise,"* ed. Henry N. Smith, Berkeley, 1957, pp. 76–77.

8.20   *Territorial Enterprise,* 6 February 1866, reprinted in *San Francisco Correspondent,* pp. 106–107. In 1868 Mark Twain mentioned C. A. V. Putnam along with Joseph T. Goodman to Jervis Langdon as a man who could testify to his character and reputation in Nevada, but added that neither "would say a damaging word against me for love or money or hesitate to throttle anybody else who ventured to do it" (Cleveland, 29 December, *Love Letters,* p. 38). Goodman wrote to Mark Twain in 1881: "Putnam is still on the *Enterprise,* aged and addicted to Bourbon, and vowing vengeance to everyone, but showing gentleness to all" (Fresno, Calif., 9 March, MTP).

9.27   *Golden Era* (San Francisco), 28 January 1866, reprinted in *The Washoe Giant in San Francisco,* ed. Franklin Walker, San Francisco, 1938, pp. 104–105.

10.4   Napier Wilt, *Some American Humorists,* New York, 1929, p. 130.

10.12 Walter Blair, *Mark Twain & Huck Finn,* Berkeley, 1960, pp. 251–253.

10.28 The evidence concerning Mark Twain's attitudes toward sex is summarized, with some psychological interpretation, in Alexander E. Jones, "Mark Twain and Sexuality," *PMLA,* 71:595–616 (September 1956).

11.1   *Writings,* VII, 17–22. This is the original title. The sketch often appears as "The Celebrated Jumping Frog of Calaveras County," and sometimes as "The Notorious Jumping Frog . . ."

12.19 *Mark Twain of the "Enterprise,"* pp. 16–19; *San Francisco Correspondent,* pp. 7–12.

12.25 *San Francisco Correspondent,* pp. 38–39.

12.28 *Writings,* IV, 145.

12.37 *Writings,* IV, 164.

13.27 Sacramento *Weekly Union,* 25 August 1866, reprinted in *Letters from the Sandwich Islands Written for the Sacramento Union by Mark Twain,* ed. G. Ezra Dane, Stanford, Calif., 1938, pp. 151–152.

14.15 Honolulu, 3 April 1866, *Letters,* I, 104.

14.32 Honolulu, 21 June 1866, *Letters,* I, 107.

14.37 Honolulu, 27 June 1866, *Letters,* I, 108–109.

15.6   Walter F. Frear, *Mark Twain and Hawaii,* Chicago, 1947, p. 17.

15.12 *Autobiography,* II, 125.

15.22 Sacramento *Daily Union,* 26 September 1866, reprinted in *Mark Twain and Hawaii,* p. 405.

15.30 *Mark Twain and Hawaii,* pp. 400, 405–406.

16.2   *Mark Twain and Hawaii,* p. 407.

17.9   Sacramento *Daily Union,* 16 November 1866, reprinted in *Mark Twain and Hawaii,* pp. 417–418.

18.9   *Mark Twain and Hawaii,* p. 127.

19.35   *Mark Twain and Hawaii*, p. 443.

19.37   Paul Fatout, *Mark Twain on the Lecture Circuit*, Bloomington, Indiana, 1960, p. 136.

20.3   Fatout, *Lecture Circuit*, p. 59.

20.10   25 October, reprinted in *Mark Twain and Hawaii*, p. 446.

23.22   *Autobiography*, I, 243. Mark Twain's plans at the time he left San Francisco are not entirely clear. His arrangements with the *Alta* concerning the *Quaker City* excursion are described by Albert B. Paine in *Letters*, I, 123, presumably on the basis of conversation. Noah Brooks, then editor of the *Alta*, said later that the paper paid Mark Twain's expenses as well as buying his letters ("Mark Twain in California," *Century*, November 1898, p. 97).

23.36   Letter to Bliss, New York, 27 January, *Letters*, I, 147–148.

23.38   *Letters*, I, 153.

24.7   Mark Twain wrote to Mrs. Mary Mason Fairbanks from Hartford on 13 March that he expected to go soon to visit the Langdons in Elmira, where he and Livy would read "500 or 600 pages of proof together—two or three weeks" (*Mark Twain to Mrs. Fairbanks*, p. 83). On 31 March he told Mrs. Fairbanks they had finished fifty pages of proof, "& it looks like it is going to take a month to finish it all" (p. 88). He left Elmira early in May, having read about five hundred pages of proof with Livy (p. 95), but returned a month later to finish the job (p. 98).

24.21   *Mark Twain to Mrs. Fairbanks*, p. 63n.

24.26   *Mark Twain to Mrs. Fairbanks*, p. 63.

24.35   Letter to "Dear Folks," Washington, 10 December 1867, in *Mark Twain, Business Man*, ed. Samuel C. Webster, Boston, 1946, p. 97; statement of Solon J. Severance, quoted in Paine, *Biography*, I, 328.

25.2   Mark Twain to Charles H. Webb, Buffalo, 26 November 1870, quoted in *"Ah Sin." A Dramatic Work by Mark Twain and Bret Harte*, ed. Frederick Anderson, San Francisco, 1961, p. vii.

25.5   *Overland Monthly*, January 1870, pp. 100–101.

25.15   The newspaper dispatches are conveniently reprinted in *Traveling with the Innocents Abroad: Mark Twain's Original Reports from Europe and the Holy Land*, ed. Daniel M. McKeithan, Norman, Okla., 1958. The burlesque story of Joseph is on pp. 220–224; that of the Prodigal Son is on pp. 245–248. Mark Twain had often signed himself "the Prodigal" in writing to Mrs. Fairbanks, but by the time he began to read proof with Livy this parable had taken on very personal implications for him (Lester G. Crossman, "Samuel L. Clemens in Search of Mark Twain—A Study of Clemens's Changing Conception of His Role as a Writer," unpublished dissertation, University of Washington, 1957, p. 524). Mark Twain wrote to Mrs. Emily A. Severance thanking her for her "training" during the *Quaker City* excursion, which had helped him in omitting from *The Innocents Abroad* "things . . . that should have been left out." "The book fairly bristled with them at first," he continued, "& it is well I weeded it as much as I did. But for you & Mrs. Fairbanks it would have been a very sorry affair" (27 October 1869, *Mark Twain to Mrs. Fairbanks*, p. 110).

NOTES

It should be pointed out that Mark Twain's sister Pamela had preceded Mrs. Fairbanks, Mrs. Severance, and Livy in the series of his feminine censors. In March 1868, in response to a letter from Pamela, he promised her there would be "no scoffing at sacred things in my book or lectures" (*Mark Twain, Business Man*, p. 100).

25.18   "Samuel Clemens in Search of Mark Twain," pp. 106–107. I have profited greatly from Mr. Crossman's analysis of Mark Twain's revisions of his newspaper dispatches.

26.3   *Writings*, II, 244–245.

26.12   William Charvat, *The Origins of American Critical Thought, 1810–1835*, Philadelphia, 1936, pp. 29–33.

26.22   [Henry Home, Lord Kames], *Elements of Criticism*, Edinburgh, 1762, III, 369.

26.31   Relevant passages are noted by Terence Martin, "Rip, Ichabod, and the American Imagination," *American Literature*, 31:137–149 (May 1959).

27.6   Mark Twain to Mrs. Fairbanks, San Francisco, 17 June 1868, *Mark Twain to Mrs. Fairbanks*, p. 28.

27.7   Leon T. Dickinson, "Mark Twain's *Innocents Abroad:* Its Origins, Composition, and Popularity," unpublished dissertation, University of Chicago, 1945, p. 148. I am much indebted in general to Mr. Dickinson's careful study.

27.15   Hartford, 1876, pp. 88–89.

27.24   Notebook 13, Oct. 1878–Jan. 1879, typescript, p. 34, MTP.

28.15   *Writings,* II, 382–383. I have corrected the text of the Definitive Edition, which has "impossible" instead of the "imposing" of the first edition in the last paragraph of the passage.

28.36   New York, 1865, pp. 449–450.

29.6   Mr. Dickinson says that *Eōthen* "was probably the most popular travel book of its kind until *Innocents Abroad*." Since its publication in 1844 *Eōthen* had gone through five English and two American editions ("Mark Twain's *Innocents Abroad*," p. 56n). A reviewer of Mark Twain's lecture about the *Quaker City* excursion—which gave prominence to the description of the Sphinx—said that the sentiment was "mostly borrowed from 'Eothen'" (John P. Irish in Iowa City *State Press*, 20 January 1869, quoted in Fred. W. Lorch, "Lecture Trips and Visits of Mark Twain in Iowa," *Iowa Journal of History and Politics*, 27:517, October 1929).

29.23   *Eōthen, or Traces of Travel Brought Home from the East*, New York, 1854, pp. 179–180.

30.17   Sacramento *Weekly Union*, 28 April 1866, reprinted in *Letters from the Sandwich Islands*, p. 41.

30.28   *Traveling with the Innocents Abroad*, p. 60.

31.15   *Traveling with the Innocents Abroad*, pp. 97–98.

31.18   Fatout, *Lecture Circuit*, p. 106.

31.30   *Writings*, I, 250–251.

32.10   *Writings*, II, 141. Despite this disclaimer, Mark Twain produced a considerable body of historical associations for Ephesus, from Alcibiades and Alexander and Antony to "troops of mail-clad Crusaders"; and for good measure he added a raucous burlesque version of the Legend of the Seven Sleepers (II, 143–148).

32.22   *Writings*, II, 262.

32.34   *Traveling with the Innocents Abroad*, p. 300.

33.9   *Writings*, II, 351.

33.25   *Writings*, II, 352–353.

34.7   Mr. Crossman makes this highly plausible suggestion ("Samuel Clemens in Search of Mark Twain," p. 224, note 90).

34.23   Lansing, Michigan, 24 December 1868, *Mark Twain to Mrs. Fairbanks*, pp. 59–60.

35.11   *Love Letters*, pp. 165–166.

35.14   Mr. Dickinson has demonstrated that this is particularly true of new episodes in the text ("Mark Twain's *Innocents Abroad*," pp. 92–95).

35.24   Franklin R. Rogers identifies the targets of the literary burlesques in *Mark Twain's Burlesque Patterns as Seen in the Novels and Narratives 1855–1885*, Dallas, 1960, pp. 43–49.

35.29   *Burlesque Patterns*, p. 59.

36.3   Gloves in Gibraltar, *Writings*, I, 60–62; the French barber, I, 108; the expedition to the Acropolis, II, 48–61; the crew's ridicule of the passengers, II, 119–122; Palestinian horses, II, 160–161; the Benton House, II, 366–368.

36.25   *Writings*, I, 302–303.

37.27   3 September 1869, quoted in *Mark Twain to Mrs. Fairbanks*, p. 110.

37.33   Boston *Transcript*, 15 December 1869, p. 1.

37.35   Quotation from Providence *Herald* reprinted in Buffalo *Express*, 9 October 1869, "Advertising Supplement."

37.37   Quotation from Rochester *Chronicle* reprinted in advertising leaflet issued by American Publishing Co., n.d., photostat in MTP.

38.8,12 Quotations from Albany *Journal* and New York *Times* reprinted in Buffalo *Express*, 9 October 1869, "Advertising Supplement."

38.26   Quotation from Syracuse *Standard* reprinted in advertising leaflet issued by American Publishing Co.

38.36   Reply to an address from the Democratic Republican delegates from Washington County, Pennsylvania (1809), in *The Complete Jefferson*, ed. Saul K. Padover, New York, 1943, p. 557. Mark Twain's commitment to the ideas of progress and American nationalism is discussed by Roger B. Salomon in *Twain and the Image of History*, New Haven, 1961. Chapter I, "Twain and the Whig Hypothesis," is especially relevant to *The Innocents Abroad*.

39.14   *Writings*, II, 42. Mr. Salomon discusses this passage and others of similar import (*Twain and the Image of History*, pp. 63–65).

39.40   *Yusef; or the Journey of the Frangi*, New York, 1855, pp. 54–55.

40.21   "The American Vandal," *Writings*, XXVIII, 21–23.

40.23   *Writings*, XXVIII, 25.

40.34   *Writings*, XXVIII, 29.

41.20   Reprinted as "A Newspaper Valedictory" in the last chapter of *The Innocents Abroad*, *Writings*, II, 401–402.

41.38   Paine, *Biography*, I, 203.

42.8   "The Facts in the Great Land Slide Case," Buffalo *Express*, 2 April

1870, p. 2. The anecdote was later included in *Roughing It, Writings,* III, 238.

42.32   *Writings,* II, 400–401.

42.35   "The Quaker City Holy Land Excursion," privately printed, n.p., [1927].

43.2   Griswold's book was published in New York in 1907. Mark Twain's copy is in MTP. Griswold sailed in the *Quaker City* but was not a member of the party on the overland trek.

43.5   The original use of the term "pilgrims" to designate all the *Quaker City* travelers was a pun, announced in the subtitle of *The Innocents Abroad*—"The New Pilgrims' Progress." They were of course pilgrims in the traditional sense because they were on their way to a shrine. But in Western usage, "pilgrim" meant "newcomer," "tenderfoot," "greenhorn"—and therefore "innocent." The specialization of "pilgrim" as a designation for the pious conservatives of the party was suggested by the fact that many of this group were members of Henry Ward Beecher's Plymouth Church in Brooklyn. The idea of the cruise, in fact, had originated in Beecher's congregation, in which the commander of the *Quaker City,* Captain Charles C. Duncan, was a prominent figure.

43.9   Mark Twain ascribes this attitude to Mollie Clemens, Orion's wife, in a letter to Howells, Munich, 9 February 1879, *Mark Twain–Howells Letters,* I, 256.

43.17   *Writings,* II, 171.

43.19   *Writings,* II, 124–126.

43.27   *Writings,* II, 173.

44.8   *Writings,* II, 227–228.

44.16   *Writings,* II, 231, 240.

44.23   *Writings,* II, 243.

44.27   *Writings,* II, 267.

44.31   *Tent Life in the Holy Land,* New York, 1865, p. 350.

45.1   *Writings,* II, 267.

45.8   *Writings,* II, 275.

46.9   *Writings,* I, 93–94. *The Plymouth Collection* was a book of hymns published for use in services in Beecher's Plymouth Church in Brooklyn.

46.26   Rogers, *Mark Twain's Burlesque Patterns,* pp. 54–55.

47.8   Strictly speaking, the three letters signed "Thomas Jefferson Snodgrass" that were contributed to the Keokuk (Iowa) *Daily Post* in 1857 are exceptions to this generalization, and some of the sketches of the 1860's, such as "Jim Smiley and His Jumping Frog," depict "Mark Twain" as relatively naïve.

47.29   *Writings,* I, 1.

48.15   *Writings,* I, 7–8.

48.28   *Writings,* I, 10.

49.5   *Writings,* I, 13–14.

49.20   *Writings,* I, 30.

50.27   *The American Novel and Its Tradition,* New York, 1957.

52.2   Buffalo, 31 August 1870, *Letters,* I, 176. This chapter draws heavily on two of my own essays: "Mark Twain as an Interpreter of the Far West: The Structure of *Roughing It,*" in *The Frontier in Perspective,* ed. Walker D. Wyman and Clifton B. Kroeber (Madison, 1957, pp. 205–228), and the Introduction to *Roughing It* in the Harper's Modern Classics series (New York, 1959, pp. xi–xxii). I also make extensive use of two unpublished dissertations: Paul S. Schmidt, "Samuel Clemens' Technique as a Humorist, 1857–1872," University of Minnesota, 1951; and Martin B. Fried, "The Composition, Sources, and Popularity of Mark Twain's *Roughing It*," University of Chicago, 1951.

52.20   The scrapbooks of Mark Twain's articles in the Virginia City *Territorial Enterprise* were kept by his brother Orion, who was serving as Territorial Secretary in Carson City. In a letter of 23 July 1862 from Esmeralda Mark Twain tells Orion he will send a clipping to be pasted in "my scrap book" (original in the collection of Samuel C. Webster, typescript in MTP; this passage is omitted from the text of the letter in *Letters*, I, 81–82). The scrapbooks apparently passed into the custody of Mark Twain's sister Pamela, in St. Louis, and Mark Twain asked for them to be sent to him in Buffalo when he began work on *Roughing It* in 1870. On 26 March he acknowledged receipt of the "coffin of 'Enterprise' files" (*Mark Twain, Business Man*, p. 112).

53.24   *Writings*, III, 2.

56.10   *Writings*, III, 155.

57.25   *Writings*, XIII, 30.

58.30   Cleveland, 24 January 1869, *Love Letters*, p. 61.

59.20   Mark Twain published yet another version, considerably expanded, in the Buffalo *Express*, 2 April 1870, p. 2.

61.24   *Writings*, IV, 4–5.

61.36   In Chapter 6 of the second volume—*Writings*, IV, 42–53.

63.28   The information about Mose is drawn from Richard M. Dorson, "Mose the Far-Famed and World-Renowned," *American Literature*, 15:288–300 (November 1943).

63.36   [Benjamin A. Baker], *A Glance at New York. A Local Drama, in Two Acts*. French's Standard Drama No. 216, New York, n.d., p. 20.

64.1   *A Glance at New York*, pp. 16–17.

64.6   *The History of Nevada*, 2 vols., Reno, Nevada, 1913, I, 269–271; *Mark Twain of the "Enterprise,"* pp. 66–67.

64.29   Chapters 10–11.

65.5   *Writings*, IV, 55.

65.17   *Writings*, IV, 57.

65.38   *Writings*, IV, 68.

66.7   Charles N. Robinson, *The British Tar in Fact and Fiction*, London, 1911, chapter 11, pp. 225–246.

66.18   *Writings*, IV, 69.

67.13   *Writings*, IV, 98–104.

67.36   Mark Twain's discussion of the Jim Blaine story is in the Autobiographical Dictation, *Mark Twain in Eruption*, p. 227.

68.9   *Writings*, IV, 103.

68.19   *Mark Twain in Eruption*, pp. 227–228.

69.35   *Writings*, IV, 113.

70.2   In 1868, to negotiate with the publishers of the *Alta California* concerning his use of the *Quaker City* dispatches in *The Innocents Abroad*.

NOTES

When he set out on his lecture tour in the Southern Hemisphere in 1895, Mark Twain lectured in the Pacific Northwest before he sailed from Vancouver.

71.16   Letters to his mother and sister, San Francisco, 20 January 1866 (misdated 1865), photostat in MTP.

71.18   Bennington, Vt., 27 November 1871, *Love Letters*, p. 166.

72.8   Hartford, 24 October 1874, *Mark Twain–Howells Letters*, I, 34.

73.19   Reprinted in *Writings*, XII, 32–33.

73.26   *Writings*, XII, 34.

74.28   *Mark Twain & Huck Finn*, p. 53.

75.19   *Writings*, XII, 32.

76.2   Mark Twain identifies Sellers with Lampton in *Autobiography*, I, 89.

76.4   Chapters 3–4, *Writings*, V, 19–38.

77.7   *Writings*, XII, 91.

77.18   Kenneth S. Lynn analyzes Longstreet's and Byrd's use of a Self-controlled Gentleman as narrator in *Mark Twain and Southwestern Humor*, pp. 64–72, 14–20.

79.7   Curtis Dahl describes the "dioramic effects" or "dissolving views" achieved by means of translucent cloth and special lighting in "Mark Twain and the Moving Panoramas," *American Quarterly*, 13:20–32 (Spring 1961).

79.21   *Writings*, XII, 77–80. Walter Blair has called my attention to the following passage in one of Mark Twain's dispatches to the *Alta California* from New York (28 May 1867): "the very blush that charms me in a lovely face, is, to the critical surgeon, nothing but a sign hung out to advertise a decaying lung. Accursed be all such knowledge. I want none of it" (reprinted in *Mark Twain's Travels with Mr. Brown*, ed. Franklin Walker and G. Ezra Dane, New York, 1940, p. 238).

80.24   In this discussion of aesthetic perception I am much indebted to Leo Marx, "The Pilot and the Passenger: Landscape Conventions and the Style of *Huckleberry Finn*," *American Literature*, 28:129–146 (May 1956).

80.35   *Writings*, XII, 50.

81.31   Bernard De Voto, "The Phantasy of Boyhood," in *Mark Twain at Work*, Cambridge, 1942, pp. 5–6. De Voto includes the text of the "Boy's Manuscript," pp. 25–44.

81.32   Franklin R. Rogers makes the plausible suggestion about David Copperfield and traces the development of the plot of *The Adventures of Tom Sawyer* in *Mark Twain's Burlesque Patterns*, pp. 101–113.

81.36   He mentioned Marsh's Comedians in the *Territorial Enterprise* (*Mark Twain of the "Enterprise,"* pp. 131–132).

82.7   Walter Blair discusses Tom's growth toward maturity as a structural pattern in "On the Structure of *Tom Sawyer*," *Modern Philology*, 37:75–88 (August 1939).

82.20   Mr. Blair emphasizes this burlesque theme (*Modern Philology*, 37:82–83).

82.25   In *Life on the Mississippi* Mark Twain describes a "low, vulgar, ignorant, sentimental, half-witted humbug" of a nightwatchman "who had absorbed wildcat literature and appropriated its marvels" (*Writings*, XII, 43).

82.38   Immediately after finishing *Tom Sawyer* Mark Twain told Howells: "It is *not* a boy's book, at all . . . It is only written for adults" (Hartford, 5 July 1875, *Mark Twain-Howells Letters*, I, 91). But when Howells read it, he wrote: "I think you ought to treat it explicitly *as* a boy's story" (Cambridge, 21 November 1875, *Mark Twain-Howells Letters*, I, 110), and Mark Twain replied: "Mrs. Clemens decides with you that the book should issue as a book for boys, pure & simple— & so do I. It is surely the correct idea" (Hartford, 23 November 1875, *Mark Twain-Howells Letters*, I, 112). No revision is implied.

83.16   *Writings*, VIII, 18–19.

84.2   *Writings*, VIII, 268–269.

84.17   *Writings*, VIII, 12.

84.36   *Writings*, VIII, 35–36.

85.22   *Writings*, VIII, 46.

86.35   *Writings*, VIII, 129–130.

87.28   *Writings*, VIII, 136–137.

89.7   *Writings*, VIII, 153.

89.25   Introduction to *The Portable Mark Twain*, New York, 1946, p. 33.

90.15   *The Oregon Trail* (Modern Library ed.), New York, 1949, p. 13.

90.24   *Writings*, VIII, 290.

90.26   *Autobiography*, II, 175.

91.10   *Writings*, VIII, 281.

91.12   *Writings*, VIII, 286–287.

92.8   *My Mark Twain*, p. 19.

92.19   *Bits of Gossip*, Westminster [London], 1904, pp. 42–43.

92.21   "My First Visit to New England," in *Literary Friends and Acquaintance*, New York, 1901, pp. 1–66.

92.24   James C. Austin, *Fields of The Atlantic Monthly. Letters to an Editor, 1861–1870*, San Marino, Calif., 1953, p. 143.

93.9   *Fields of The Atlantic Monthly*, p. 369 (the sum is erroneously set here at a thousand dollars); Henry C. Merwin, *The Life of Bret Harte*, Boston, 1911, p. 232.

93.16   *Mark Twain-Howells Letters*, I, 10–11. In *My Mark Twain* (p. 3) Howells incorrectly associates the witticism with his review of *The Innocents Abroad*.

93.27   Unsigned editorial in the Worcester *Gazette*, reprinted in *Harvard Library Bulletin*, 9:157 (Spring 1955).

93.32   In a letter to Mark Twain, Cambridge, 3 December 1874, *Mark Twain-Howells Letters*, I, 46.

93.38   Hartford, 8 December 1874, *Mark Twain-Howells Letters*, I, 49.

94.13   This incident is discussed in more detail in my article " 'That Hideous Mistake of Poor Clemens's,' " *Harvard Library Bulletin*, 9:145–180 (Spring 1955).

95.3   The text of the introduction was published in the Boston *Journal*, 18 December 1877, p. 3.

95.21   In a letter to her from Buffalo, 27 September 1869, *Mark Twain to Mrs. Fairbanks*, p. 107.

NOTES

95.22 The text of the speech is in *Harvard Library Bulletin*, 9:176–180, and (with minor changes) in *Writings*, XXVIII, 63–68.

97.3 The toast to General Grant is described in Paine, *Biography*, II, 656–657.

97.12 "Jane Austen," DV 201, MTP.

97.32 *Writings*, XXVIII, 71–74.

98.20 *My Mark Twain*, pp. 60–61.

98.31 18 December 1877: *Advertiser*, p. 1; *Globe*, p. 8; *Traveller*, p. 1; *Transcript*, p. 4.

99.6 Hartford, 23 December 1877, *Mark Twain–Howells Letters*, I, 212.

99.11 Cambridge, 19 December 1877, in *Life in Letters of William Dean Howells*, ed. Mildred Howells, 2 vols., Garden City, New York, 1928, I, 243.

100.6 Mark Twain's letter is in *Harvard Library Bulletin*, 9:164.

101.9 The editorial of the Worcester *Gazette* was reprinted in the Boston *Traveller*, 26 December 1877, p. 1. The other newspaper comments are quoted in *Harvard Library Bulletin*, 9:148, 157–161.

105.22 Holland, *Lessons in Life*, pp. 312–313.

105.39 The Holland letter is in the Boston *Transcript*, 18 December 1877, p. 3; quoted in *Harvard Library Bulletin*, 9:170–171.

106.9 *My Mark Twain*, p. 59.

106.23 James R. Lowell, *Complete Writings*, 16 vols., Cambridge, 1904, XI, 8.

106.25 Stedman's comment is quoted by Walter Blair in "The Popularity of Nineteenth-Century American Humorists," *American Literature*, 3:175–194 (May 1931).

106.34 William Garrett, *Reminiscences of Public Men in Alabama*, quoted in Walter Blair, "Introduction," *Native American Humor*, pp. 108–109.

107.3 "Civilisation in the United States," *Nineteenth Century*, 23:489 (April 1888).

107.33 *My Mark Twain*, p. 168.

108.4 Mark Twain's letter to Lang is in *Letters*, II, 526–528.

108.10 The story papers and the sensation fiction they published are described by Mary Noel in *Villains Galore. The Heyday of the Popular Story Weekly*, New York, 1954.

108.24 Rogers, *Burlesque Patterns*, especially chapter 4, "The Craft of the Novel," pp. 95–151.

108.31 The Buffalo Bill play and burlesque are described in Henry N. Smith, *Virgin Land: The American West as Symbol and Myth*, Cambridge, 1950, pp. 105–106.

108.34 The text of *Across the Continent* is included in *Davy Crockett & Other Plays*, ed. Isaac Goldberg and Hubert Heffner, Princeton, 1940, pp. 65–114.

109.3 The comments of Everett and Baird are quoted in Noel, *Villains Galore*, p. 289.

109.7 Beecher's contributions to the *Ledger* are described in Noel, *Villains Galore*, pp. 232–236. Paxton Hibben deals with *Norwood* in *Henry Ward Beecher: An American Portrait*, New York, 1927, esp. p. 220.

109.13 Noel, *Villains Galore*, pp. 229–230.

109.17   *Golden Era,* 28 January 1866, pp. 1, 6. Miss Braddon's novel was en-
titled *Rupert Godwin.* It had been serialized in London, Paris, and
New York before the *Golden Era* began to run it in San Francisco
("Publishers' Announcement" in *Rupert Godwin,* 3 vols., London, 1867,
I, v). The *Golden Era* had previously run two other novels by Miss
Braddon, and was currently serializing—along with *Our Mutual Friend*
—Pierce Egan's *The Fair Lilias; or Life in Death,* a noticeably Gothic
affair.

109.35   Child praised the Whittier dinner speech (*My Mark Twain,* p. 62).
Perry wrote enthusiastically to Howells about *The Innocents Abroad*
and also published a highly favorable comment on *Huckleberry Finn*
(*Mark Twain–Howells Letters,* II, 603n).

110.3   Ellen Emerson's statement about her father and Holmes's letter to
Mark Twain are in *Harvard Library Bulletin,* 9:165–167.

110.6   The phrases occur in Howells' review of *The Innocents Abroad,*
reprinted in *My Mark Twain,* p. 110.

111.4   Mark Twain's comments on the Whittier dinner speech are quoted
in *Harvard Library Bulletin,* 9:174–175.

113.2   This chapter makes constant use of Walter Blair's impressive *Mark
Twain & Huck Finn.* But my reading of *Huckleberry Finn* has of
course been influenced also by other books and articles. I should mention particularly chapter 15 in Daniel G. Hoffman's *Form and Fable
in American Fiction* (New York, 1961), which deals expertly with
the folklore in the novel.

114.23   "When Was Huckleberry Finn Written," *American Literature* 30:1–
25 (March 1958).

115.25   The story is preserved in the form of galley proof of type set by the
Paige machine, DV 303, MTP. Quotations © copyright 1962 by the
Mark Twain Company.

115.36   *Mark Twain & Huck Finn,* p. 151.

116.7   *Writings,* XIII, 112.

116.12   *Writings,* XIII, 130.

117.18   *Writings,* XIII, 2.

117.23   *Writings,* XIII, 9.

117.33   *Writings,* XIII, 30.

118.3   *Writings,* XIII, 143.

118.10   *Writings,* XIII, 169.

118.28   *Writings,* XIII, 227–228.

118.32   *Writings,* XIII, 160.

119.21   In *Mark Twain and Southwestern Humor* (pp. 216–219) Kenneth
Lynn points out that Mark Twain's dawning recognition of moral
depth in Huck's character created a difficulty for him at this point.
Mr. Lynn's analysis has led me to modify my earlier view of the problem of plot construction in the novel.

119.35   *Writings,* XIII, 294.

120.33   *Writings,* XIII, 122–124.

121.5   *Writings,* XIII, 296.

121.15   *Writings,* XIII, 294–295.

121.31   Mr. Blair called to my attention the revision of this passage.

NOTES

123.20   The thunderstorm: *Writings,* XIII, 67–68; dawn on the river: XIII, 163–165.
123.30   The fog: *Writings,* XIII, 112–116; the snake-bite: XIII, 73–74.
124.8   *Writings,* XIII, 4.
125.9   Huck's planting of false clues: *Writings,* XIII, 45–47; deception of the slave hunters: XIII, 125–126; deception of the Grangerfords: XIII, 137–138.
125.29   The Widow Douglas: *Writings,* XIII, 146; "borrowing": XIII, 130.
126.2   Pap's economic philosophy: *Writings,* XIII, 44.
126.13   *Writings,* XIII, 36–38.
126.26   *Writings,* XIII, 38–39.
127.18   *Writings,* XIII, 40–41.
127.29   *Writings,* XIII, 25.
128.11   *Writings,* XIII, 33.
128.20   *Writings,* XIII, 27–28.
129.33   *Writings,* XIII, 303, 304.
130.12   *Writings,* XIII, 304.
130.18   *Writings,* XIII, 323.
130.33   *Autobiography,* I, 102–103.
131.12   *Writings,* XV, 271–272.
131.20   To an unidentified person, quoted in *The Portable Mark Twain,* p. 774.
131.33   *Writings,* XV, 276–277.
132.7   *Writings,* XIII, 321.
132.13   "The Facts Concerning the Recent Carnival of Crime" is in *Writings,* XIX, 302–325.
132.16   Paine, *Biography,* I, 142–144.
132.19   Paine, *Biography,* I, 456–457.
133.4   *Mark Twain & Huck Finn,* p. 151.
133.19   *Writings,* XIII, 310.
134.5   Nat, the Phelps's slave: *Writings,* XIII, 346–347; counting the spoons: XIII, 353–354; the ratholes: XIII, 352–353; Sister Hotchkiss: XIII, 386–389.
134.14   Case-knives: *Writings,* XIII, 341.
134.30   *Writings,* XIII, 359.
135.3   The Sherburn episode: *Writings,* XIII, 195–204.
135.15   The shooting of Smarr is described by Dixon Wecter in *Sam Clemens of Hannibal,* Boston, 1952, pp. 106–109.
135.17   In addition to the version of the shooting and attempted lynching in *Huckleberry Finn,* Mark Twain described the episode in his *Autobiography* in 1898 (I, 131) and in the unpublished manuscript "Villagers of 1840–3" (DV 47, MTP). In "The United States of Lyncherdom" (1901), he mentions seeing "a brave gentleman deride and insult a mob and drive it away" (*Writings,* XXIX, 245). Walter Blair suggests that the description of a shooting in a footnote to Chapter 40 of *Life on the Mississippi* also draws on Mark Twain's memory of the shooting of Smarr (*Mark Twain & Huck Finn,* p. 306).
135.23   *Writings,* XIII, 195.

135.31 Walter Blair fixes the date of composition of Chapter 21 as "probably . . . before March 19, 1883," and says that the rest of the novel was written after June 15, 1883 (*American Literature*, 30:20). Except for a sequence corresponding to part of Chapter 12 and all of Chapters 13 and 14, the manuscript preserved in the Buffalo Public Library begins with Chapter 22. The manuscript of Chapters 15–16 has not survived.

136.1 *Mark Twain & Huck Finn*, pp. 310–311.

136.6 *Mark Twain & Huck Finn*, pp. 292–294.

136.30 Paul Baender, "Mark Twain's Transcendent Figure," unpublished dissertation, University of California (Berkeley), 1956.

138.2 In "Mark Twain: An Inquiry" (*North American Review*, February 1901), reprinted in *My Mark Twain*, p. 174. Elsewhere in the essay Howells says, "I who like *The Connecticut Yankee in King Arthur's Court* so much have half a mind to give my whole heart to *Huckleberry Finn*" (p. 173).

138.5 The earliest musical comedy version, by Richard Rodgers and Lorenz Hart (1927), was the first Rodgers-Hart musical to run over four hundred performances. In 1943 they prepared an "up-dated version" of *A Connecticut Yankee* in which the Yankee was a lieutenant in the Navy and Sandy a WAC corporal (Stanley Green, *The World of Musical Comedy*, New York, 1960, pp. 145–146, 159). There was a silent movie of the *Yankee* in 1921 (Daniel Blum, *A Pictorial History of the Silent Screen*, New York, 1953, p. 205), and talking versions in 1931 (starring Will Rogers) and 1949 (a musical, with Bing Crosby) (Daniel Blum, *A Pictorial History of the Talkies*, New York, 1958, pp. 36, 239, 245).

138.10 *Main Currents in American Thought*, 3 vols. in 1, New York, 1930, vol. III, *The Beginning of Critical Realism in America*, p. 97.

139.22 *Writings*, XIV, 31.

139.24 The burlesque *Hamlet* is in MTP (DV 320).

139.34 *Notebook*, p. 171, corrected by reference to the original notebook in MTP.

140.24 "Borrowing" horses: *Writings*, XIV, 343; devices to baffle pursuers: XIV, 343–344; Morgan's talking himself out of a tight place: XIV, 369; conscience a nuisance: XIV, 153. It is significant also that Mark Twain later ascribed to the Yankee "the good heart" that he saw in Huck (letter to his daughter Clara, Hartford, 20 July 1890, *Love Letters*, p. 257; cf. his description of *Huckleberry Finn* as a book "where a sound heart & a deformed conscience come into collision & conscience suffers a defeat," Notebook 28a [I], typescript, p. 35, 1895, MTP).

141.23 *Writings*, XIV, 175.

142.9 *Writings*, XXVII, 131–132.

142.17 Howells mentions the project in a letter to Mark Twain, Auburndale, Mass., 18 January 1886, *Mark Twain-Howells Letters*, II, 550.

142.22 Hartford, 16 November 1886, *Mark Twain to Mrs. Fairbanks*, pp. 257–258.

142.31 Elmira, 22 August 1887, *Mark Twain-Howells Letters*, II, 595.

NOTES

143.16   The discussion of protective tariffs is at *Writings*, XIV, 323–328. The examination of candidates for commissions in the army (*Writings*, XIV, 238–247) illustrates the need for civil-service reform.

143.39   *Writings*, XIV, 174.

144.24   *Writings*, XIV, 105.

145.11   *Writings*, XIV, 62–63.

145.22   *Writings*, XIV, 139.

145.26   *Writings*, XIV, 143.

145.33   *Writings*, XIV, 144.

146.2   *Writings*, XIV, 167–169.

146.11   Cambridge, 22 October 1889, *Mark Twain–Howells Letters*, II, 616.

146.18   *Harper's*, January 1890, p. 320.

146.27   New York, 7 July 1889, quoted in *Mark Twain–Howells Letters*, II, 609.

146.32   Philip S. Foner, *Mark Twain Social Critic*, New York, 1958, p. 176.

146.36   In a letter to Mark Twain, New York, 12 November 1889, *Mark Twain–Howells Letters*, II, 612.

147.9   "Decorations of Sixth Century Aristocracy": *A Connecticut Yankee*, New York, 1889, p. 326. The illustration was one of those chosen for reproduction in the prospectus issued by the Charles L. Webster Co. (New York, 1889, p. 3 of the section of publisher's comments).

147.23   *The Standard* (New York), 1 January 1890 (vol. II, no. 1), p. 10.

147.29   Quoted in Paine, *Biography*, II, 888.

147.30   *My Mark Twain*, p. 166.

148.21   Boston *Sunday Herald*, 15 December 1889, p. 17.

148.22   The drawing of Jay Gould as a slave driver is at p. 465 of the first edition.

148.32   Richard Hofstadter, *The Age of Reform: From Bryan to F.D.R.*, New York, 1955, p. 91.

149.9   *Plumas National* (Quincy, California), 5 July 1890, p. 2.

149.12   Tennyson as Merlin: p. 41 of the first edition; the Prince of Wales as a "chucklehead": p. 297.

149.21   A bishop kicking a king: p. 218 of the first edition; "High Church": p. 559.

149.31   *Harper's*, January 1890, p. 320.

149.36   *Mark Twain–Howells Letters*, II, 622.

150.17   Roger B. Salomon makes the point in *Twain and the Image of History*, p. 103. In a forthcoming book entitled "Mark Twain: Statesman without Salary" Louis J. Budd emphasizes Mark Twain's basic conservatism in political and economic matters.

150.23   *Century*, 39:77.

150.28   The mass of the nation: *Writings*, XIV, 237.

151.3   *Writings*, XIV, 5.

151.11   *Writings*, XIV, 237.

151.17   *Writings*, XIV, 5.

151.30   "The Significance of the Frontier in American History," reprinted in *The Early Writings of Frederick Jackson Turner*, ed. Everett E. Edwards, Madison, 1938, pp. 227–228.

152.4   In a conversation reported in Paine, *Biography*, II, 887–888.

152.8   *Writings,* XIV, 52. Later, Mark Twain forgets the Yankee's passion for chromos and has him remark that the workmanship of the crude pictures commemorating miraculous cures wrought by the water of the well in the Valley of Holiness "would have made a chromo feel good" (*Writings,* XIV, 199).

152.13   *Writings,* XIV, 18.

152.19   The reference to Fielding and Smollett is at *Writings,* XIV, 32.

152.23   J. Lawrence Laughlin, Professor of Economics in the University of Chicago, was a special target of Populist abuse (Clinton Keller, "Children of Innocence: The Agrarian Crusade in Fiction," *Western Humanities Review,* 6:366, Autumn 1952).

152.33   "Twain and the Whig Hypothesis," in Salomon, *Twain and the Image of History,* pp. 20–32.

152.35   "On Progress, Civilization, Monarchy, etc.," Paine 102b, MTP, quoted in Salomon, *Twain and the Image of History,* p. 27.

153.9   The comparison is Mr. Salomon's: his chapter on *A Connecticut Yankee* is entitled "The Fall of Prometheus."

153.18   The essay is reprinted, with explanatory comment, by Paul J. Carter, Jr., in "Mark Twain and the American Labor Movement," *New England Quarterly,* 30:382–388 (September 1957).

154.18   *Writings,* XIV, 60.

154.25   *Writings,* XIV, 76–77.

154.33   *Writings,* XIV, 398.

155.12   Mark Twain's praise of Quincy is at *Writings,* XII, 461–462.

155.28   *Writings,* XIV, 93–94.

156.8   *Writings,* XIV, 449.

156.15   Notebook 20, Aug. 20, 1885–Jan. 20, 1886, typescript in MTP, p. 33.

156.21   *Autobiography,* I, 99.

156.27   *Autobiography,* I, 110.

156.35   *Writings,* XIV, 10.

157.18   *Writings,* XIV, 1–2, 7–8.

157.26   *Writings,* II, 42.

157.37   Leo Marx, "The Machine in the Garden," *New England Quarterly,* 29:27 (March 1956).

158.6   Bernard Bowron, Leo Marx, and Arnold Rose, "Literature and Covert Culture," *American Quarterly,* 9:382–383 (Winter 1957).

158.28   *Writings,* XIV, 78–79. Allen Guttmann has called attention to the implications of the volcano image and to other evidences of Mark Twain's mixed feelings about Hank Morgan ("Mark Twain's Connecticut Yankee: Affirmation of the Vernacular Tradition," *New England Quarterly,* 33:232–237, June 1960).

159.11   *Writings,* XIV, 205–207.

159.26   18 January 1890, clipping in MTP.

159.35   13 January 1890, clipping in MTP.

160.20   The images quoted or paraphrased occur, in order, on the following pages: *Writings,* XIV, 55, 59, 74, 116, 160, 251.

160.30   *Writings,* XIV, 164–165.

161.20   *Writings,* XIV, 102–103.

161.28   *Writings,* XIV, 301.

NOTES

162.4   *Writings*, XIV, 303.

162.6   The reference to Southern poor whites is at *Writings,* XIV, 298–299.

162.8   *Writings,* XIV, 103.

162.30   *Writings,* XIV, 429–430.

162.33   *A Connecticut Yankee,* New York, 1889, p. 363. Beard mistranscribes the text, substituting "this" for "that."

163.12   The Yankee remarks, "I never care to do a thing in a quiet way; it's got to be theatrical or I don't take any interest in it" (*Writings,* XIV, 310–311). Later he says that he must always choose a "picturesque" means of achieving his purposes: "it is the crying defect of my character" (*Writings,* XIV, 376).

163.28   *Writings,* XIV, 213.

163.37   *Writings,* XIV, 235.

164.18   *Writings,* XIV, 36–37.

164.22   *Writings,* XIV, 42–43.

164.36   *Writings,* XIV, 45–46.

164.39   *Writings,* XIV, 50.

165.6   *Writings,* XIV, 58.

165.10   *Writings,* XIV, 215–217.

165.14   Eliot's remark is in "American Literature and the American Language," *Washington University Studies,* New Series, Language and Literature, no. 23, St. Louis, 1953, p. 17.

165.24   The quoted phrases occur on the following pages: *Writings,* XIV, 65, 66, 103, 347, 430.

165.32   Comparisons of mobs to waves occur at *Writings,* XIV, 50, 214, 294, 304, 357.

165.39   *Writings,* XIV, 396.

166.7   *Writings,* XIV, 196.

166.14   *Writings,* XIV, 218.

166.21   *Writings,* XIV, 385.

166.26   *Writings,* XIV, 386.

166.30   Commenting on a dramatization of *A Connecticut Yankee* by Howard Taylor (which was never produced) Mark Twain wrote to his daughter Clara in July 1890: Taylor "has captured but one side of the Yankee's character—his rude animal side, his circus side; the good heart & the high intent are left out of him; he is a mere boisterous clown, & oozes slang from every pore. I told Taylor he had degraded a natural gentleman to a low-down black-guard" (Hartford, *Love Letters,* pp. 257–258).

166.32   The tournament is described at *Writings,* XIV, 387–396.

167.31   The notebook entries are discussed in John B. Hoben, "Mark Twain's *A Connecticut Yankee:* A Genetic Study," *American Literature,* 18:205–212 (November 1946).

168.2   Prospectus for *A Connecticut Yankee,* New York, 1889, "Publishers' Announcement," p. 77.

168.15   *Writings,* XIV, 272–273.

168.24   *Writings,* XIV, 425–426.

168.35   *Writings,* XIV, 435.

169.16   *Writings,* XIV, 443–444.

169.20   Cambridge, 10 November 1889, *Mark Twain–Howells Letters,* II, 619.

169.22   *Harper's,* January 1890, p. 320.

169.24   Letter from Howells to Mark Twain, Kittery Point, Maine, 15 August 1908, *Mark Twain–Howells Letters,* II, 833–834.

171.7   *Writings,* XIV, 133, 143–144.

171.20   *Writings,* XIV, 150.

171.22   *Writings,* XIV, 103.

172.25   *Writings,* XXVII, 287–304, especially pp. 303–304. The sketch was published posthumously in *Harper's* in 1912.

172.31   *Writings,* XIV, 154.

173.15   *Writings,* XVI, 208–209.

173.18   *Writings,* XVI, 209.

174.36   *Writings,* XVI, 3.

175.9   *Writings,* XVI, 5.

175.30   *Writings,* XVI, 52.

175.38   *Writings,* XVI, 272–275.

176.6   *Writings,* XVI, 98.

176.15   *Writings,* XVI, 139–140.

176.25   *Writings,* XVI, 4.

177.4   *Writings,* XVI, 18–19.

177.34   *Writings,* XVI, 123.

178.7   *Writings,* XVI, 126.

178.16   *Writings,* XVI, 15.

178.29   *Writings,* XVI, 11.

179.16   *Writings,* XVI, 22–23.

180.13   Daniel M. McKeithan, "The Morgan Manuscript of Mark Twain's *Pudd'nhead Wilson,*" *Essays and Studies on American Language and Literature* (Uppsala), 12:33–34 (1961).

180.27   *Writings,* XVI, 209.

180.30   Mrs. Anne P. Wigger, "The Composition of Mark Twain's *Pudd'nhead Wilson* and *Those Extraordinary Twins:* Chronology and Development," *Modern Philology,* 55:93–102 (November 1957), especially pp. 93–94.

181.9   New York, 12 January, *Love Letters,* p. 291.

181.30   *Writings,* XVI, 201.

181.37   Paul Baender notes transcendent elements in Wilson ("Mark Twain's Transcendent Figure," p. 85).

182.35   *Writings,* XVI, 202.

183.15   *Writings,* XXIII, 5. Hadleyburg does not seem to be in the South, but the rumor that a girl "carried a spoonful of negro blood in her veins" has created a scandal in the village (*Writings,* XXIII, 27).

183.19   *Writings,* XXIII, 33.

183.26   *Writings,* XXIII, 56.

183.34   *Writings,* XXIII, 53.

184.23   *Writings,* XXIII, 18.

185.4   Mark Twain's opinion of *Joan of Arc* is recorded in Paine, *Biography,* II, 1034.

NOTES

185.5   This phrase is Mark Twain's in his essay "Saint Joan of Arc," *Writings,* XXII, 326.

185.18   The essay is in *Mark Twain at Work,* pp. 105–130.

185.34   *Writings,* XXVII, 140.

186.3   The MS of the last chapter is in DV 327, MTP.

186.16   In a letter from Vienna, 13 May 1899, *Mark Twain–Howells Letters,* II, 698–699.

186.18   *Writings,* XXVII, 20.

187.15   *Writings,* XXVII, 50.

187.25   *Writings,* XXVII, 52–53.

188.2   *Writings,* XXVII, 16–17. I have discussed this passage in "Mark Twain's Images of Hannibal: From St. Petersburg to Eseldorf," *Studies in English* (University of Texas), 37:3–23 (1958).

INDEX

INDEX

INDEX

INDEX

A great deal has been learned about Mark Twain since Van Wyck Brooks in *The Ordeal of Mark Twain* and Bernard DeVoto in *Mark Twain's America* debated his achievement as a writer. Especially within the past few years, significant studies have been devoted to his ideas and to specific themes in his work. But no one has drawn together these manifold scholarly findings in an interpretation of Mark Twain's entire career. Henry Nash Smith, viewing Mark Twain with the eye both of the critic and of the historian, surveys the development of his style and thought through all the major books.

Mr. Smith's primary concern is the continuing interaction between the writer's view of the world and his attitude toward his fictional materials. Since Mark Twain habitually used the creative process to test the validity of his observation of life, this proves to be a most rewarding method. The book proceeds chronologically from the journalism that culminated in *The Innocents Abroad* to the brief moment of triumph and equilibrium achieved part way through *Huckleberry Finn,* and on to the years of black despair whose statement Mark Twain finally managed in *The Mysterious Stranger.*

Seeing Mark Twain constantly in the context of the cultural traditions, changes, and battles of his times, the author keeps his writing free of jargon and never narrows his focus to exclude the general reader. The dramatic, tragic story of Mark Twain's growth and ultimate disillusion emerges step by step as it is reflected in his writing. At the same time it becomes evident that Mark Twain's own literary and